POLITICS AND CONSTITUTIONALISM

SUNY series in American Constitutionalism
Robert J. Spitzer, editor

POLITICS AND CONSTITUTIONALISM

The Louis Fisher Connection

EDITED BY

Robert J. Spitzer

State University of New York Press

Published by
State University of New York Press, Albany

For information, address State University of New York Press,
State University Plaza, Albany, N.Y., 12246

Production by Diane Ganeles
Marketing by Michael Campochiaro

Library of Congress Cataloging-in-Publication Data

Politics and constitutionalism : the Louis Fisher connection / Robert J.
    Spitzer, editor.
        p.   cm. — (SUNY series in American constitutionalism)
    Includes bibliographical references and index.
    ISBN 0-7914-4639-5 (alk. paper). — ISBN 0-7914-4640-9 (pbk. : alk. paper)
    1. Constitutional law—United States. 2. Fisher, Louis. I. Spitzer,
Robert J., 1953– II. Series.
KF4550.A2 P64 2000
320.473—dc21   99-049908
                                                                CIP

10 9 8 7 6 5 4 3 2 1

To Teresa Wilson

proving that the rule of law
is for everyone

Contents

viii   *Contents*

Preface

I first met Lou Fisher in Washington, D. C., in 1986 at a day-long session, called a "short course," a day before the start of the American Political Science Association's (APSA) Annual Meeting, which convened at the magisterial Supreme Court building. It was billed as a behind-the-scenes look at the court, including a tour of the building and time with some court personnel. As I sat in the lobby that morning in late August, who should I spy strolling in but Mr. Fisher. Since my days as a graduate student, I had deeply admired Fisher's writings, especially his first two books on presidential-congressional relations and budgeting. This admiration, I should confess, was built on the practical fact that these books proved to be indispensable resources for my graduate "A" exam in American politics—a sure indication of their value. Fisher and I had been introduced at an earlier time, but I did not expect him to recall that brief encounter. He did. We wound up spending the day together, chatting about a variety of subjects when opportunity allowed.

Two things struck me about this day. One was the fact that Fisher, a Washington insider who had written often about the courts, would deign to spend the day on this cook's tour of the court for academics. Yet here he was, interested in everything, enjoying the day. Second, I was disarmed by Lou's quiet demeanor and easy manner. He was unpretentious, friendly, and a good listener. Not long after, I summoned my courage and asked Lou to write an introduction to what became my book on the presidential veto. He readily complied. Since that time, I have imposed on Lou's friendship often for information and insight on all manner of political subjects. Moreover, I have relied even more heavily on his prolific writings to inform my own work.

Fisher's route to political science and government service was by no means direct. His undergraduate major was in chemistry, and after receiving his B.S. in 1956, he pursued graduate work in that same field for a brief time at Johns Hopkins before opting out, eventually switching to political science after a stint in the military and some other miscellaneous jobs. Completing his graduate work at the New School for Social Research in New York City, where Lou earned his Ph.D. in 1967, he found his way to the Library of Congress three years later. While he has always kept his hand in teaching, the core of Lou's professional life has been his link to Congress and government service. That his contributions to our understanding of the Constitution, the separation of powers, and the law have been so significant is a testament both to his intellectual tenacity and to the intellectual opportunities that can arise from governmental service. That Fisher has served his government with distinction is readily evident from his frequent testimony before, and other activities connected with, Congress. That Fisher has made a landmark contribution to political science's understanding of the governing process is evident by the existence of Fisher's many writings and of course by the existence of this book.

For this book, I thank the good people of SUNY Press, particularly Acquisitions Editor Zina Lawrence and Acting Director Priscilla Ross, the forbearance of the contributors, and especially the far-sightedness of my friend and contributor David Gray Adler, with whom I first discussed this idea. My thanks also to Jerry O'Callaghan, Deb Dintino, Mellissa Mitchell, Aaron Mitchell, Shannon Long, Steve Long, Alexis Long, Jinny Spitzer, Skye Wilson, and to Tess, to whom this book is lovingly dedicated.

1

Introduction

Robert J. Spitzer

Louis Fisher's prolific body of writings about the American Constitution, institutions, and the law stands as an enormous contribution to the study and appreciation of American politics from a modern institutionalist perspective. It has accomplished this goal in part because Fisher's writings are central to political science's contribution to these respective fields of study. Yes, many in political science study constitutional law, Congress, the presidency, the courts, public law, and other related subfields. Fisher's distinctive mark has come not only from his versatility with all of these subfields, but with his integrative study of their intermix, interaction, and balance. As Fisher has written, "To study one branch of government in isolation from the others is an exercise in make-believe."[1] His contributions are both all the more impressive, and underappreciated, because his professional life has simultaneously straddled two disciplines, political science and law. For this fact alone, a book honoring Fisher's body of work is a timely testament to the power and scope of his writings.

Yet Fisher's work has served at least two other important contributions. A second contribution has been to pioneer the much-vaunted return to institutions that has swept political science in the last two decades. For his part, Fisher has received disproportionately little credit for his work as a pioneer of the return to institutions, beginning as it did with the 1972 publication of his first book, *President and Congress.*[2] In this book, Fisher examined the two branches of government pertaining to legislative power, spending power, taxation, and war power. At a time when most political science was obsessed with political/behavioral dynamics behind formal power (following, for example, Richard Neustadt's paradigm from *Presidential Power*),[3] here was Fisher urging his readers to return to the Constitution, the Federalist Papers, and the legal-structural arrangments that gave rise to these institutions and therefore to modern policy disputes. Admittedly, Fisher's institutionalist orientation is reminiscent of the "old institutionalism" of the late nineteenth and early twentieth centuries by virtue of what Fisher's work does not do; in particular, it does not reflect the drive to generate grand theory buttressed by close empiricism; it does not embrace an all-encompassing definition of institutions, extending to any "sets of relationships" or even "informal networks"; and it does not flee from normative concerns.[4] These latter traits, however, compose only a subset of modern institutionalism.[5]

The core of the new institutionalism recognizes that the key unit of politics is the institution; it incorporates special attention to historical analysis and context; it emphasizes the interplay of forces rather than the isolated study of single institutions; it understands the importance of particular cases, but reaches for generalizability; and it seeks to explore the interplay of interests, ideas, and institutions by understanding that institutions are the fountainheads of political decision making and choice.[6] These are all values that identify Fisher's work.

A third contribution of Fisher's work emanates more directly from his career path than from his publications, in that his career represents a vanishing breed—the symbiosis of career government service and significant scholarship. Following the pattern of other disciplines, political science has become increasingly specialized, compartmentalized, empirical, and abstractly (some might say obtusely) theoretical. Practitioners and theorists continue to share some common ground and common resumes, especially in fields like international relations. Yet the prevailing trend has been toward progressive bifurcation of the academy and the political world.

Fisher's writings are not those of the self-serving memoirist or the petty bureaucrat. They grapple with issues of great consequence, including such specific matters as budgeting, executive reorganization, impoundment, the veto power, and executive privilege. These practical governing problems are then framed in larger constitutional terms as they pertain to the separation of powers, institutional power, democratic values, and the express normative question of what constitutes good policy and good governance. In his award-winning book on budgeting,[7] for example, Fisher chronicled the history and modern consequences of the federal budget process by examining statutory shifts in budget authority. The tale of shifting budgetary authority is interesting and valuable in its own terms. Yet its consequences for presidential power and interbranch relations do not escape Fisher's eye. Nor does the lesson that politics not only drives, but is driven by, institutional change. Fisher has dealt with these issues as an expert attached to the Library of Congress who is called upon by Congress to explicate key issues and offer sound judgments. Despite the dictates of an occupation that encourage a narrow policy focus, Fisher's writings match, if not exceed, those of any emanating from the academic/scholarly community. Political scientists who train and teach in the academic world, as well as those found in government service, would do well to appreciate Fisher's leadership-by-example in his lifelong devotion to the intersection of government service and the scholarly enterprise.

Based on Fisher's prodigious scholarly contributions, this book stands on at least two vital principles. The first is that modern politics is as firmly rooted in timeless constitutional principles and institutional procedures today as it was one or two centuries ago. From federalism to foreign policy, constitutional meaning sheds a bright and vivid light on modern political dilemmas. This observation is readily accepted as a truism, yet it is too often absent, even shockingly absent (aside from obligatory bows) from contemporary political analysis.

The second principle upon which this book stands is that the evolution, interpretation, and meaning of the Constitution, and the doctrine that flows from it, is not the sole province of the courts (or of lawyers). Rather, it arises from all the branches of government. This observation is by no means new. For example, a study appearing in the *Harvard Law Review* in 1958 chronicled twenty-one instances between 1945 and 1957 when Congress acted to reverse court rulings.[8] Writing a few years later, Alexander Bickel noted that constitutional meaning and interpretation may arise from "fruitful interplay between the Court and the legislature or the executive. . . ."[9] Writing more recently, Fisher has stated in definitive terms that "The Supreme Court is not the sole or even dominant agency in deciding constitutional questions. Congress and the President have an obligation to decide constitutional questions."[10] Still, the idea that the legislative and executive branches contribute to

constitutional law operates, for the most part, below the radar
screens of most constitutional scholars and the analysis they generate. Fisher's important (and also award-winning) book, *Constitutional Dialogues*, establishes the point, yet his continues to be a
nearly lone voice. Part of the reason for this is reflected in the
attitudes of courts themselves, the nature of their opinions, and the
vast legal profession that stands behind the courts. For example, in
the important 1997 Supreme Court case of *City of Boerne v. Flores*,
a case that receives treatment in more than one chapter in this
book, Justice Anthony Kennedy wrote in the majority opinion that
Congress lacks the power "to determine what constitutes a constitutional violation" and that the power to interpret the Constitution
"remains in the Judiciary."[11] Without denying the courts' central
role in constitutional interpretation, to accept without question or
analysis Justice John Marshall's *obiter dictum* that the courts alone
are "to say what the law is"[12] (which Kennedy approvingly quotes
in *Boerne*) is to commit two errors.

The first is to deny the just-stated fact that constitutional interpretation can and should involve all of the branches of government. The second, and more subtle error, is that it accepts and
perpetuates a false dichotomy between law and politics. This false
dichotomy operates as a dividing line between the executive and
legislative branches, on the one hand, and the courts on the other.
Even if we agree that the executive and legislative branches are
the "political" branches, it surely does not follow that the judicial
branch is not also a political branch. One can acknowledge that
court politics and behavior, broadly defined, are different from the
other branches. Nevertheless, the courts are political, as is the law
itself. Some within the legal community have sought to advance
the proposition that courts and the law are more than grand legal
edifices. Notably, the school of legal realists defines law as the
product of "the behavior patterns of judges and other officials"[13]
rather than as an abstract, olympian ideal.

A clear evidence of the legal/judicial community's desire to cling
to the law-politics dichotomy as a way to minimize, if not deny the
political quality of law is reflected in law school training that continues to downplay the inherently political nature of the law, constitutional interpretation, and judicial behavior, a fact long
acknowledged by critics of legal education from Jerome Frank[14] to
Ralph Nader.[15] On court application of judicial review to constitutional interpretation, Frank is blunt in asserting that the entire
process is "a peculiar kind of political agency" and that the "judicial

veto [his name for judicial review, a process he viewed as akin to legislative law-making] is basically political."[16]

One may argue, contrary to Frank, that the "law-and-courts-as-above-politics" paradigm is a necessary, even justifiable conceit, in order for courts to retain their institutional legitimacy. I do not quibble with this need, but I do quibble with the analytical backwash that results from the perpetuation of this defective paradigm. To its credit, political science has provided a key corrective. David O'Brien, among many political scientists who study the courts and the Constitution, has stated the matter succinctly, noting that "The [Supreme] Court stands as a temple of law," but also that "it remains a fundamentally political institution."[17] Political science has properly and correctly identified the political nature of the courts, and the political consequences of the law. What it has mostly overlooked, however, is the political nature of law itself. In part, this is because the courts, the Constitution, and the law continue to be viewed mostly through the eyes of the legal profession which, despite the efforts of some in political science and law, perpetuates the fictions that law is not political, and that politics and law are separate and distinct. As to the former assertion, some students of public policy have noted that law, as the expression of the coercive power of the state, coincides precisely with the definition of public policy. Theodore J. Lowi has summarized the paradox this way:

> Anyone who studies political systems today must be struck by the presence of the state in all avenues of life.... Although political science is rich in theories that help give meaning to political experience, none of these has tried to construct a politics on the basis of the state and its functions.[18]

Lowi understands that law and policy are synonyms and that they are authoritative expressions of the state. The analysis of state structures and power is a fitting and sufficient definition of politics. Even viewed from the legal community, one can discern acknowledgement of the inherently political nature of law. Robert S. Summers and his colleagues describe five qualities of law: law as a grievance-remedial instrument, as a penal-corrective instrument, as an administrative-regulatory instrument, as an instrument for organizing and conferring public benefits, and as an instrument for facilitating private arrangements.[19] All encapsulate policy objectives, just as all are political. The foremost political scientist/

constitutional-legal scholar of our century, Edward S. Corwin, stated
the appropriate goal for his time and ours:

> The real destiny of political science is to do more expertly
> and more precisely what it has always done; its task is
> criticism and education regarding the true ends of the state
> and how best they may be achieved.[20]

This is where institutionalists of the Fisher tradition come in. In
the tradition of Corwin, institutionalists (as I have discussed in
connection with Fisher's work, and therefore as applicable to the
contributors to this volume) understand that politics arises from law,
and that law is also political. Further, they appreciate the interactive institutional process that produces modern constitutional meaning. The Constitution created the branches of government; the
branches, in turn, continue to vest meaning in the document. These
new institutionalist perspectives are themes that guide this book.

The distinguished contributors to this volume are uniquely
situated to analyze these questions. As devoted institutionalists, all
study and value court rulings, legal standards, precedent, and institutional analysis. Yet they also understand and appreciate politics. The confluence of these analytic values is uncommon, a fact
that adds insight and import to this book. While the chapters to
come are not designed to cover every element of Fisher's work, they
all arise from, or respond to, Fisher's perspectives as seen in the
scholarship of the respective authors.

The question of who gets the last word, constitutionally speaking, is one that pervades most of the chapters in this book. In his
chapter, Neal Devins turns the standard argument concerning judicial exclusivity on its head. The common defense of judicial exclusivity is that this branch is best positioned and disposed to preserve
and defend core constitutional values. Yet such an assumption,
Devins argues, actually marginalizes the Constitution because the
document benefits from the energetic buffeting of political and social
forces articulated through the executive and legislative branches.
This process makes the Constitution both more durable and more
relevant.

In opposition to Devins, and in part to Fisher, Michael J.
Glennon squarely confronts the question of "coordinate review"—

that is, the degree to which the other branches of government possess a right to determine constitutional meaning—by according it a lesser status. By considering coordinate review among the branches in the realm of foreign affairs, Glennon argues that the "political" branches do have such a power, especially when the courts are silent on constitutional issues, but that the executive and legislative branches do take a back seat in the matter in instances when the courts assert doctrine. Beyond the matter of who may interpret the Constitution, Glennon also examines the "what" of interpretation; that is, what sources of information provide the wellspring for interpretation?

The idea that the Constitution is, and should be, the product of coordinate construction among the three branches is Nancy Kassop's point of departure. This approach not only widens the scope of who interprets the Constitution, Kassop argues, but sensitizes us to emphasize constitutional accommodations rather than higher profile, but more corrosive, controversies. Further, it reminds us that judicial independence is both indispensable and fragile. Beyond this, the courts are no less prone to error than the other branches. Since they do "get it wrong" at least sometimes, the other branches, as well as the states, complement what must ultimately be an incremental, modest, stepwise process of constitution building.

David Gray Adler complements this theme by examining some of the misbegotten constitutional doctrine surrounding the exercise of the war power. Beginning with a discussion of the related concept of judicial finality, which largely owes its existence to court trumpeting and legal community dogma, he proceeds to analysis of executive warmaking. Adler's analysis would seem to undercut the wisdom of involving the other branches in a constitutional dialogue, considering the extent to which modern presidents have asserted fictional Constitution-based war powers. Yet the larger lesson is that the best hedge against constitutional error is greater, not lesser, involvement.

Undergraduate students of American government often consider federalism to be a tedious, arcane, even archaic concept little connected to modern politics. As Dean Alfange Jr.'s chapter on the Supreme Court and federalism reveals, nothing could be further from the truth. In a sweeping historical survey of court treatment of federalism as it has affected congressional power, Alfange levels a severe, even damning appraisal of recent Supreme Court cases that have sought to rob Congress of what he argues are reasonable, proper, and otherwise settled congressional exercises of power over the states. This judicial "arrogance of power," pivoting in recent cases on the votes of five justices, turns on its head the otherwise reasonable proposition that Congress has, by Constitution, law, and history, every reasonable right to assure the effectiveness of its legislation over matters of national policy (while also recognizing the propriety of state autonomy).

In a democracy, governmental secrecy is a paradoxical concept. Writing in *The Federalist Papers*, John Jay noted that "perfect *secrecy* and immediate *dispatch* are sometimes requisite." Writing in the same set of essays, Alexander Hamilton identified the incompatibility of democracy and secrecy as applied to the House of Representatives—the governing body closest to the people—when he noted that the very idea of "*secrecy*, and dispatch, are incompatible with the genius of a body so variable and so numerous."[21] While undoubtedly necessary for the conduct of (especially foreign) policy, secrecy is also inimical to bedrock democratic values of accountability and openness. In his chapter on secrecy, Loch K. Johnson argues forcefully that the balance scales have too much and too far favored needless secrecy over democratic values and practices. Unsurprisingly, the chief culprit has been the executive; since the early 1970s, "evasion and duplicity" have been the norms of Executive branch behavior not only in war consultation, but in a wide panoply of executive-led foreign policy ventures. That pragmatism, or a just outcome, fails as justification is seen in a lengthy pattern of failed policies marked by embarrassment and unpopularity. Johnson is unblinking in his solution—honoring of "original constitutional boundaries."

If the courts are not entitled to a monopoly over constitutional interpretation, neither are lawyers. Robert J. Spitzer takes the legal profession's near monopoly over constitutional interpretation as his point of departure. The study of the Constitution and law are bedrocks of political science, and political scientists continue to make important contributions to this field. Nevertheless, the legal profession is typically viewed as that which is most well situated to offer legal interpretation and meaning, especially with regard to constitutional questions. Spitzer cites two disparate areas of constitutional interpretation—pertaining to an interpretation of the president's veto power in Article I and pertaining to the Second Amendment of the Bill of Rights—to show that legal analysis in these two areas, as developed by lawyers in law journals, can too easily produce alarmingly flawed analysis, as is true in both of these cases. Worse, this defective analysis too easily serves as a primary buttress for wayward public policy. Spitzer concludes with an appeal to political science to renew its commitment to constitutional-legal analysis.

The voluminous and important writings of Louis Fisher inform the analysis of this book's contributors, and therefore bring the volume's contributors together. It is fitting, therefore, that he provide summative and analytic comment on some of the many strands of analysis spun by the foregoing writers.

Finally, I note that the present work began when most of these authors assembled for a panel organized and held to honor Fisher's work at the 1997 Annual Meeting of the American Political Science Association (APSA). The contributors thank the APSA for authorizing the panel.

Notes

1. Louis Fisher, *The Politics of Shared Power: Congress and the Executive,* 3rd ed. (Washington, D.C.: CQ Press, 1993), p. ix.

2. Louis Fisher, *President and Congress* (New York: Free Press, 1972).

3. Richard E. Neustadt, *Presidential Power* (New York: Wiley, 1960).

4. These particular elements of the new institutionalism are discussed in Philip J. Ethington and Eileen L. McDonagh, "The Common Space of Social Science Inquiry," *Polity* 28 (Fall 1995): 85–90; Theda Skocpol, "Why I am an Historical Institutionalist," *Polity* 28 (Fall 1995): 105; Morris Fiorina, "Rational Choice and the New(?) Institutionalism," *Polity* 28 (Fall 1995): 108.

5. Hugh Heclo discusses the enduring debate between the positivists (or empiricists, for lack of a better term) and the contextualists (or qualitativists), arguing that the extreme positions of both offer unproductive resolution. Instead, Heclo asserts that "It is squarely in the Weberian spirit to stake out an intermediate epistemological position where we expect accounts and explanations to be relative to context but leave ourselves ample room for exposing more general processes and historical types." This resolution serves equally well as a summary of Fisher's work. "Ideas, Interests, and Institutions," in *The Dynamics of American Politics*, ed. by Lawrence C. Dodd and Calvin Jillson (Boulder, Colo.: Westview Press, 1994), p. 370.

6. See Dorothy Ross, "The Many Lives of Institutionalism in American Social Science," *Polity* 28 (Fall 1995): 117–123; Karen Orren and Stephen Skowronek, "Beyond the Iconography of Order: Notes for a 'New Institutionalism,'" in *The Dynamics of American Politics*, pp. 311–330; Skocpol, "Why I am an Historical Institutionalist"; Heclo, "Ideas, Interests, and Institutions."

7. Louis Fisher, *Presidential Spending Power* (Princeton, N.J.: Princeton University Press, 1975).

8. "Congressional Reversal of Supreme Court Decisions: 1945–1957," *Harvard Law Review* 71(1958): 1324–37. The article noted that six of the twenty-one instances were not the result of direct confrontation between the branches, but rather occurred because "Congress was able to take into account policy factors that the Court could not properly have considered." (1326)

9. Alexander M. Bickel, *The Least Dangerous Branch* (Indianapolis, Ind.: Bobbs-Merrill, 1962), p. 206.

10. Louis Fisher, *Constitutional Dialogues: Interpretations as Political Process* (Princeton, N.J.: Princeton University Press, 1988), p. 5.

11. *City of Boerne v Flores*, 138 L Ed 2d 624 (1997), at 638, 641.

12. *Marbury v Madison*, 1 Cranch 137 at 177 (1803).

13. Lon L. Fuller, *The Morality of Law* (New Haven, Conn.: Yale University Press, 1964), p. 191. Fuller concludes his book with a plea for "an analysis of the social processes that constitute the reality of law." (p. 242) A classic expression of legal realism is Jerome Frank, *Law and the Modern Mind* (New York: Tudor Pub. Co., 1936). For more on this and other theories of legal philosophy, see Surya Prakash Sinha, *Jurisprudence: Legal Philosophy in a Nutshell* (St. Paul, Minn.: West Pub., 1993).

14. Jerome Frank, *Courts on Trial* (New York: Atheneum, 1970), Chap. XVI. Frank's criticism echoes his broader critique of law, known as legal realism, which seeks to demythologize and demystify law, emphasizing instead the social, psychological, and political forces that explain judicial decisions.

15. Ralph Nader, "Law Schools and Law Firms," *The New Republic*, 11 October 1969, p. 21. See also Duncan Kennedy, *Legal Education and the Reproduction of Hierarchy: A Polemic Against the System* (Cambridge, Mass.: Afar, 1983).

16. Frank, *Courts on Trial*, p. 311.

17. David M. O'Brien, *Storm Center: The Supreme Court in American Politics* (New York: Norton, 1990), p. 13.

18. Theodore J. Lowi, "The State in Politics," in *Regulatory Policy and the Social Sciences*, ed. by Roger G. Noll (Berkeley, Calif.: University of California Press, 1985), p. 67.

19. Robert S. Summers, et al., *Law: Its Nature, Functions, and Limits* (St. Paul, Minn.: West Pub., 1986), p. 27.

20. Edward S. Corwin, "The Democratic Dogma and the Future of Political Science," *American Political Science Review* 23(August 1929): 592.

21. Alexander Hamilton, James Madison, and John Jay, *The Federalist Papers* (New York: New American Library, 1961), #64, p. 392; #75, p. 452.

2

The Last Word Debate Revisited

Neal Devins

Imagine the rights of women without *Roe v Wade*; the rights of racial minorities without *Brown v Board of Education*; or the rights of criminal defendants without *Miranda v Arizona*. For those who see the courts as powerful, vigorous, and potent proponents of change, that world would be horrific.[1] Indeed, the political furor over Clarence Thomas, Robert Bork, and other Supreme Court nominees is largely informed by the belief that Supreme Court justices wield enormous political power. This belief also explains, as Justice Antonin Scalia complained, why the justices are subject to "carts full of mail from the public, and streets full of demonstrators, urging us—their unelected and life-tenured judges . . .—to follow the popular will."[2] Nevertheless, nearly two hundred years after *Marbury v Madison* declared that it is the Court's "province and duty" to say "what the law is," the question of whether Supreme Court rulings bind elected officials remains controversial.

Starting with Ronald Reagan's 1986 elevation of William Rehnquist to chief justice, a vigorous debate has emerged over the potency of judicial decision making. Arguing that Supreme Court decisions do not bind government officials "henceforth and forevermore," Reagan Attorney General Edwin Meese sought to limit the impact of Court decisions on abortion, religious exercise, and states' rights.[3] More recently, the Clinton Education Department has sparked controversy by investigating the University of Texas for complying with a federal appeals court decision prohibiting affirmative action in admissions.[4]

The willingness of the Reagan and Clinton administrations to discount judicial decisions they dislike underscores the potency of social and political forces in defining constitutional values. The Supreme Court is well aware of these forces. It sometimes calibrates its decisions to limit political reprisals. Moreover, when it declares itself the final word on the meaning of the Constitution, chances are that the Court feels especially challenged by the other branches.

Take *City of Boerne v Flores*, the Court's most recent invocation of judicial finality. The Religious Freedom Restoration Act, which *Boerne* invalidated, was a direct challenge to Court efforts to limit First Amendment protections to governmental conduct that targeted religion. When Bill Clinton signed the Act, he spoke unabashedly of "this act revers[ing] the Supreme Court" and of his conviction that elected government's view of religious liberty "is far more consistent with the intent of the Founders than [is] the Supreme Court."[5] Congressional sponsors of the measure condemned the Court's "degradation," "devastation," and "virtual elimination" of religious freedom.[6] To Supreme Court justices, these are fighting words and, as such, it is not surprising that the Court decided to fight back. Citing *Marbury*, the *Boerne* Court declared that "[t]he power to interpret the Constitution in a case or controversy remains in the Judiciary."[7] More striking, after proclaiming horror at the prospect that "[s]hifting legislative majorities could challenge the Constitution," *Boerne* suggests that popular government's role in affecting constitutional change is limited to "the difficult and detailed amendment process."[8]

Boerne's invocation of *Marbury* is hardly unusual. For most of its history, the Supreme Court has gone to great lengths to remind the American people that it alone delivers the final word on the Constitution's meaning. In 1857, the Court was sufficiently confident in its "high and independent character" that Associate Justice John Catron informed President-elect James Buchanan that, in the matter of *Dred Scott*, the Court would "decide and settle a controversy which has so long and seriously agitated the country."[9] One hundred years later, the Court conveyed a similar message in a quite different context. Responding to efforts by Arkansas governor Orval Faubus to stop court-ordered desegregation in Little Rock, the Court proclaimed that *Marbury* "declared the basic principle that the federal judiciary is supreme in the exposition of the law of the Constitution."[10]

This view, that constitutional truth derives solely from nine individuals (or a majority of them) sitting on the Supreme Court, also figured prominently in the abortion controversy. In its 1992 decision reaffirming the "central holding" of *Roe v Wade-Planned Parenthood v Casey*, the Court claimed the authority to resolve the abortion dispute, invoking "the Nation's commitment to the rule of law" and declaring that "the Court's interpretation of the Constitution calls the contending sides of a national controversy to end their national division by accepting a common mandate rooted in the Constitution."[11] One of *Roe's* fiercest critics, Robert Bork, echoed this theme, writing in 1990 that "the Constitution is the trump card in American politics, and judges decide what the Constitution means. When the Supreme Court invokes the Constitution . . . the democratic process is at an end."[12]

This portrayal of the Court as a player shaping policy through decisions having a nationwide impact, is anything but surprising. But the corresponding belief that Supreme Court decisions are the "last word" in constitutional disputes is overly parochial, ultimately shortsighted, and factually inaccurate. The Court may be the ultimate interpreter in a particular case, but not always the larger issue of which that case is a part. Congress, the White House, government agencies, interest groups, the general public, and the states all play critical roles in shaping constitutional values.

The above proposition is hardly novel. Indeed, for much of his long and distinguished career, Louis Fisher has called attention to the ways elected officials and the public at large participate in "constitutional dialogues" with the Court.[13]

Through meticulous research and penetrating analysis, Fisher has demonstrated that the courts hardly ever speak the last word on issues that matter to the nation. Rather than risk reprisals from the elected branches, sometimes courts purposefully steer clear of issues. Lou's work on war powers makes this point. Other times, after a decision proves politically unworkable, courts moderate, or overturn, their handiwork. Lou's examination of the Court's overruling its child labor and flag salute decisions highlights the power of populist resistance. Finally, through his work on the legislative veto decision, Lou has shown the willingness of elected officials to ignore constitutional rulings by the courts.

Thanks in part to this scholarship, legal academics no longer buy into the customary identification of the Supreme Court as the exclusive source of constitutional law.[14] Nevertheless, the myth of judicial exclusivity persists. The popular press treats Court rulings as definitive, law school casebooks typically identify constitutional law as the work of the Supreme Court, and lawmakers express doubt over their power to disagree with the Court.

This essay, like many before it, will show constitutional decision making to be a dynamic process involving all parts and levels of government. Yet, even if it was understood that the Court had the last word on the Constitution's meaning, judicial exclusivity would marginalize the Constitution.[15] Absent the constraints imposed by social and political forces, the Court's constitutional judgments will be less relevant and hence less stable. Demonstrating that the tugs and pulls of politics make the Constitution more relevant and more durable is this essay's larger objective.

I. Cross Currents in Constitutional Law

The historical record provides overwhelming evidence that other parts of government challenge the Court's constitutional reasoning, and that the Court is influenced by these challenges as well as the broader social currents which surround it. As noted by Ruth Bader Ginsburg a year before her appointment to the Supreme Court, judges "play an interdependent part in our democracy. They do not alone shape legal doctrine . . . they participate in a dialogue with other organs of government, and with the people as well."[16]

Marbury v Madison, the supposed foundation of judicial supremacy, nicely illustrates how politics and constitutional decision making are inextricably linked to each other.[17] When *Marbury* was decided, the Supreme Court and its chief justice, John Marshall, were under attack. Court foe Thomas Jefferson had just been elected president and, at his urging, Secretary of State James Madison openly challenged the judiciary's power to subject executive branch officers to court orders. Specifically, when William Marbury challenged Madison's failure to deliver to him a judicial commission, Madison refused to present a defense, thereby forcing the Court to decide the case without the benefit of the executive's arguments. Further complicating matters, were the Court to rule for Marbury, Marshall believed that his political enemies would push for his impeachment. Marshall took the impeachment threat seriously, contending that it would be better for the elected branches to reverse a Court opinion by statute than to impeach Supreme Court justices.

Marshall's challenge, therefore, was to craft an opinion that would both support judicial power over the elected branches and avoid a head-to-head confrontation between the judiciary and the executive. The solution was to first acknowledge the merits of Marbury's challenge, but then conclude that the Court was without jurisdiction to resolve the dispute. Along the way, the Court was also able to establish judicial review, holding unconstitutional the statute that granted it jurisdiction in the *Marbury* dispute.

Chief Justice Marshall's tactics in *Marbury* reveal that Supreme Court decision making cannot be divorced from its political context. Indeed, at the time of *Marbury*, constitutional decision making was dominated by the elected branches. Without a body of Supreme Court decisions to look to, Congress and the president had no choice but to engage in definitive constitutional interpretations. Correspondingly, when the courts did speak, elected officials did not treat these decisions as final.

In 1801, Thomas Jefferson declared the Alien and Sedition Act (which criminalized speech critical of the government) a constitutional "nullity" and pardoned everyone prosecuted under it. Asserting that judicial supremacy would transform the Constitution into "a mere thing of wax" that the courts "may twist and shape into any form they please," Jefferson placed no stock in Court decisions upholding the Act.[18]

A more dramatic example of the elected branches controlling constitutional decision making occurred in 1832, when President Andrew Jackson vetoed legislation rechartering the Bank of the United States. The fact that a unanimous Supreme Court had approved the Bank's chartering in *McCulloch v Maryland* was irrelevant: "The opinion of the judges," proclaimed Jackson, "has no more authority over Congress than the opinion of the Congress has over the judges, and on that point the President is independent of both." "Each public official who takes an oath to support the Constitution swears that he will support it as he understands it, and not as it is understood by others."[19] For this reason, Jackson— albeit in another context—is reputed to have said, "John Marshall has made his decision, let him enforce it."

Another insight into three-branch interpretation comes from the bitter struggle over slavery. Through *Dred Scott v Sandford*, the Court intended to "definitive[ly]" settle the issue of slavery. By holding that the right to own a slave was "distinctly and expressly affirmed in the Constitution,"[20] however, the Court deepened the schism that ultimately resulted in Civil War.

Dred Scott's status as the last word on slavery was immediately called into question, most notably by Abraham Lincoln. For

Lincoln, Court decisions were necessarily binding on the parties themselves *but* could not bind elected government to judicially imposed policymaking. Otherwise, the "people will have ceased to be their own rulers" if government policies are "to be irrevocably fixed by the decisions of the Supreme Court."[21]

The Supreme Court again found itself under sharp attack during the so-called *Lochner* era, a period from 1905 to 1937 in which the Court, in striking down about two hundred social and economic laws, both narrowly construed the authority of Congress and the states to regulate commerce and broadly construed the due process rights of employers. The Court's actions were universally condemned as a symbol of unprincipled judicial overreaching, and the *Lochner* era helped prompt President Franklin Delano Roosevelt's plan to enlarge the Court (from nine to fifteen justices) and pack it with jurists sympathetic to his New Deal reforms.

Roosevelt's Court-packing plan proved to be a political debacle.[22] Nevertheless, the Court buckled to popular opinion thanks to Roosevelt's victory in all but two states in 1936, as well as to populist attacks on the Court. Shortly after the defeat of the Court-packing plan, the Court announced several decisions accepting of New Deal programs. In explaining this transformation, Justice Owen Roberts recognized the extraordinary importance of public opinion in undoing the *Lochner* era: "Looking back, it is difficult to see how the Court could have resisted the popular urge for uniform standards throughout the country—for what in effect was a unified economy."[23]

The fact that judges, as Justice Benjamin Cardozo put it, cannot escape "the great tides and currents which engulf" the rest of us should comes as no surprise.[24] As such, it was inevitable that decisions like *Dred Scott* and *Lochner* would eventually collapse under the weight of changing social conditions. *Brown v Board of Education*, in contrast, reveals what can be accomplished when a court pays attention to those social and political forces that may be unleashed by its decisions.

Today, it seems inconceivable that *Brown's* basic declaration of racial equality tested the limits of judicial authority. When *Brown* was decided, however, segregation was so ingrained in the South that the outlawing of dual school systems promised social turmoil and massive resistance. To minimize Southern resistance, the justices sought to improve the acceptability of their decision by speaking in a single moderate voice. Specifically, *Brown* contains no judgmental rhetoric nor does it call for the immediate dismantling of segregated school systems.[25]

The story of school desegregation is revealing for other reasons. After the Court's monumental decision in *Brown*, Congress and the executive have framed most of the debate. By 1964, there was a growing recognition on Capitol Hill that *Brown's* promise of equal educational opportunity was rendered meaningless by Southern resistance. The solution was the 1964 Civil Rights Act, which, among other things, authorized Justice Department participation in school desegregation litigation and demanded that federal grant recipients be nondiscriminatory.[26] More significant, by pumping out billions of dollars of education aid, Congress supplied sufficient incentive for many school systems to comply with federal nondiscrimination standards. Between 1963 and 1968, the percentage of black children in all-black schools in the South dropped from 98 percent to 25 percent.[27]

Unlike *Brown*, where elected government reforms gave meaning to the Court's decision, the approval of mandatory busing remedies in *Swann v Charlotte-Mecklenburg Board of Education* is one of the Court's most criticized rulings. After two decades of congressional and White House resistance to mandatory reassignments, the Court has ceded to elected-branch desires and returned much of school desegregation to the control of state and local government. Specifically, the Rehnquist Court has made clear that federal courts should be willing to terminate desegregation orders, placing increasing emphasis on judicial restraint and extolling the virtue of local school board control.[28] At the same time, these rulings neither require nor encourage district court judges to terminate school desegregation injunctions. Consequently, although rejecting district court efforts to include suburban school systems in a Kansas City, Missouri, desegregation order, the Court did not interfere with intrusive district court orders requiring state-subsidized housing construction in Yonkers, New York, and imposing a statewide tax levy to support desegregation in Kansas City.

This give-and-take process reveals the extraordinary importance of social and political forces in shaping Court doctrine. The saga of abortion rights likewise underscores the interactive nature of constitutional decision making. Like *Brown*, *Roe v Wade* served as a critical trigger to the recognition of abortion rights. For example, when *Roe* was decided, a vigorous right-to-life movement successfully blocked pro-choice legislative reform efforts in Michigan, North Dakota, and elsewhere.[29] Consequently, although 64 percent of Americans supported the liberalization of abortion laws at that time, *Roe* nonetheless invalidated the laws of forty-six states.

Roe, too, prompted elected government into action.[30] From 1973 to 1989, 306 antiabortion measures were passed by forty-eight states. Congress and the White House also took aim at *Roe.* Through funding and other restrictions, the federal government revealed its hostility to expansive abortion rights. More significant, the Reagan and Bush administrations called for *Roe's* reversal.

As with court-ordered busing, two decades of elected government resistance (and the appointment of Supreme Court justices) resulted in the Court's returning much of this divisive issue to the states. By reaffirming "abortion rights" while repudiating *Roe's* stringent trimester test in favor of a more deferential "undue burden" standard, *Planned Parenthood v Casey* signalled the Court's willingness to uphold state regulation—if not prohibition—of abortion.

Abortion and school desegregation, like slavery before them, make a mockery of claims that Supreme Court decisions are authoritative and final. A permanent feature of our constitutional landscape is the ongoing volleys between elected government and the courts.

II. Judicial Exclusivity and Political Stability

Constitutional dialogues between the courts and elected government often result in more vibrant and durable constitutional interpretation. In particular, a final interpretive authority of the Constitution will make our most fundamental text stagnant and irrelevant, rather than preserve and honor it. In other words, the Constitution becomes more relevant and more stable when all branches and levels of government do battle with one another.

Courts and elected officials should both be activists in shaping governmental policy, in large measure, because judges and politicians sometimes react differently to social and political forces. Congress, for example, focuses its "energy mostly on the claims of large populous interests, or on the claims of the wealthy and the powerful, since that tends to be the best route to reelection."[31] Courts, in contrast, are less affected by these pressures, for judges possess life tenure. Accordingly, because special interest group pressures affect courts and elected officials in different ways, a government-wide decision-making process encourages a full-ranging consideration of the costs and benefits of different policy outcomes.

This politicization of constitutional discourse, while contributing to partisan value-laden constitutional interpretation, is better than the alternatives—legislative or judicial supremacy. Legislative supremacy, as *Marbury* recognized, would blur the line separating the Constitution from ordinary laws. Moreover, subject to the pressures of reelection, "legislatures are too likely to get caught up in the passions of the moment, be they flag burning, alleged communists in the State Department, to the need to really sock it to various types of criminal defendants."[32] For progressives and conservatives alike, lawmakers' propensity to do that which is politically expedient makes legislative supremacy unpalatable.

Judicial exclusivity, like legislative supremacy, creates more problems than it solves. "When technologies are changing rapidly, when facts or values are unclear and when democracy is in a state of moral flux, courts [with limited factfinding capacity and inability to respond quickly to changing circumstances] should recognize that they may not have the best or final answers."[33] Moreover, lacking the powers of purse and sword, as *Casey* recognized, the Court's authority is necessarily tied to "the people's acceptance of the Judiciary."[34]

No doubt, this politicization of constitutional discourse will contribute to partisan value-laden constitutional analysis.[35] Nevertheless, complex social policy issues are ill suited to the winner-take-all nature of litigation. Emotionally charged and highly divisive issues are best resolved through political compromises that yield middle-ground solutions, rather than through an absolutist and often rigid judicial pronouncement. Witness the ongoing controversy over the separation of church and state. On one side of the divide, separationists claim that government may only employ secular means to achieve secular ends. On the other side, revisionists claim that the prohibition against the establishment of religion only bars the establishment of a national religion by the federal government.

Strict adherence to either separationist or revisionist thinking leads to unacceptable results. Strict compliance with separationist thinking would place religion at a positive disadvantage compared to secular worldviews or cultural expressions. Separationist theory, if carried to its logical extreme, would require the removal of "In God We Trust" from our currency and the words of some of the great works of art at our publicly funded museums; an end to tax exemption for religiously affiliated institutions as well as churches; and the elimination of chaplains from the armed services and religion from the curriculum of our state universities. Revisionists, by ignoring the dangers inherent in close church-state entanglement, commit similar error. Application of their theory would allow the states to limit public funds, public employment opportunities, and so on, to the sect of its choosing without violating the Establishment Clause.

The practical difficulties of validating either separationist or revisionist positions highlight the dilemma that courts face in resolving constitutional disputes. Were court decisions to have last-word status, this dilemma would be far worse. Because winner-take-all litigation does not favor middle-ground approaches, politically workable solutions often require elected government intervention. Witness, for example, *Immigration and Naturalization Service v Chadha*.[36] Its 1983 invalidation of the so-called legislative veto[37] has been disregarded by both the White House and Congress. Neither Congress nor the executive branch found it workable because of the static model of government offered by the Court. Agencies yearned for discretionary authority to advance their policy agendas; Congress needed to check its legislative delegations. Consequently, in the fourteen years since *Chadha*, well over three hundred legislative veto provisions have been enacted into law.[38]

More striking, ten years after it upheld the independent counsel in *Morrison v Olson*, lawmakers, legal academics, and pundits generally agree that the statute is constitutionally suspect. Yet, thanks to *stare decisis* and other limitations, it is unlikely that the Court will reconsider its handiwork. That task, instead, is reserved to elected officials. Since Court decisions are necessarily bound by both lawyers' arguments and the available facts, it is inevitable that the Court will make mistakes—mistakes that only majoritarian institutions can cure.

Judicial supremacy yields unworkable solutions, not a more equitable world. "Government by lawsuit," as Justice Robert Jackson warned, "leads to a final decision guided by the learning and limited by the understanding of a single profession—the law."[39] Alexander Bickel puts the matter more directly—"doubt[ing] the Court's capacity to develop 'durable principles' " and therefore doubting "that judicial supremacy can work and is tolerable."[40]

To be sure, those who believe that Congress is not "ideologically committed or institutionally suited to search for the meaning of constitutional values"[41] may question the practicality of this dynamic decision-making model. Populist constitutional interpretation, however, serves as an important foil for the Court. In so doing, elected government interpretation makes the Constitution more relevant and more durable.

The saga of abortion rights underscores the appropriately interactive nature of constitutional decision making. *Planned Parenthood v Casey*, by paving the way for significant state regulation of abortion, makes clear that the Court will bend to the social and political forces which surround it. *Casey*, however, did not trigger an antiabortion revolution. According to Alan Guttmacher Institute studies, "antiabortion legislators [have] heeded [*Casey*] . . . and curtailed their attempts to make abortion illegal."[42] In 1994, for example, no legislation was introduced to outlaw abortion. Furthermore, in the two years following *Casey*, one-third of abortion-related legislative initiatives would have guaranteed the right to abortion. Finally, of the handful of abortion-restricting regulations adopted since *Casey*, all involve restrictions approved by the Court—waiting periods, informed consent, and parental notification.

Casey appears to have stabilized, if not resolved, the abortion dispute. While the Supreme Court eviscerated *Roe*'s trimester standard, the post-*Casey* calm reveals that *Roe* shaped elected government attitudes. Contrary to the pre-*Roe* period, during which forty-six states either prohibited or severely limited abortion access, abortion rights are now a secure feature of our constitutional landscape.

Without question, to a pro-choice advocate, *Casey*'s balance sells out important interests of women, and, to a pro-lifer, it permits moral outrages to continue. But there is no realistic alternative to *Casey*'s balancing act. The political upheaval that followed *Roe* reveals the unworkability of a strident pro-choice jurisprudence. But a jurisprudence allowing the prohibition of abortions is equally unworkable. In the years before *Roe*, when nontherapeutic abortions were prohibited in nearly early stage, abortions were almost as common as they are today.[43] Ultimately, abortion is too divisive for either pro-choice or pro-life absolutism to rule the day. Absent the constitutional dialogue that followed *Roe*, however, the politically unworkable trimester standard would have remained in place.

III. Conclusion: How to Challenge the Court

Elected officials must not shy away from their responsibility to interpret the Constitution and, when necessary, challenge the Court. Complex social policy issues, especially those that implicate constitutional values, are best resolved through "the sweaty intimacy of creatures locked in combat."[44]

City of Boerne v Flores, invalidating legislative efforts to define
the content of First Amendment religious liberty protections, does
not call into question elected government's broad authority to limit
the effect of Supreme Court decisions.[45] To begin with, *Boerne* says
nothing about Congress's authority to control federal programs or
its power to place conditions on the receipt of federal funds (including the denial of federal funding to disfavored activities). Moreover,
while specifying that Congress's authority to enforce the Fourteenth
Amendment is limited to "legislation which deters or remedies
constitutional violations," the Court acknowledged that "the line
between measures that remedy or prevent unconstitutional actions
and measures that make a substantive change in the governing
law is not easy to discern."[46] Correspondingly, in recognizing that
"Congress must have wide latitude in determining" whether corrective legislation is, in fact, remedial, *Boerne* acknowledged Congress's
power to engage the Court in constitutional dialogues.[47]

Boerne, moreover, also makes clear that elected officials need
to engage the Court in a dialogue, not a shouting match. Rather
than encourage dialogue over the Constitution's meaning, the Religious Freedom Restoration Act (RFRA) sought to silence the Court.
Specifically, because the RFRA calls for "the most demanding test
known to constitutional law,"[48] the Court's role in defining the
parameters of First Amendment religious liberty protections was
limited to clarifying ambiguous language in the RFRA and not
interpreting the Constitution. Backed into a corner, the Court fought
fire with fire. Telling Congress that "[o]ur national experience
teaches that the Constitution is preserved best when each part of
the government respects both the Constitution and the proper actions and determinations of the other branches,"[49] the Court invalidated the statute and celebrated its status as ultimate interpreter
of the Constitution.

Over time, *Boerne*'s suggestion that Court constitutional interpretations are final and definitive will give way to those social and
political forces which prompted the RFRA in the first place. After
all, the breadth of support for the RFRA both within and outside
of Congress makes it "difficult to imagine a piece of legislation that
could more powerfully demonstrate a societal consensus concerning
the meaning of a constitutional provision."[50] While the RFRA went
too far—taking this consensus and shoving it down the justice's
throats—*Boerne* hardly forbids subsequent legislative entreaties.
Indeed, *Boerne*'s author, Anthony Kennedy, informed lawmakers at
his confirmation hearing that they "would be fulfilling their duty"

by limiting the effects of Supreme Court decisions that they think are "wrong under the Constitution."[51]

∞∞

No single institution has the final word on constitutional questions. What is "final" at one stage of our political development may be reopened at some later date, leading to fresh interpretations and overrulings of past judicial doctrines. Admittedly, as Walter Murphy wrote, "[t]here is a magnetic attraction to the notion of an ultimate constitutional interpreter just as there is a magnetic pull to the idea of some passkey to constitutional interpretation that will, if properly turned, always open the door to truth, justice and the American way."[52] But just as finality is not the language of politics, constitutional decision making too is a never-ending process. Whether the issue is abortion, race, or the rights of religious minorities, judges and lawmakers are likely to shape the Constitution and each other.

This process of "ambition counteracting ambition" is central to our system of divided government. "We do not accept," as Louis Fisher put it, "the concentration of legislative power on Congress or executive power on the President. For the same reason, we cannot permit judicial power and constitutional interpretation to reside only in the courts."[53] Moreover, contrary to suggestions that judicial supremacy is necessary to stave off "interpretive anarchy,"[54] social and political forces outside the courts help make the Constitution more relevant, more vital. Bickel described the courts as engaged in a "continuing colloquy" with political institutions and society at large, a process in which constitutional principle is "evolved conversationally not perfected unilaterally."[55] By empowering "we the people" through their elected representatives, it also makes the Constitution more vibrant, more durable, and more democratic.

Notes

1. For an argument that courts do not matter, see Gerald N. Rosenberg, *The Hollow Hope* (1991). Rosenberg's analysis, while significant and provocative, is not persuasive. This chapter, in part, will show that courts play an integral—if not determinative—role in constitutional decision making. For more detailed treatments of Rosenberg, see Neal Devins,

Judicial Matters, 80 Calif. L. Rev. 1027 (1992); Peter Schuck, *Public Law Litigation and Social Reform*, 102 Yale L. J. 17663 (1993).

2. *Webster v Reproductive Health Services*, 492 US 490, 535 (1989) (Scalia, J., concurring).

3. Edwin Meese, *The Law of the Constitution*, 61 Tulane L. Rev. 983 (1987).

4. Terrence J. Pell, "Texas Must Choose Between a Court Order and a Clinton Edict," *Wall Street Journal*, 2 April 1997, sec. A-15.

5. President's Remarks on Signing the Religious Freedom Restoration Act of 1993, 2 Pub. Papers 2000 (Nov. 16, 1993).

6. 139 *Congressional Record* H2360 (daily ed. May 11, 1993) (statement of Rep. Schumer); *Id.* at H2361 (statement of Rep. Orton); *Id.* at H2359 (statement of Rep. Nadler).

7. 117 S.Ct. 2157, 2166 (1997).

8. *Id.*

9. John B. Moore, ed., 10 *The Works of James Buchanan* 106 n.1 (1908–11).

10. *Cooper v Aaron*, 358 US 1, 18 (1958).

11. 505 US 833, 867 (1992).

12. Robert H. Bork, *The Tempting of America: The Political Seduction of the Law* 3 (1990).

13. Fisher's books include *Constitutional Dialogues* (1988), *Constitutional Conflicts Between Congress and the President* (3d ed., 1991), *Presidential War Power* (1995), *Political Dynamics of Constitutional Law* (with Neal Devins) (2d ed., 1996), *The Politics of Shared Power* (4th ed., 1998).

14. Robert F. Nagel, *Judicial Power and American Character: Censoring Ourselves in an Anxious Age* (1994); Neal Devins, ed., Elected Branch Influences in Constitutional Decisionmaking, 56 Law & Contemp. Probs., Autumn 1993, at 1, 3–4; Barry Friedman, *Dialogue and Judicial Review,* 91 Mich. L. Rev. 577 (1993); Michael J. Klarman, *Rethinking the Civil Rights and Civil Liberties Revolutions,* 82 Va. L. Rev. 1 (1996); Sanford Levinson, *Could Meese Be Right This Time?*, 61 Tul. L. Rev. 1071 (1987); Michael Stokes Paulsen, *The Most Dangerous Branch: Executive Power to Say What the Law Is,* 83 Geo. L.J. 217 (1994); David A. Strauss, *Presidential Interpretation of the Constitution,* 15 Cardozo L. Rev. 113 (1993); Robin West, *The Aspirational Constitution,* 88 Nw. U. L. Rev. 241 (1993); Mark Tushnet, "The Constitution Outside the Courts" (unpublished manuscript).

15. Larry Alexander and Fred Schauer make precisely the opposite argument in their article *On Extrajudicial Constitutional Interpretation.* 110 Harv. L. Rev. 1359 (1997). For Alexander and Schauer, judicial supremacy is necessary to stave off "interpretive anarchy." This chapter, while not a response to their article, explains why I think the Alexander-Schauer position is incorrect.

16. *Speaking in a Judicial Voice,* 67 N.Y.U. L. Rev. 1185, 1198 (1992).

17. See Fisher and Devins, *supra* note 13 at 25–35.

18. Albert Bergh, ed., 11 *Writings of Thomas Jefferson* 215.

19. James D. Richardson, ed., 3 *A Compilation of the Messages and Papers of the President,* 1789–1897, 144.

20. 60 US 383, 451 (1856).

21. 7 *Papers of the President,* 1789–1897, 3210.

22. See William Leuchtenberg, *The Constitution in the Age of Roosevelt* 132–62 (1995).

23. Owen Roberts, *The Court and the Constitution* 61 (1951).

24. Benjamin Cardozo, *The Nature of the Judicial Process* 168 (1921).

25. On *Brown's* Limits, see J. Harvie Wilkinson III, *The Supreme Court and Southern School Desegregation, 1955–1970: A History and Analysis,* 64 Va. L. Rev. 485 (1978).

26. Pub. L. No. 88-352. For further discussion, see Fisher & Devins *supra* note 13 at 242–56.

27. See Gary Orfield, *Public School Desegregation in the United States, 1968–1980,* 5 (1983).

28. *Board of Education v Dowell,* 498 US 237, 248 (1991); *Freeman v Pitts,* 503 US 467, 490 (1992).

29. See David J. Garrow, *Liberty and Sexuality* 576–77 (1993).

30. For a case study treatment, see Neal Devins, *Shaping Constitutional Values,* 56–120 (1996).

31. Steven G. Calabresi, *Thayer's Clear Mistake,* 88 Nw. U.L. Rev. 269, 273 (1993).

32. *Id.*

33. Cass Sunstein, "Supreme Caution: Once Again the High Court Takes Only Small Steps," *Washington Post,* 6 July 1997, sec. C-1.

34. *Planned Parenthood v Casey,* 120 L. Ed. 2d 674, 707 (1992).

35. See Louis Michael Seidman and Mark V. Tushnet, *Remnants of Belief* (1996).

36. 462 US 919 (1983).

37. The legislative veto is a procedure by which departments or agencies would make proposals that would become law unless rejected by a majority vote of one or both houses of Congress.

38. See Louis Fisher, *The Legislative Veto: Invalidated, It Survives,* 56 Law & Contemp. Probs. 273 (Autumn 1993).

39. Robert H. Jackson, *The Struggle for Judicial Supremacy: A Study of a Crisis in American Power Politics* 291 (1941).

40. Alexander Bickel, *The Supreme Court and the Idea of Progress* 99 (1970).

41. Owen M. Fiss, *Foreward: The Forms of Justice,* 93 Harv. L. Rev. 1, 10 (1979).

42. *State Reproductive Health Monitor* (New York: Alan Guttmacher Inst.), May 1994, at ii.

43. See Rosenberg, *supra* note 1 at 178–80.

44. Alexander M. Bickel, *The Least Dangerous Branch,* 261 (1962).

45. For an elaboration of why I think *Boerne* is of limited reach, see Neal Devins, *How Not to Challenge the Court,* 39 Wm. & Mary L. Rev. (forthcoming 1998).

46. *Boerne,* 117 S. Ct. at 2164.

47. *Id.*

48. *Id.* at 2171.

49. *Id.* at 2172.

50. Daniel O. Conkle, *The Religious Freedom Restoration Act: The Constitutional Significance of an Unconstitutional Statute,* 56 Mont. L. Rev. 39, 89 (1995).

51. *Nomination of Anthony M. Kennedy to be Associate Justice of the Supreme Court of the United States: Hearings Before the Senate Comm. on the Judiciary,* 100th Cong. 223 (1987) (statement of Anthony Kennedy, Supreme Court nominee).

52. Walter F. Murphy, *Who Shall Interpret? The Quest for the Ultimate Constitutional Interpreter,* 48 Rev. Politics 401, 417 (1986).

53. *Constitutional Dialogues* at 279.

54. Alexander & Schauer, *supra* note 15 at 1379.

55. Bickel, *supra* note 43 at PIN.

3

Diplomacy, Foreign Affairs, and Coordinate Review

Michael J. Glennon

I am honored to pay tribute to one of the preeminent legal scholars of our era. Louis Fisher, through a quarter of a century of testimony and lecture, article and memo, has done as much as anyone to close the gap between the world of thought and the world of action, in an era when the academy seems more and more isolated from government.

Fisher's most enduring contribution to the law of diplomacy lies, I believe, in demonstrating the inexorable link between constitutionalism and foreign policy. In repeated controversies over the years involving the most profound national commitments, he has reminded presidents and legislators and judges—many who would have preferred to have forgotten—that our first loyalty is to the United States Constitution; that we cannot play constitutional hopscotch to reach a preordained policy outcome; and that to do so weakens not only the Constitution but the foreign policy that is supposedly advanced.

Of course, opinions differ as to what the Constitution actually means in those interbranch disputes. And opinions differ, too, concerning whose interpretation is authoritative. *Marbury v Madison* generated a widespread belief that the Constitution is what the Supreme Court says it is. Marshall told us that it is "emphatically the province and duty of the judicial department to say what the law is."[1] That observation seems, at least at a civics-book level, to resolve the issue: the courts are the final arbiter of the Constitution. But suppose the courts have not spoken; is the President or Congress under any constitutional obligation in the face of judicial silence? For that matter, are the political branches bound by the Supreme Court's interpretation of the Constitution? When—if ever— are they coequal interpreters of the document?

Viewed through the prism of Fisher's prodigious scholarship, foreign affairs disputes present rich material for examining these questions. United States courts have been uncharacteristically silent in the international realm; because the parties frequently are found to lack standing, or because the action is deemed not ripe for review, or because the case is thought to present a political question, courts often dismiss foreign affairs disputes as "nonjusticiable"—i.e., as not suitable for judicial resolution. Even when the judiciary does settle a dispute, it is sometimes contended that the controversy resolved by the courts in an earlier dispute is always necessarily different from the one presented to the courts in a later controversy, or that that court's decision is not controlling and that the political branches have a "coordinate" right to construe the Constitution. Because the stakes in foreign affairs disputes are often enormous, many in Congress and the Executive Branch find such approaches attractive.

In this essay, I examine two central questions that are a focus of Fisher's scholarship. The first inquiry—the "what" question— concerns sources of constitutional power. What sources ought governmental decision makers properly look to for the purpose of interpreting the Constitution? The second inquiry—the "who" question—concerns the identity of the final arbiter of the Constitution's meaning, if there is a final arbiter, raising the recurrent debate over "coordinate review."

As will be seen, I emphatically agree with Fisher that acts of all three branches affect the Constitution's meaning. I suggest, in fact, that law and political science are not oppositional categories, and I will attempt to show that constitutional law in fact *subsumes* political science as well as history. I am led to conclude that the political branches can be bound by constitutional principles even in the face of judicial silence. On the other hand, when the courts do speak, I would accord their decisions greater weight than would Fisher; for reasons that I will outline, I have reservations about his approach to the question of coordinate review.

⊙⊙

Is Congress or the president under any constitutional obligation when the courts say (or have said) nothing? At the outset the answer depends on one's view of what law is. If there is no law absent judicial articulation, then there is no point in proceeding further. The matter is relegated to the give-and-take of politics. If, on the other hand, law does exist even if the courts don't say so, then a constitutional obligation may attach.

Holmes believed that law was merely "the prophesies of what the courts will do."[2] This version of positivism (if not legal realism) was hardly new, having been expressed in a perhaps stronger form by John Austin. Austin, in the so-called imperative theory, contended that law was a command by sovereign to subject—a habit of obedience to commands—and that absent a sanction or penalty imposed on violators, the law was not law.[3] The Austinian position held sway for some years, but now seems to have been quite thoroughly refuted. H. L. A. Hart showed that what we mean by law does indeed exist beyond the realm of command backed by coercion; law does not require an authoritatively imposed penalty in the event of its violation, let alone an authoritative reiteration or interpretation by a court.[4] So the alternative to judicially articulated rules is now a lawless vacuum. Consider a perennially favorite law school hypothetical:

> You are asked, as an adviser to the president, whether it would be constitutional to name Richard Nixon the Duke of San Clemente. You realize that no one would likely have standing to challenge the validity of the act. You also realize that the act is expressly prohibited by the text of the Constitution. Would you advise the president, because no court will ever rule his act invalid, that he can lawfully proceed to name Nixon Duke?

Probably not. The president is bound by constitutional norms even though those norms are not judicially enforced. A case such as *Goldwater v Carter*[5] therefore does not tell us that the president is constitutionally free to terminate a treaty without congressional consent; it merely tells us that the courts will not tell us whether he may. I therefore disagree with Fisher when he asserts broad latitude on the part of the political branches operating in the face of judicial silence. He writes: "When courts decide to duck a case by using threshold devices of standing and other techniques, the political branches have the first and last word on constitutional issues. Indeed, they have the only word."[6] Not so, in my view; the political branches may have the first, last—and only—word in such a situation, but their discretion is not unlimited; as I will point out, traditional sources of constitutional power still circumscribe that discretion by providing parameters within which good faith constitutional interpretation must occur. The president therefore may be precluded constitutionally from terminating a treaty in just the manner that the president is constitutionally precluded from naming a duke.

May be precluded; how do we know whether he/she *is* precluded? I have suggested elsewhere that analysis of this question might benefit from the consideration of what is known in international law as the doctrine of sources. The notion is that the underlying question concerns rules about rules[7]—to what sources we may properly resort in determining whether a purported rule is really a rule, really law. In the international legal system there exists a codified list of sources to which resort is permissible. This list is set out in an annex to the United Nations Charter, called the Statute of the International Court of Justice. Article 38 of the Statute lists the following as proper reference points: "(a) international conventions, whether general or particular, establishing rules expressly recognized by the contesting states; (b) international custom, as evidence of a general practice accepted as law; (c) the general principles of law recognized by civilized nations; (d) . . . judicial decisions and the teachings of the most highly qualified publicists of the various nations, as subsidiary means for the determination of rules of law."[8]

I suggest that the U.S. constitutional system is sustained by a similar set of sources of authority—that, in asking, say, whether the president can act alone to terminate a treaty, we are in reality asking, initially, to what source(s) we might properly refer to an answer. If the first source is not dispositive, we might then refer to a second, and then, if it won't do the trick, to a third. I refer to these tiers of sources as primary, secondary, and tertiary. Primary sources are the text of the Constitution and case law. The secondary source is constitutional custom. And the tertiary sources are the intent of the framers and functional considerations. When a rule is validated by one or more of those sources—when a candidate meets the qualifications for rulehood—then it is properly regarded as a constitutional norm.[9] The recent debate over "originalism" can be seen as an argument over whether the framers' intent counts as a source and, if so, how much.

To continue with the same example, the text of the Constitution is silent with respect to treaty termination; in contrast to the power to make treaties, which is conferred upon the president and two-thirds of the Senate, the Constitution does not in words confer power to terminate treaties upon the president, the president and the Senate, the Senate alone, the Congress, or the president and the Congress. But the absence of an explicit textual grant of the power to terminate treaties does not mean that there is no constitutional law on the matter. Rather, it means that resort to extrinsic sources is necessary.

What source properly comes next? I will not rehearse the entire argument here; suffice it to say that my next stop is case law. Even though the text is not dispositive—*because* the text is not dispositive—the courts may have had occasion to interpret the text. If they have had such occasion, it would be untoward to give controlling weight to custom, the framers' intent, or functional considerations, all of which presumably were taken into account by the courts in fashioning the announced rule.

If, on the other hand, the courts have not had occasion to consider the issue, I refer next to constitutional custom. At this point the analysis becomes a bit more elaborate. As in international law, not every practice constitutes a custom, much less one that takes on normative status. I consider a series of acts a practice only if the acts are consistent and carried out over a sufficiently long period of time, during an era of relative normalcy. I regard a practice as a custom only if it is seen as a juridical norm by all pertinent parties to its potential creation. And I think of a custom as having normative weight only if it originated in the days when the Founding Fathers ran the government, thus giving some evidence that this custom is what they intended. In effect, this combines the probative weight of two sources of authority. And if the courts have said nothing and if no constitutional custom exists—which turns out to be true of treaty termination—then I still do not conclude that there is no constitutional law on the matter. Rather, I suggest that resort to two final, or tertiary sources, is then appropriate, and that it is difficult to establish any priority between them.

One tertiary source is the framers' intent. I place it tied for last on the list of sources for reasons that are well known. No "official" records were kept, beyond, of course, the text upon which the Founding Fathers agreed. Their true "intent," to the extent known, might well be said to rest only upon the text that they produced. James

Madison, the principal notetaker, did so unofficially. Though Madison kept notes, these were not published until forty years later. Several others also recorded their recollections, but we do not know whether they are accurate or complete. Nor do we know how many delegates were present when the reported remarks were made, or whether those delegates agreed or disagreed with the reported comments. Finally, a strong case can be made that the real "framers" are not the Philadelphia delegates at all but the delegates to the state-ratifying conventions—those who actually voted on the Constitution.

The other tertiary source is functional: taking institutional considerations into account, which branch, in light of its structure and composition, is best suited to handle the matter? Is speed or secrecy critical? If so, the Executive may be best suited to handle the job. Is deliberation and diversity of opinion important? If so, Congress may be preferred. In the case of treaty termination, I conclude that institutional features of the Executive predominate, and that the termination of treaties by the president, acting alone, is thus constitutionally appropriate.

Whether powers are plenary or concurrent is analyzed in the same way. For example, the president may have power constitutionally to terminate a treaty if Congress also has power to do so, but only if the act is carried out before Congress has acted. In such an instance, the two branches have concurrent power. In *Goldwater,* the president terminated the treaty in the face of congressional silence concerning the desirability of termination, so I would view his act as constitutionally permitted. However, some presidential powers are not subject to congressional control; these are plenary. Congress too is possessed of powers not exercisable by the Executive without prior congressional approval. These are plenary powers of Congress and include the power to choose to place the nation at war and the power to appropriate funds for governmental expenditure. Rather like the commerce clause, there are thus additional double-edged constitutional provisions that at once both permit and prohibit. As the commerce clause permits Congress to regulate commerce among the states, so too it prohibits the states from regulating some such commerce without congressional approval. As the appropriations, war and treaty clauses permit Congress (or the Senate) to authorize certain presidential acts, so too they prohibit the president from carrying out those acts (placing the nation at war, expending funds without congressional approval, making a treaty) without approval.

Plenary powers are distinguished from concurrent powers in the same manner—by reference to text, cases, custom, intent, and function. Thus one concludes that the power to pardon resides in the Executive, and that that power is exclusive, because it has been affirmed by the Supreme Court. One concludes that the power to recognize and to de-recognize foreign governments resides in the president, and exclusively in the president, because that power has been exercised exclusively by the chief executive, without congressional challenge, since the reception of Citizen Genet (and recognition of the government of revolutionary France) by President George Washington. And, one concludes, the Senate has power to condition its consent to treaties, notwithstanding presidential objection, because it has done so numerous times without challenge by the Executive since it conditionally approved the Jay Treaty in 1793.

It is these sources that courts draw upon when they interpret the Constitution. In some cases, such as *Dames & Moore v Regan*[10] and *Haig v Agee,*[11] the Supreme Court has relied heavily upon custom, apparently viewing it as determinative. In others, such as *Myers v United States*[12] and *Humphrey's Executor v United States,*[13] the Court has given controlling weight to the framers' intent. In *United States v Nixon*[14] and *United States v Curtiss-Wright Export Corp.,*[15] on the other hand, the Court relied upon functional considerations in allocating power. And it is from these same sources that the political branches can and do draw when they interpret the Constitution. While many members of Congress were dissatisfied with President Gerald Ford's pardon of Richard Nixon, or with President Jimmy Carter's de-recognition of the Republic of China and recognition of the People's Republic of China, not one member proposed legislation that would have overturned either act, probably because each act was seen (for different reasons) as falling within the scope of the present's plenary powers. Congress, as noted above, had never seriously challenged the president's sole recognition power, and when Congress did challenge an exercise of the pardon power, the Supreme Court found that power to be exclusively presidential.[16]

It is debatable whether congressional procedures for addressing constitutional questions are sufficiently reliable.[17] No formalized procedure exists in either house of Congress for addressing constitutional questions. There is no requirement, for example, that

a committee report contain a section on constitutional issues analogous to the section on budgetary impact. (Actually, that might be
a good idea.) Few would quarrel with the suggestion that legislative consideration of constitutional questions is, consequently,
uneven. Congress held substantial hearings on some recent controversies, such as those concerning treaty interpretation, treaty termination, and amendment of the War Powers Resolution. In those
hearings, constitutional issues were examined at least as fully as
they would be in judicial pleadings or oral argument. On the other
hand, specific "hot potato" issues, such as the invasion of Panama
or Grenada, receive virtually no serious congressional attention.[18]
Politically, some matters are more easily considered in the abstract.
What is not debatable, however, is that the same sources available
to the courts to determine the meaning of the Constitution are as
readily available to Congress and the president, which is worth
emphasizing before reviewing those constitutional provisions that
arguably relate to coordinate review.

Those are several such provisions. The president, upon being
inaugurated, swears to "preserve, protect, and defend" the Constitution. It also obliges him to "take care that the laws be faithfully
executed." The Constitution denominates itself as the supreme law
of the land. Members of Congress, too, take an oath to support the
Constitution; like the president, they, too, are often required to
engage in the act of interpretation ancillary to compliance.

It is not novel, therefore, to think that a president might properly regard himself or herself as being constitutionally precluded
from naming a duke or breaching a Senate-added treaty condition—
even though the source from which that conclusion obtains is something other than case law. Nor would it be novel to think that members
of Congress ought to view themselves as constitutionally precluded
from purporting to countermand the recognition of a foreign government or to negotiate a certain treaty—even though the source is,
again, not case law. Both political branches have an obligation to
honor the Constitution and to engage in the preliminary act of interpretation, even when the courts are silent. Introducing *Constitutional Dialogues,* Fisher put it succinctly: "[C]onstitutional law is not
a monopoly of the judiciary."[19]

But suppose the courts are not silent? Are the political branches
permitted to interpret the Constitution in a manner inconsistent
with the interpretation of the Supreme Court? Could Congress

validly conclude that, constitutionally, the Supreme Court was wrong in *INS v Chadha*,[20] that the legislative veto is in fact constitutional, and proceed to enact additional legislative vetoes (as it has actually done)? Could a subsequent president validly conclude that, constitutionally, the Court was wrong in *United States v Nixon*,[21] that the claim of executive privilege should always trump the demands of the criminal justice system, and that a president may refuse to turn over subpoenaed materials to a federal prosecutor?

A similar claim was made in *Cooper v Aaron*,[22] where the legislature of Arkansas contended, in effect, that it was not bound by the Supreme Court's finding in *Brown v Board of Education*[23] that "separate but equal" schools violated the Fourteenth Amendment. The Supreme Court forcefully dismissed the legislature's argument in words that are worth recalling at length. The Court said:

> What has been said, in the light of the fact developed, is enough to dispose of the case. However, we should answer the premise of the actions of the Governor and Legislature that they are not bound by our holding in the Brown case. It is necessary only to recall some basic constitutional propositions which are settled doctrine. [*18] Article VI of the Constitution makes the Constitution the "supreme Law of the Land." In 1803, Chief Justice Marshall, speaking for a unanimous Court, referring to the Constitution as "the fundamental and paramount law of the nation," declared in the notable case of Marbury v. Madison, 1 Cranch 137, 177, that "It is emphatically the province and duty of the judicial department to say what the law is." This decision declared the basic principle that the federal judiciary is supreme in the exposition of the law of the Constitution, and that principle has ever since been respected by this Court and the Country as a permanent and indispensable feature of our constitutional system. It follows that the interpretation of the Fourteenth Amendment enunciated by this Court in the Brown case is the supreme law of the land, and Art. VI of the Constitution makes it of binding effect on the States "any Thing in the Constitution or Laws of any State to the Contrary notwithstanding." Every state legislator and executive and judicial officer is solemnly committed by oath taken pursuant to Art. VI, cl. 3, "to support this Constitution." Chief Justice Taney, speaking for a unanimous Court in 1859, said that this requirement reflected the framers' "anxiety to preserve it [the Constitution] in

full force, in all its powers, and to guard against resistance to or evasion of its authority, on the part of a State. . . ." Ableman v. Booth, 21 How. 506, 524. No state legislator or executive or judicial officer can war against the Constitution without violating his undertaking to support it. Chief Justice Marshall spoke for a unanimous Court in saying that: "If the legislatures of the several states may, at will, annul the judgments of the courts of the United States, and destroy the rights acquired under those judgments, the constitution itself becomes a solemn mockery. . . ." United States v. Peters, 5 Cranch 115, 136. A Governor who asserts a power to nullify a federal court order is similarly restrained. If he had such power, said Chief Justice Hughes, in 1932, also for a unanimous Court, "it is manifest that the fiat of a state Governor, and not the Constitution of the United States, would be the supreme law of the land; that the restrictions of the Federal Constitution upon the exercise of state power would be but impotent phrases. . . ." *Sterling v. Constantin*, 287 U.S. 378, 397–398.[24]

There seems an intuitive appeal to this argument for deference to the courts, socialized as we are in a culture of judicial supremacy. Surely, one might think, the Court need not reassess a rule every time the need arises to apply it. Chaos would reign. As Justice Frankfurter said, concurring in *Cooper*: "To yield to such a claim would be to enthrone official lawlessness, and lawlessness if not checked is the precursor of anarchy."[25]

On the other side, though, are considerations that the majority opinion does not address. These relate to the utility and method of constitutional change. We have, it is often said, a living Constitution. Its meaning changes over the years; it "was intended to endure for the ages."[26] The implication of the *Cooper* Court's opinion seems to be that governmental officials, in swearing to uphold the Constitution, undertake an obligation not to challenge settled doctrine. No legislator, it may be inferred, may constitutionally vote for a measure which if enacted would be unconstitutional. The Court takes care to use the word "state" to modify those legislators bound by this requirement, but there is no reason to believe that its reasoning would not apply to federal legislators as well; the issue is not in the end the supremacy of the federal government as against state governments, but the supremacy of the United States

Supreme Court as against all other governmental entities, state and federal.

Let us try for a moment to ignore the obvious and recurring gray-area problem: it is of course not always clear what the Court regards as constitutional and what it does not. So debates rage in pages such as these over the validity of the War Powers Resolution, or of state-imposed term limits on federal officials, or of "hate speech" limitations. The reach of the *Steel Seizure Case*[27] and *Powell v McCormack*[28] and *Brandenberg v Ohio*[29] is not self-evident; also out there are *United States v Curtiss-Wright Export Corp.*,[30] *United States v New York State Department of Taxation and Finance*,[31] and *Beauharnais v Illinois*.[32] It might be said that the obligation to obey attaches only to the "manifest Constitution," as Alexander Bickel called it, but this solution has a whiff of Yogi Berra in it, echoes of eliminating close calls at first base by moving the bag ten feet farther down the baseline. Where words are the medium of exchange, shades of gray are inevitable, and merely shifting the point of dispute does not transform gray into black or white. The problem is not resolved by concluding that the obligation to obey attaches only when it is clear, since the same argument is simply moved ten feet further, to whether the doctrine is clear or unclear. Calling something "manifest" does not make it manifest. So the analysis stays tidier if focus remains on the *Cooper* Court's implicit assumption that, four years after *Brown,* school desegregation was no longer a gray-area issue in that all officials of all governmental units have an indisputable obligation to obey its unreiterated rulings. The import thus seems to be that Congress cannot constitutionally keep enacting legislative vetoes in the face of *Chadha,* that states cannot criminalize flag-burning after *Texas v Johnson*,[33] and that states cannot require parental consent for abortions after *Roe v Wade*.[34]

Ah, there's the rub: we *can't* ignore the gray-area problem. Many of the key issues that confront state and federal legislators, judges and executive officials do not have a self-evident constitutional answer. Is the president bound to "take care" that the provision of the War Powers Resolution mandating withdrawal from hostilities after sixty days be "faithfully executed?" Reasonable people differ. Is a state legislator constitutionally precluded from voting for a parental-consent requirement after *Roe*? Difficulty arises not simply because of the gray-area problem—not simply because of doctrinal indeterminacy—but because of the *judiciary's* unpredictability even when the law is determinate. Judges change their minds. They die and are replaced. New presidents are elected and appoint new judges who interpret the Constitution differently. To what extent may a conscientious governmental official take the courts' unpredictability into account in deciding what to "obey"? Would not an iron-clad obligation to adhere to "existing case law" freeze the Constitution's evolution, providing no possibility to adaptation to changed times and circumstances? Did governmental officials at the time owe unquestioning obeisance to *Dred Scott*[35] or *Plessy v Ferguson*?[36] For how long after a case is decided must it be respected?

The tension underpinning these questions suffuses the constitutional system. We can permit litigation espousing theories that break new ground—but at the cost of compelling the courts to entertain frivolous claims.[37] We can permit challenge to existing rules—but at the cost of undermining their legitimacy. We can have constitutional movement—but at the cost of stability. The debate over coordinate constitutional review is, in the end, a debate over fundamental societal values, over creativity versus order, over innovation versus predictability. To the extent that interpretive authority is centralized, to the extent that the locus of power is the courts, to the extent that their construction of the Constitution counts more than that of coordinate branches, we choose one set of values over another. Trade-offs are inevitable.

Those trade-offs were reflected in the recent debate over amendment Rule 11 of the Federal Rules of Civil Procedure. The earlier rule was seen as permitting excessive, abusive litigation, even though it required an attorney to certify that to the best of his/her knowledge the pleadings were "well-grounded." The rule was rarely invoked, resulting in an amendment that imposed a supposedly more stringent standard of "reasonableness." This was expected to result in more rigorous application of the standard[38]—though critics claimed that the deference of frivolous claims was purchased by infringing attorneys' creativity.

Surprisingly, though, this value tension is seldom articulated at the constitutional level, and when it is, lower courts have gleaned little guidance from *Cooper*. In two recent cases the issue was placed in high relief by divided circuits. *Lear Siegler, Inc., v Lehman*,[39] a controversy in which the United States Senate and House of Representatives both intervened, involved a refusal by the secretary of the navy to comply with provisions of a law (the Competition in Contracting Act, or "CICA") on the ground that the law was unconstitutional. The power to disregard unconstitutional statutes, the

Executive argued, flows from the president's duty to uphold the Constitution and to faithfully execute the laws.

The Ninth Circuit Court of Appeals found this position "utterly at odds with the texture and plain language of the Constitution, and with nearly two centuries of judicial precedent. . . ."[40] The court concluded that "[t]o construe this duty to faithfully execute as implying the power to forbid their execution perverts the clear language of the 'take care' clause."[41]

In the same year, the Third Circuit seemingly came to an opposite conclusion. In *West Indian Co., Ltd. v Government of the Virgin Islands*[42] the Third Circuit Court of Appeals held that the executive was free not to defend in court a statute that it regarded as unconstitutional. However, the executive authority in question was the executive of the Virgin Islands, not the United States. Further, the alleged duty to represent flowed not from the United States Constitution but from territorial law. And, of course, refusal to defend a statute in court is less confrontational than an outright refusal to comply with it.

The *Cooper* Court did not recognize (let alone attempt to reconcile) these competing approaches. Justice Frankfurter did address them in his concurrence, but his comments raise more questions than they resolve. They too are worth recalling in some detail. He wrote:

> Being composed of fallible men, [the Supreme Court] may err. But revision of its errors must be by orderly process of law. The Court may be asked to reconsider its decisions, and this has been done successfully again and again throughout our history. Or, what this Court has deemed [37] its duty to decide may be changed by legislation, as it often has been, and, on occasion, by constitutional amendment. "But from their own experience and their deep reading in history, the Founders knew that Law alone saves a society from being rent by internecine strife or ruled by mere brute power however disguised. 'Civilization involves subjection of force to reason, and the agency of this subjection is law.' (Pound, *The Future of Law* (1937) 47 Yale L. J. 1, 13). The conception of a government by laws dominated the thoughts of those who founded this Nation and designed its Constitution, although they knew as well as the belittles of the conception that laws have to be made, interpreted and enforced by men. To that end, they set apart a body of men,

who were to be the depositories of law, who by their disciplined training and character and by withdrawal from the usual temptations of private interest may reasonably be expected to be 'as free, impartial, and independent as the lot of humanity will admit.' So strongly were the framers of the Constitution bent on securing a reign of law that they endowed the judicial office with extraordinary safeguards and prestige. No one, no matter how exalted his public office or how righteous his private motive, can be judge in his own case. That is what courts are for." United States v. United Mine Workers, 330 U.S. 258, 307–309 (concurring opinion). The duty to abstain from resistance to "the supreme Law of the Land," U.S. Const., Art. VI, para. 2, as declared by the organ of our Government for ascertaining it, does not require immediate approval of it nor does it deny the right of dissent. Criticism need not be stilled. Active obstruction or defiance is barred.[43]

If "active . . . defiance is barred," was enforcement of the Alien and Sedition Acts required? Had the Acts not been repealed, and had President Thomas Jefferson entertained (as he apparently did) a good-faith belief that those laws violated the First Amendment, would he nonetheless have been "barred" from construing the Constitution for himself, from (in his view) complying with his oath to "preserve, protect, and defend" the Constitution, and from declining to prosecute seditious newspaper editors? Should it matter that the courts had not spoken, that the validity of the Acts had not been adjudicated? Frankfurter seemed to think it did. He continued:

Our kind of society cannot endure if the controlling authority of the Law as derived from the Constitution is not to be the tribunal specially charged with the duty of ascertaining and declaring what is "the supreme Law of the Land." (See President Andrew Jackson's Message to Congress of January 16, 1833, II Richardson, Messages and Papers of the Presidents (1896 ed.), 610, 623.)[44]

So could one rightly conclude that, since the "tribunal specially charged" with doing so had not ascertained and declared that the Alien and Sedition Acts were valid, no enforcement duty attached? Was Jefferson free to engage in coordinate review because the Supreme Court had not, in effect, "occupied the field"?

It depends, Frankfurter seemed to say, on (1) whether the opinion addressed an underlying moral issue; and (2) whether the Supreme Court was closely divided: "Particularly is this so where the declaration of what "the supreme Law" commands on an underlying moral issue is not the dubious pronouncement of a gravely divided Court but is the unanimous conclusion of a long-matured deliberative process."[45] What constitutes an underlying moral issue is beyond the scope of this essay. Frankfurter did know one when he saw one, though, and underlying moral issues have nothing to do with mere custom, habit, or feeling:

> Local customs, however hardened by time, are not decreed in heaven. Habits and feelings they engender may be counteracted and moderated. Experience attests that such local habits and feelings will yield, gradually though this be, to law and education. And educational influences are exerted not only by explicit teaching. They vigorously flow from the fruitful exercise of the responsibility of those charged with political official power and from the almost unconsciously transforming actualities of living under law.[46]

People (and the legislators and executives they elect) may be wrong—morally wrong—in their customs, habits or feelings. However, they can always be educated morally, if not by schools (which hadn't seemed up to the task before *Brown*) then by law—as promulgated by, well, Felix Frankfurter. Why do he and other members of the Supreme Court have this power? Because in contrast to other governmental officials, who inevitably inject their own personal views into the process of constitutional interpretation, judges are above that pedestrian enterprise; the Constitution that *they* give us is pure, immune from the genetic and environmental influences that color the construction of the Document by lesser interpreters: "The Constitution is not the formulation of the merely personal views of the members of this Court, nor can its authority be reduced to the claim that state officials are its controlling interpreters."[47]

That is, to put it mildly, a peculiar view to be propounded by, of all people, Felix Frankfurter, the Frankfurter of deference to the outcome of political processes, the Frankfurter who dissented in *Baker v Carr*,[48] warning that what was there asked of the Court was "to choose among competing bases of representation—ultimately, really, among competing theories of political philosophy. . . ."[49] Frankfurter's rationale seems internally contradictory: if the Constitution does *not* derive from the "merely personal views" of its judicial expounders, how can they ever be "gravely divided" on what " 'the supreme Law' commands on an underlying moral issue"? Might Frankfurter think that abortion is not an "underlying moral issue"? Was not the judgement of the Arkansas legislature in *Cooper* also the "conclusion of a long-matured deliberative process"? Why is their interpretation of the Constitution trumped by the Court's?

It does not do, again, to say that the reason is that the Court (in *Brown*) had already occupied the field. Constitutional norms concerning segregation existed before *Brown*, just as constitutional norms concerning censorship existed before *Near v Minnesota*.[50] Had the Alien and Sedition Acts remained on the books, it is not self-evident that Jefferson's construction was wrong, or that every president to hold office before *Near* would have been obliged to prosecute sedition. Law existed before the Court said so; Jefferson acted on that belief in pardoning Republican newspaper editors convicted under the Acts (and in declining to prosecute editors who scurrilously attacked him during the presidential campaign of 1800).

Does it follow, by extension, that notions of "coordinate review" permit a president to decline to comply with any law that he/she believes in good faith to be unconstitutional? One rationale sometimes enlisted in support of that proposition is, ironically, a variation of Frankfurter's. The Supreme Court, it is suggested, would never have occasion to rule upon the constitutionality of a law or practice unless a case or controversy were created by executive noncompliance. So executive lawlessness merely creates a "test case" and thus upholds the constitutional scheme by giving an otherwise quiescent judiciary the requisite case or controversy to say what the law is.[51]

But precisely the opposite is often true: executive noncompliance can create non-justiciable disputes, as did (arguably) executive noncompliance with the Incompatibility Clause in *Schlesinger v Reservists Committee to Stop the War* and with the Taxing and Spending Clause in *United States v Richardson*.[52] It was, indeed, executive *compliance* with the law that ultimately resulted in the invalidation of the legislative veto. Had the Executive ignored the law and declined to regard itself as bound by the House resolution overturning the attorney general's stay of Chadha's deportation, Chadha's name would not be on that case because he would have been delighted with the result. It was far from clear, under standing doctrine prevalent at the time, whether any legislator would have been able to challenge the Executive's noncompliance. Similarly, executive *compliance* with a law can be the only way to get the courts involved. If, for example, the Alien and Sedition Acts had never been repealed, there is no question that they would ultimately have been held invalid when executive enforcement availed the right plaintiff the opportunity to challenge the Acts. "Ultimately" in that case may have been a long time; it was over a hundred years until the Supreme Court began to enforce the First Amendment. But the point is that the claim cannot be sustained that "coordinate review" by the Executive—executive law violation—is a necessary predicate for review by the courts. Executive law violation is not necessary for the Constitution to have play at the joints, and in some circumstances presidential breach can effectively preclude the very judicial review necessary for constitutional adaptation.

Back to the "ultimately" problem for a moment. Why should *any* period of enforcement be required? If Congress enacts a statute that, say, requires the immediate exile of all journalists who criticize former Speaker Newt Gingrich, is the president constitutionally obliged to enforce it *even once*—hoping that it is quickly struck down by the courts? The president, again, takes an oath to support the Constitution, which requires that he "take care" that this statute be "faithfully executed"; that duty is not imposed only with respect to statutes that the president *likes*. The chief executive is given an opportunity to escape enforcement responsibility—he/she can veto the law. And the veto can be carried out for any reason, including the belief that the bill is unconstitutional.

But if Congress overrides the veto, might the president's duty to support the Constitution require *non*-enforcement of a manifestly unconstitutional statute? If the courts have as yet said nothing about the statute, and if the sources on which they ultimately will rely are also available to the president, why is it wrong to think the president has a constitutional responsibility to engage in "coordinate review" until the courts provide final guidance? If there is "constitutional law" in the absence of explicit judicial articulation, why, for that matter, is it wrong to believe that the hypothetical statute is actually not "law" at all, since the applicable principle inheres in the implicit constitutional prohibition *against* such a statute?

Perhaps it is wrong because Congress also has made an implicit judgment about the constitutionality of the statute—concluding that it is valid—and because there is no principled reason to give controlling weight to the president's constitutional judgment over that of Congress, whose members, after all, also swear to

uphold the Constitution. This is not the same as the president
engaging in "coordinate review" of the Constitution to find it unlawful to name Nixon duke. There, no competing interpretation of
the Constitution existed. Here, two different and inconsistent interpretations of the Constitution exist, each made by a co-equal
branch of the federal government; on what principled basis should
one prevail?[53]

Jefferson's answer would seemingly have been that the Executive should prevail. Because each branch has a right to interpret the
Document within its own sphere of operation, and because law-*making*
is a legislative function, Congress had a constitutional right to enact
the law, and the law can properly be said to "exist." But because
enforcement is an executive function, the president has the constitutional right to decline to enforce a law that he/she believes in good
faith to be unconstitutional. And the judiciary may be able to engage
in self-protective review, as it did in *Marbury* in striking down an
impermissible modification of its jurisdiction, but to go beyond self-
protection in invalidating statutes is not permitted.

Jefferson's approach is the paradigm for latter-day models of
"coordinate review." Yet it doesn't work, not only because it deprives Congress of any meaningful role—what power does it take
to enact a statute that is only paper?—but because it also deprives
the courts of any meaningful role. Under it, nearly all of the 120-
some cases striking down federal laws were wrongly decided; if an
individual is convicted of violating an unconstitutional statute, that
individual's recourse is to seek a pardon from the Executive. Whatever theoretical merits such a system might have had in the eighteenth century, the United States' constitutional system has evolved
beyond any possibility of returning to it.

Lincoln's idea of denying the Court's opinions *stare decisis* effect would provide a broader ambit for judicial review. Under it, the
courts would not be limited to self-protection and could still, say,
strike down the Alien and Sedition Acts. But only the parties to a
case would be bound to comply with the Court's holding, meaning
that the Court would have to spend a great deal of time reconsidering and reiterating. In the minds of some, this evidently remained
a live option until 1958, when the Court in *Cooper* declined the
invitation.

Both Jefferson and Lincoln tried to find a way to deal with the
possibility of abuse inherent in any system with platonic guardians. Who guards the guardians? Their answer was to seek to set
up a system of circular authority of limited, overlapping powers, so

as to blur the answer as to which branch had the last word. We have, again, moved beyond their efforts—few today doubt that the judiciary are the final arbiters of the law in the United States—but not all are happy with the result.[54] And the alternative—giving the president power to trump Congress, or vice versa—too often makes the more powerful party the judge of its own case.

If institutional disinterest is the central advantage that the judiciary has over the "coordinate" political branches in constitutional review in foreign affairs disputes, each of the political branches would be seen as responsible for partaking in an obligation to get disputes before the courts—to frame the issue for judicial review—and for persuading the courts to undertake review on the merits notwithstanding the absence of a traditional "Hofeldian" plaintiff. Until this year, the Supreme Court balked at addressing the issue of congressional standing, although lower federal courts had considered the question. In my view, the Supreme Court should have affirmed the view taken by those lower federal courts that found standing in congressional plaintiffs who challenged executive noncompliance with the law. Broader standing rules would give the Court the chance to say "what the law is" without necessitating the prosecution of violators of statutes such as the hypothesized statute prohibiting criticism of Speaker Gingrich. It would also permit the resolution of these thorny issues without allowing the Executive to perform acts of doubtful validity where it has a stake in the outcome. Few principles are as central to Anglo-American jurisprudence as that prohibiting the judging of one's own case; judicial abstention merely enhances the possibility of executive self-dealing.

To illustrate the way this approach would work in the context of the War Powers Resolution, upon introducing the United States armed forces into hostilities in, say, Somalia, the president would issue a report to Congress stating flatly that this has been done. (No president has challenged the validity of the reporting requirement *per se*.) In the same report the president would forthrightly state his/her belief that the Resolution's sixty-day time period is unconstitutional and that he/she will not comply with it. At that point, congressional plaintiffs should have standing to challenge the president's refusal to comply with the law. The issue would then be ripe for review and could be placed before the courts for resolution.

If the Supreme Court in such a situation denies standing to the congressional plaintiffs, the president would then be required to make a judgment whether executive compliance or noncompliance will create a plaintiff with standing. In the Gingrich-criticism hypothetical, for example, compliance would bring a rapid test case, as it would (as discussed above) in cases like *Chadha.* Statutes can, in fact, provide for fast-track judicial review.[55]

I have argued elsewhere against broad use of the political question doctrine in foreign affairs cases.[56] Professor Thomas Franck has extended the argument against judicial abstention—judicial abdication—to other situations where the courts seek to duck their responsibility to say what the law is.[57] The task of the political branches is, in the end, to recognize that their function is political, not adjudicative, and to join issue in such a manner as to make judicial resolution of a dispute easier rather than harder and sooner rather than later. For the Executive Branch, this would in some situations suggest executive enforcement of a law it considers unconstitutional; in other circumstances, it would mean executive nonenforcement. For Congress these obligations entail a good-faith effort on the part of every member to assess the constitutional implications of each vote. The objective of each branch in each situation must be to get the issue decided where it should properly be—in the courts—and not to present the other, and the courts, with an unreviewable fait accompli that aggrandizes its own power, erodes the province of a coequal branch, and undermines the constitutional order. The law's paramount business is to preclude anarchy; articulation of the rules by which a people must live, at least in a society mindful of the interdependence of liberty and order, is the first telltale sign of civilization, and, in our own, the final obligation of the courts.

Notes

1. *Marbury v Madison,* 1 Cranch 137 (1803) at 176.

2. O. W. Holmes, *The Path of the Law* 9 (2d ed. 1951).

3. Austin, *The Province of Jursiprudence Determined* 133 (1954 ed.)

4. H. L. A. Hart, *The Concept of Law* 222–225 (1961). Law, Hart wrote, imposes duties on those who make it as well as those who do not; it applies to the governors and the governed alike. Second, some of those duties are like orders, he pointed out, but others are not. Laws concerning contracts, wills, and marriage, for example, are not backed by threat but are still commonly seen as law. Third, contrary to Austin's belief, some legal rules are brought into existence by nothing analogous to explicit prescription. Some customs, such as not wearing a hat in church, for example, are not legally recognized; others are. Finally, lawmakers in the

modern legislative system enjoy continuing authority that is not dependent upon mere habit, which is necessarily backward-looking. Citizens regard legislatively made rules as legitimate even though they have not yet had an opportunity to obey those rules.

5. 444 US 996 (1979).

6. Louis Fisher, *Constitutional Dialogues: Interpretation as Political Process* 5 (1988).

7. "Secondary" rules, Hart calls them. A "rule of recognition" is such a rule, describing what attributes are required before a candidate for rulehood is accepted as a rule.

8. 59 Stat. 1055 (1945), TS No. 993.

9. M. Glennon, *Constitution Diplomacy*, ch. 2 (1990).

10. 453 US 654 (1981).

11. 453 US 280 (1981).

12. 272 US 52 (1926).

13. 295 US 602 (1935).

14. 418 US 683 (1974).

15. 299 US 304 (1936).

16. *Ex Parte Garland,* 71 US (4 Wall.) 333 (1867).

17. For the argument that they are not, *see* Paul Brest, *Congress as a Constitutional Decisionmaker and Its Power to Counter Judicial Doctrine,* 21 Ga. L. Rev. 57 (1986).

18. They should. *See* Louis Henkin, *The Legality of the United States Action in Panama,* Colum. J. Transnat'l L. 293 (1991).

19. Louis Fisher, *Constitutional Dialogues: Interpretation as Political Process* 5 (1988).

20. 462 US 919 (1983).

21. 418 US 683 (1974).

22. 358 US 1 (1958).

23. 347 US 483 (1954).

24. *Cooper v Aaron,* 358 US at 17–19.

25. *Id.* at 22.

26. *McCulloch v Maryland,* 4 US (Wheat) 316, 415 (1819).

27. *Youngstown Sheet and Tube v Sawyer,* 343 US 579 (1952).

28. 395 US 486 (1969).

29. 395 US 444 (1969).

30. 299 US 304 (1936).

31. U.S. v N.Y. State Department of Taxation and Finance, 1992 US Dist. Lexis 18482, Dec. 4, 1991 decided.

32. 343 US 250 (1952).

33. 491 US 397 (1989).

34. 410 US 113 (1973).

35. *Dred Scott v Sanford,* 19 How. (60 US) 393 (1957).

36. 163 US 537 (1896).

37. *See generally* Snyder, *The Chill of Rule 11,* 11 Litigation 16 (Winter, 1985).

38. *See generally* Note, Rule 11: *Has the Objective Standard Transgressed the Adversary System?* 38 Case Western Reserve L. Rev. 279, 283 (1987).

39. 842 F. 2d 1102 (9th Cir. 1988).

40. 842 F. 2d at 1121.

41. *Id.* at 1124.

42. 844 F. 2d 1107 (3rd Cir. 1988).

43. 358 US at 24.

44. 358 US at 24.

45. 358 US at 25.

46. 358 US at 25.

47. *Cooper v Aaron,* 358 US 1, 25–26 (1958).

48. 369 US 186 (1962).

49. *Id.* at 369 US at 300 (Frankfurter, J., dissenting).

50. 283 US 697 (1931).

51. Set aside the hypocrisy with which the argument has occasionally been made. The Reagan administration, for example, while claiming to welcome an opportunity to give the courts an opportunity to pass upon the validity of the War Powers Resolution, in fact resisted adjudication on the merits in arguing the nonjustifiability of *Lowry v Reagan.*

52. 418 US 166 (1974).

53. Perhaps the most prominent foreign affairs dispute in which this issue arises concerns the War Powers Resolution. One of the central disputes of the last twenty years—the constitutionality of the War Powers Resolution—has at bottom involved precisely this question. Is the president permitted constitutionally to disregard the Resolution's sixty-day time limit in a good-faith belief that it is unconstitutional?

54. Raoul Berger, *Government by Judiciary* (1977).

55. *See, e.g., Compare* 2 U.S.C. §437h(a) (1970 ed., Supp. IV) (facilitating judicial review of Federal Election Campaign Act) *with* Buckley v Valeo, 424 US 1 (1976) (construing that provision as "intended to provide judicial review to the extent permitted by Art. III," *id.* at 11–12).

56. Michael Glennon, *Constitutional Diplomacy* (1990).

57. Thomas M. Franck, *Political Questions/Judicial Answers* (1992).

4

The Courts and the Political Branches: Interpretation, Accommodation and Autonomy

Nancy Kassop

At the heart of the intersection of law and politics is the notion of "first principles"—those core concepts that form the foundations of republican government. "Law" emanates from the words and texture of the Constitution, while "politics" fuels the debate over the meaning and application of those phrases. Who has the responsibility for interpreting "first principles," how is it done, and what are its consequences?

These are the questions with which Louis Fisher has grappled over the last thirty years. Those of us who "came of age" in political science during the 1970s, and who were drawn to the study of separation of powers, inevitably gravitated to Fisher's work in the field.[1] What we have discovered in the intervening years is that what began as an examination into basic questions of constitutional allocation of power in his early work has developed into a much richer and more nuanced explanation of institutional roles and responsibilities. Perhaps, more (or, at least, earlier) than any other scholar toiling in these fields, Fisher's approach to the proper balance of institutional authority posits a "constitutional dialogue," a continuing conversation among the branches that truly intermixes law with politics.[2]

He sees a fluidity in the relations among the president, Congress, and the courts, and includes the states and the public, as well, in this ongoing, alternating pattern of action and reaction among the players until a consensus develops that brings an issue to its rest.

> Judicial decisions rest undisturbed only to the extent that Congress, the President, and the general public find the decisions convincing, reasonable, and acceptable. Otherwise, the debate on constitutional principles will continue.[3]

His view influences all three branches, but breaks the most ground in its treatment of the contours of federal judicial power, challenging the more popularly accepted and traditional notion of judicial supremacy, and substituting in its place the process of coordinate construction. The ramifications of this alternative approach are substantial: they result in the diffusion of the very source of constitutional interpretation, and profoundly affect the dynamics of interbranch behavior. In short, Fisher's contribution does nothing less than (1) change our understanding of "who" interprets the Constitution, (2) sensitize us to look for the "accommodations" rather than the conflicts in the resolution of institutional and political controversies, and (3) remind us of the fragile nature of judicial independence, requiring constant, vigilant protection from the efforts of the political branches to infiltrate its sphere. It is these three concepts of interpretation, accommodation, and autonomy that figure most prominently in Fisher's work on the judiciary and its role in a democratic system, and that will be addressed here.

Institutional Roles and Responsibilities

Ask anyone "What is the role of the Supreme Court?" and you will most likely get a reflexive answer. The standard reply would be that (1) it is the ultimate interpreter of the Constitution, (2) it monitors the separation of powers among the branches, and (3) it safeguards individual and minority rights against the tyranny of the majority. But throughout Fisher's work runs a consistent thread that challenges each of these answers. He marshals examples to show how easily all three of these statements can be rebutted: (1) the Court has *no* monopoly on interpretation, and is joined in this function by other branches, other levels, and other institutions; (2) separation of powers is a *political* construct that depends for its balance not on the courts but on contemporary political imponderables and, mostly, on the will of each branch to protect its respective powers and to use them responsibly; and (3) the Court has done a poor job of guarding individual liberties, while other branches and players have amassed a far better record in this area.

Rather, Fisher sees a dispersal of the power and roles that are traditionally assumed to belong to the Court (and *solely* to the Court). With more institutions performing these roles—and often doing them better than the Court—the result is a smaller, narrower, more limited role for the Court than most might ascribe to it. While acknowledging a reduced role for the judiciary, Fisher, at the same time, has no hesitation in stating that judicial decision-making is necessarily and unashamedly, "lawmaking."[4] He gleefully replies to the disapproving comment in (then) Justice Rehnquist's dissent in *Roe v Wade* (1973) that the Court's "conscious weighing of competing factors . . . is far more appropriate to a legislative judgment than to a judicial one" by noting that the weighing and balancing of competing factors (e.g., national security interests vs. individual rights, Congress'ss investigatory power vs. president's claim of executive privilege, law enforcement vs. privacy) is the *primary* way in which the courts do their job.[5] Constitutional law is, after all, a "process" to Fisher, engaging all three branches and born out of "defining political values, resolving political conflict, and protecting the integrity and effectiveness of the political process."[6] The Court is no less (and no more) a player in that process than its executive and legislative partners, and, similarly, performs its part of the task in much the same "piecemeal" manner of "compromise, expediency and ad hoc action."[7]

I. Interpretation: Judicial Review vs. Coordinate Construction

Fisher wastes no time in showing that the principle of judicial review that automatically tops the list of functions of the federal courts (for most people, except Scalia) has been wrongly understood to mean that the courts have exclusive power to interpret the Constitution. Even such august decisions as *Marbury v Madison* (1803), *Cooper v Aaron* (1958), *Baker v Carr* (1962), and *U.S. v Nixon* (1974) lose their potency as examples of this principle, when he can extract wording from each to show that even these decisions contain explicit acknowledgement that judicial interpretations are just one among many that can be validly offered.[8] With *Marbury*, Fisher argues that Marshall's much-quoted words that it is "emphatically the province

and duty of the judicial department to say what the law is" do not
suggest an exclusive province for the courts, and do not prevent
other branches from contributing their views.[9] Language in *Cooper*
and in *Baker*, respectively, describing the Supreme Court as "supreme in the exposition of the law of the Constitution," and "ultimate interpreter of the Constitution," does not mean that other
interpreters may not weigh in with their views.[10] And, wording in
Nixon that "each branch ... must initially interpret the Constitution ..." suggests plainly that *all* branches possess the right (if not
the duty) to engage in constitutional interpretation.[11]

Fisher presents further evidence to prove that Chief Justice
John Marshall did not believe in judicial supremacy and did not
exercise judicial review again during his tenure on the Court after
Marbury. Fisher notes that the highly charged political circumstances
in which *Marbury* was decided may have had far more to do with
Marshall's use of judicial review than any deeply held belief that
this power belonged exclusively to the courts. Accordingly, Fisher
assigns a much more limited role to judicial review and to the decision most often cited as its jurisprudential birthplace.[12]

In fact, he posits that far from grounding Marshall's legacy on
his use of judicial review to strike down an act of Congress, it is
more accurate to see it in precisely the opposite terms, since the
chief justice's other claim to fame arose from his consistent support
for broad congressional power in decisions such as *McCulloch v
Maryland* (1819) and *Gibbons v Ogden* (1824).[13] In terms of the
impact on the development of a truly national political and economic system, establishing the broad contours of congressional power
would seem to be of the highest magnitude when assessing
Marshall's influence.

Beyond Marshall and *Marbury*, Fisher catalogues presidents,
framers, justices, and other commentators who lend support to the
principle and use of coordinate construction, in contrast to judicial
supremacy. Prominent among these are Madison, Hamilton,
Jefferson, Jackson, Lincoln, and Chief Justice Warren.[14] All are on
record as accepting the validity of constitutional interpretation by
Congress and the president. Later sections of this chapter will
address the point that interpretation by the Court may even be less
effective than when done by the other branches. For now, a recent
pair of Supreme Court decisions provides an intriguing example of
what can happen—and of what can go astray—in the dynamic
world of constitutional interpretation by coordinate branches. It is
worth a digression.

Employment Division v Smith *and* City of Boerne v Flores:
The Court versus Congress

Among those who have publicly expressed an understanding of coordinate construction is Justice Anthony Kennedy at his Senate confirmation hearings in 1987. Fisher compared the responses of three Reagan-era Supreme Court appointments (Rehnquist to chief, Scalia and Kennedy) to questions about judicial supremacy, and found, to his pleasure, that nominee Kennedy was particularly convincing in his explanation of the power of all three branches to make independent judgments on matters of constitutional interpretation. In a revealing exchange with Senator Arlen Specter, Kennedy made the point quite forcefully that a Senator had the power (and the duty) to challenge a Supreme Court decision with which he disagreed by introducing legislation to overturn the ruling.[15]

Imagine Fisher's disappointment, then, at the announcement of the decision in *City of Boerne v Flores* (1997), with Kennedy writing for the Court that the 1993 Religious Freedom Restoration Act (RFRA) passed by Congress in its effort to overturn the 1990 *Employment Division v Smith* ruling exceeded Congress's power. In essence, Congress had done exactly what Kennedy had advocated to Specter in his confirmation hearings—Congress had used its legislative power to register its disapproval of the Court's 1990 decision that had sharply reduced the protection of the First Amendment's free exercise clause by a restrictive interpretation of that liberty.

RFRA established a statutory cause of action under Section 5 of the Fourteenth Amendment to enforce a broader protection of religious liberty, but the Court, speaking through Kennedy, held that Congress's enforcement power under this section is only "remedial" and "preventive" in nature, and may not be used for the purpose of changing the "substantive" meaning of a constitutional right. The distinction between a "remedial" or "preventive" purpose, on the one hand, and a "substantive" one, on the other, is murky, at best, and, "incoherent," at worst, according to David Cole.[16] Cole criticized the *Boerne* decision as one where the Court announced its monopoly on constitutional interpretation, based on the presumption that "the Constitution has a determinate meaning that only the Supreme Court can divine."[17] But he noted that interpreting constitutional provisions is a dynamic process, resulting in "reasonable disagreements." And, he adds, "that should counsel considerable deference to Congress's interpretation."[18] Cole ends his analysis of the decision with an explanation of coordinate construction that should be music to Fisher's ears:

> But the 14th Amendment's drafters chose to give Congress explicit enforcement power under Section 5 because they were unwilling to trust entirely in the Supreme Court to protect constitutional liberties. . . . They thought empowering two branches of government to protect basic rights and liberties was better than leaving it to one. *Boerne* cuts Congress out of the process, and leaves the definition of liberty to one branch, the judiciary. . . . [19]

As an editorial aside, Cole adds, "And given the political identity of this Court, that is the most troubling result of the term, not only for religion, but for all constitutional liberties."[20]

Cole's remark provides a perfect lead-in to the most well-known Fisherism—that the courts often get it wrong when they interpret the Constitution, and that they do not deserve the reputation or the public's trust in them for protecting individual liberties against majority invasion. But there is one more feature of *Boerne* that illustrates an aspect of judicial behavior as described by Fisher that bears mention. This is the act of "judicial invitation" to Congress and the president, the states, or future litigants to take up the gauntlet and either provide an institutional counterresponse to a decision (as for Congress, the president or the states), or bring a future case (as for litigants) to give the courts a chance to address the issue another time but in a slightly different form.

Fisher notes the use of this tactic (1) in the 1890s when the Court issued an implicit invitation to Congress to overturn the "original package doctrine" of *Leisy v Hardin* (1890), (2) when Congress responded with the McCarran Act in 1945 to the Court's ruling in the *U.S. v Southeastern Underwriters Association* (1944) case that only Congress could exempt the insurance industry from the Sherman Antitrust Act, and (3) with the interaction in 1987 between Congress, the Court, and the FCC over the constitutionality of the fairness doctrine in broadcasting.[21]

Another familiar example of judicial invitation occurred in *Miranda v Arizona* (1966), where the Court, after issuing its own procedural requirements for custodial interrogation by police of criminal suspects, added:

> It is impossible for us to foresee the potential alternatives for protecting the privilege which might be devised by Congress or the states in the exercise of their creative rule-

making capacities. Therefore, we cannot say that the Constitution necessarily requires adherence to any particular solution for the inherent compulsions of the interrogation process as it is presently conducted. Our decision in no way creates a constitutional straitjacket which will handicap sound efforts at reform, nor is it intended to have this effect. We encourage Congress and the states to continue their laudable search for increasingly effective ways of protecting the rights of the individual while promoting efficient enforcement of our criminal laws. However, unless we are shown other procedures which are at least as effective in apprising accused persons of their right of silence and in assuring a continuous opportunity to exercise it, the following safeguards must be observed....[22]

Similarly, Fisher richly recounts the sequence of cases and events leading up to the Supreme Court's decision in *West Virginia State Board of Education v Barnette* (1943), which, among the many facets to this case that distinguish it within American constitutional jurisprudence is that it provides another useful example of "judicial advertising." This arose out of the signaling to future litigants by Justices Black, Douglas, and Murphy in *Jones v Opelika* (1942) that they were prepared to reconsider their 1940 decision in *Minersville School District v Gobitis*.[23]

City of Boerne v Flores is the latest of these "judicial invitation" cases. In his opinion for the Court in *Employment Division v Smith*, Scalia leaves open the possibility that the democratic process could yield legislation that would permit broader protection for religious freedom than the Court in its *Smith* decision is willing to provide. It is an open "invitation" to states and to Congress to devise other ways to protect the values in the Bill of Rights.

Just as a society that believes in the negative protection accorded to the press by the First Amendment is likely to enact laws that affirmatively foster the dissemination of the printed word, so also a society that believes in the negative protection accorded to religious belief can be expected to be solicitous of that value in its legislation as well. It is therefore not surprising that a number of States have made an exception to their drug laws for sacramental peyote use....[24]

He does, however, issue a caution that the practices of a religious minority may not win public approval in the political process, that

... leaving accommodation to the political process (may) place at a relative disadvantage those religious practices that are not widely engaged in; but that unavoidable consequence of democratic government must be preferred to a system in which each conscience is a law unto itself or in which judges weigh the social importance of all laws against the centrality of all religious beliefs.[25]

Congress followed Scalia's suggestion, responding to a broad coalition of groups with an interest in religious liberty who viewed the *Smith* decision with alarm in that it opened the door to far greater government intrusion into religious practices. The Religious Freedom Restoration Act passed both houses of Congress in 1993 with near-unanimous approval, restricting government from substantially burdening religious exercise except when it can prove a compelling interest and uses the least restrictive means in reaching that interest. The effect of the law was to overturn *Employment Division v Smith*. But Kennedy, speaking for the Court in *Boerne*, found that

> When the political branches of the Government act against the background of a judicial interpretation of the Constitution already issued, it must be understood that in later cases and controversies the Court will treat its precedents with the respect due them under settled principles, including *stare decisis*, and contrary expectations must be disappointed. RFRA was designed to control cases and controversies, such as the one before us; but as the provisions of the federal statute here invoked are beyond congressional authority, it is this Court's precedent, not RFRA, which must control.[26]

He reminded Congress that although the Court will extend much deference to the legislature to determine what action under Section 5 of the Fourteenth Amendment is needed to secure those guarantees, Congress's power is not unlimited, and the courts will be the ultimate judge if that power exceeds its constitutional authority, as it did here.[27] It remains to be seen if Congress will try to legislate once more in this area or will try to enact a constitutional amendment to overturn *Smith*.[28]

II. Sharing the Power: Interpretation by other Branches, Levels, and Institutions

One of Fisher's hallmark contributions to the study of constitutional law is his firm belief in interpretation outside of the courts. He carefully compiles historical examples of interpretation by other actors. He looks to Congress, the president, and state legislatures and courts, and, also, admonishes all of us as responsible citizens to monitor the actions of our government to insure that constitutional principles are being enforced. The sharing of interpretive power by other actors makes possible the constant interaction among them and the continual action-reaction pattern that is a far more accurate and realistic description of the governmental process than a stiffly hierarchical one that posits the finality of an issue at the door of the courts.

Interpretation by Congress and the President
(or, "Courts Often Get it Wrong")

Fisher has uncovered numerous examples where either Congress or the president, and at times, both, have exercised independent judgment on matters of constitutional interpretation. Sometimes, these actions were taken without any reference to a judicial decision, purely on the initiative of the branch, and other times, they either precipitated or countered a judicial action. Under either scenario, the evidence is clear that both branches recognize their coequality with the judiciary in determining the meaning of constitutional provisions.

Recognition of authority is one thing, but it does not guarantee that a branch will exercise that power when necessary. Perhaps, nothing troubles Fisher more than when a branch—and it is most often, if not always, Congress—fails to use its authority to protect its institutional prerogatives or, worse, "passes the buck" to the courts, assuming that if a constitutional irregularity has arisen, the judicial branch will address the breach. Separation-of-powers matters, in particular, provoke this behavior in Congress, as when it provides for expedited review or congressional standing in such laws as the Line-Item Veto Act of 1996. These procedural shortcuts, enveloped in legislation, serve as "green lights" to members that they can go ahead and enact a law which may include constitutionally questionable sections, but that they can assume that the courts will judge the validity of the law, thus, removing the obligation from Congress to do so. Fisher propounds the point that each branch has a duty to explore and resolve to its satisfaction any constitutional questions *before* it takes formal action. The possibility of judicial review will always be present, but the larger reality is that most laws will *not* be reviewed by the courts for their constitutionality. Thus, the burden falls far more heavily on Congress and the president to undertake their own obligation in good faith.[29]

A. *Interpretation by the President.* Fisher cites Jefferson, Jackson, and Lincoln as early examples of presidents who believed in and acted according to coordinate construction. Jefferson's distaste for the Sedition Act of 1798 was well known, but since there was no chance that the law would be struck down by Federalist judges, Jefferson waited for the law to expire in 1801, and then took executive action to terminate any punishment or prosecution under the law. IIe declared that the law had been unconstitutional and, as such, was null and void and, further, noted that judges and presidents were "equally independent" to act according to each one's determination of the constitutionality of its own actions.[30] Congress acted in concert with Jefferson on this matter in that it passed private bills to compensate individuals who had paid fines under the law, and it expressly noted in a House committee report that the law had been unconstitutional.[31]

Jackson employed principles of coordinate construction to justify his veto in 1832 of the bill to recharter the Bank of the United States, the institution whose constitutionality had been upheld in the Court's 1819 *McCulloch* decision. In his veto message, he noted that there was no more reason for judges to control the actions of Congress or the president "when acting in their legislative capacities" than for the political branches to control the judiciary when acting within *its* sphere, and that the Court should prevail only when "the force of (its) reasoning" deserved such respect.[32] Moreover, he recognized that the oath of office taken by each officer obligates that person to *his* understanding of the Constitution, and not to that of others, thus, also, underscoring the independent nature of constitutional interpretation by each branch.[33]

Fisher points to Lincoln's remarks about the *Dred Scott v Sandford* (1857) decision during the Lincoln-Douglass debates and in his Inauguration Address, illustrating that Lincoln recognized that the Court's interpretations of constitutional matters were not superior, but were, instead, equal, to the president's or Congress's, and that the public also shared responsibility for determining whether the Court's views were acceptable.[34] Perfectly consistent with Fisher's view of coordinate construction is Harold Hyman's characterization of the skepticism of mid-nineteenth century Americans about leaving public law to the lawyers or officials. Fisher quotes Hyman: "Like politics, with which it was inextricably joined, the Constitution was everybody's business."[35]

Equally significant was Lincoln's view that Supreme Court decisions controlled only the parties to the case, not the larger policy issue.[36] In order to maintain some semblance of legal order, one would have to agree, at a minimum, that parties are obligated to obey a judicial decision. But the question of wider or universal application of a ruling is a more politically charged and determinative one: the "universal application" approach is based on judicial supremacy, while the "parties-only" approach permits the use of coordinate construction. Fisher acknowledges that *too* stringent a reliance on independent interpretation could produce political and legal disorder in the system, but the operative principles that drive his philosophy are those of moderation, accommodation, and reasonableness.[37] Such a foundation allows him to advocate the use of coordinate construction, with the confidence of knowing that, in the end, political factors, loosely defined but within a constitutional structure and process, will govern the outcome of any particular dispute.

Fisher also notes that the *Dred Scott* example is another one where, as with Jackson and the Sedition Act, a president's independent construction of the invalidity of a Court ruling was soon followed by an interpretation by Congress that also refused to accept the legitimacy of the decision.[38] First, Congress enacted legislation in 1862 that prohibited slavery in the territories, directly countering *Dred Scott*, and as Fisher reports, with no utterance in the debate of any objection to congressional overturning of a Court decision. And, ultimately, with a firmness that could not be mistaken, ratification of the 13th, 14th, and 15th Amendments put to rest any doubt of the illegitimacy of *Dred Scott*. All branches participated, and the voice of the people was heard and heeded.[39]

In turning to a few modern examples of presidential interpretation, however, we might take pause a bit in recognizing that there are, indeed, times when the nation turns to the Court for a redressing of an imbalance of power among the branches. Fisher may acknowledge these as more the exception than the rule, and that only when conditions have reached crisis proportions and the political branches are locked in battle against each other do we turn to the courts for a graceful resolution. Moreover, he would argue that even the Court's decisions here were not the "final" ones, as subsequent political actions were taken to flesh out the ultimate conclusion in these cases.

The two examples that come to mind here are Truman's seizure of the steel mills in 1952 and Nixon's claim of absolute executive privilege in 1974.[40] Both presidents certainly engaged in independent construction of their executive powers under the Constitution, and both watched as the Supreme Court ruled those interpretations invalid under the specific circumstances of each case. There is cause to suggest that, in both cases, the presidents "lost the battle but won the war": the case can be made that the Court in *Youngstown Sheet and Tube Company v Sawyer* (1952) did *not* rule that a president may never exercise inherent powers in an emergency nor did it rule in *U.S. v Nixon* (1974) that a president may never claim executive privilege to keep information from a prosecutor or Congress. In fact, the Court, in both cases, lent its support to those very two claims, albeit under different factual circumstances than the ones there. But the larger historical significance of both cases is that they brought to the nation some measure of an authoritative decision in each case at a time when the antagonists could not reach a resolution on their own.

It *is* true that, in both cases, subsequent political actions further clarified the Court decisions, but it would be difficult to overstate the importance of the Court's actions here in defusing the respective crises. Sometimes, the Court *does* get it right—and the other branches need to be nudged along by the principled actions of "the least dangerous branch."

Before leaving the examination of presidential interpretation, the most recent manifestation of coordinate construction by executives must be noted, and its ramifications explored. President Reagan began the practice of issuing bill-signing statements in which he identified certain provisions as unconstitutional and unenforceable, and directed federal agencies not to implement them. The effect was to either revise or invalidate sections of a law *after* the legislative process had been completed. There is nothing remarkable about presidents using the bill-signing process to register displeasure with some sections of a law, but the leap that the Reagan administration accomplished over past use of this practice was its success, spearheaded by Attorney General Meese, in getting these statements published in the *United States Code Congressional and Administrative News (USCCAN)* so that courts might refer to them when engaging in statutory interpretation. In this sense, Meese hoped that courts would look to "executive intent" of the law as a counterweight to the traditional notion of legislative intent.

Does this practice accord with Fisher's idea of coordinate construction? Lower federal courts during the Reagan era answered with sharply worded rulings that such action usurped both legislative *and* judicial powers, in that the president unconstitutionally arrogated to himself both the lawmaking and judicial reviewing authority.[41]

Is this not a clear conflict between the branches where each is exercising its prerogative to interpret the Constitution, and where those interpretations simply differ? Does Fisher accept this practice as a legitimate part of the coordinate construction process? Why or why not? And why, if the courts invalidated this presidential action during the Reagan administration in very sharp terms, did the Bush administration, under the guidance of White House Counsel C. Boyden Gray, continue to employ and expand this tactic?[42]

B. *Interpretation by Congress.* A major contribution by Fisher to the discipline is his steady reminder to all of us that Congress is a vital source of constitutional interpretation, that it performs that function perhaps more frequently than the courts, and that it has a better record, overall, than the courts on protecting individual liberties and on understanding the operative institutional dynamics of separation of powers. Not only have his writings in this area served to sensitize *us* to the need to look beyond the courts for interpretive guidance, but, equally, his daily work with members of Congress from his position at the Congressional Research Service gives him an ideal venue from which to urge lawmakers that they have a solemn responsibility to reflect carefully and to consider the constitutional questions *before* they act. Fisher's extensive testimony, memos, reports, and consultations with members, especially in the war powers and budget areas, may be his greatest legacy to Congress, as an institution. For us as scholars, the breadth of examples and illustrations that he has amassed on the general topic of interpretation by Congress is daunting and should be sufficient proof to anyone of Congress's coequal role with the courts as to the interpretive function.

1. INDIVIDUAL LIBERTIES

Certain issues surface repeatedly in his writings to illustrate those striking examples where judicial decisions have been inhospitable to individual rights, and where Congress has acted to correct the damage inflicted by the Court.

In the post-Civil War period, Fisher points to the *Civil Rights Cases of 1883* and the Court's rulings in the 1870s on women's rights as two sets of decisions that were unhelpful in expanding equal rights.[43] In the first set, the Court ruled that Congress's effort in 1875 to grant equal access to blacks to public accommodations exceeded its authority under the 13th and 14th Amendments. It took almost eighty years, until the passage of the Civil Rights Act of 1964, to undo the damage inflicted by the Court in that decision.

The Court's decision in *Bradwell v Illinois* (1873) narrowly interpreted the 14th Amendment's privileges and immunities clause, finding that it did not protect a woman's right to practice law. Congress, however, took a different approach, and within six years, enacted a law that permitted women who satisfied certain professional criteria to be admitted to practice before the U.S. Supreme Court. Technically, this law did not overturn *Bradwell*, but it did provide a broader opportunity than the Supreme Court was willing to grant for women to practice in the legal profession. Fisher plumbs the Senate debate and uncovers eloquent passages from senators who recognize the imperative of equal rights for women at the same time that the Court was unable to agree.[44]

The same pattern of judicial narrow-mindedness followed by congressional recognition of fairer rights for women occurred a century later, and this time, Congress squarely acted to overturn a decision with which it disagreed. The Court ruled in *General Electric v Gilbert* (1976) that Title VII of the Civil Rights Act of 1964 did not require employers to include pregnancy within their medical disability coverage for employees. Thus, male and female workers could be covered for any medical disability except pregnancy-related conditions. It took Congress a scant two years to enact the Pregnancy Discrimination Act of 1978 to reverse this decision by amending Title VII and making explicit that discrimination on the basis of pregnancy was sex discrimination and, thus, prohibited under Title VII.[45]

Fisher examines the congressional efforts to pass legislation regulating child labor, first under the commerce power, and then under the tax power, and the resulting two Supreme Court decisions invalidating them in 1918 and 1922, respectively, as illustrating yet another example of congressional-judicial-congressional interplay.[46] A try at a constitutional amendment in 1924 yielded unsuccessful results, but the changes on the Court wrought in the aftermath of the Court-packing plan in 1937 gave Congress one more chance. The Fair Labor Standards Act of 1938 included a section regulating child labor under the commerce power (again), and the Court sustained it unanimously in *U.S. v Darby* (1941).[47]

Fisher turns to the behavior of the Court during wartime for two especially dramatic examples of a restrictive judicial view of individual rights.[48] He vividly documents the flag salute cases and the Japanese-American cases to illustrate where "the Court got it wrong" (*very* wrong), and other institutions and actors rose to the challenge to rebuke the Court.

Fisher's view on the unfolding of the flag salute cases is particularly instructive because it shows the contribution not only of Congress but of the public and the states, as well as constitutional "interpreters." He details the spiraling of events that began with the decision in *Minersville School District v Gobitis* (1940), upholding a compulsory flag salute law in Pennsylvania against the First Amendment challenge by Jehovah's Witnesses and sparking a protest against the ruling from an aroused public opinion that understood the protections of the First Amendment better than the Court. States also reacted to the decision, and Fisher has uncovered state court decisions in flag salute cases from New Hampshire, New Jersey, Kansas, and Washington that ran contrary to *Gobitis* and that found greater protection for religious liberty in state constitutions than the U.S. Supreme Court had found in the Bill of Rights. Congress entered the scene in 1942 with legislation that permitted a much more relaxed approach to respect for the flag than a rigid salute, thus, undermining the basis of the decision. With the announcement in *Jones v Opelika* (1942) that three justices had reconsidered their earlier position, and the personnel changes on the Court, the stage was set for the judicial overruling that came in *West Virginia State Board of Education v Barnette* (1943). But Fisher is emphatic that the credit for changing the Court's ruling here belongs to the public for its instinctual understanding that the Court misinterpreted the Constitution.[49]

The Japanese-American cases of 1943 and 1944 provide a particularly shameful episode of all *three* branches acting in concert to deprive individuals of equal rights.[50] President Franklin Roosevelt issued Executive Order 9066 on February 1942, authorizing the creation of designated military areas on the West Coast, to be further regulated by military authorities, as necessary. This led to the establishment of a curfew and, ultimately, the exclusion of 112,000 persons of Japanese ancestry from these areas. A month later, Congress passed a law that criminalized any violation of these military orders. *Hirabyashi v U.S.* (1943) grew out of the violation of the curfew, and *Korematsu v U.S.* (1944) arose out of the refusal of a Japanese-American to leave a designated area. When these cases reached the Supreme Court in 1943 and 1944, respectively, the Court had little difficulty in sustaining convictions in both cases against the charge that the government's actions (Congress *and* the president) were discriminatory on the basis of race. Thus, here we find all three branches acting consistently in interpreting the Equal Protection Clause of the 14th Amendment— they just all happen to be wrong. Justice Jackson's dissent in *Korematsu* is notable for its caution to the courts that far more damaging to liberty than the military orders themselves is "a judicial construction of the due process clause that will sustain this order . . . " where "the Court for all time has validated the principle of racial discrimination in criminal procedure and of transplanting American citizens."[51]

By 1980, Congress formally acknowledged the mistake made by the government in these cases after a two-year commission had examined the facts, and by 1988, Congress had passed legislation that provided reparations of $20,000 to each of the surviving Japanese-Americans who had been interned. Even coordinate construction could not bring the nation to its senses during a wartime environment, and the eventual recognition of past damage came very late in the day.[52]

Two final examples round out Fisher's offerings of cases where Congress has had to "mop up" after the Court. *Zurcher v Stanford Daily* (1978) is illustrative of the dilemma where the Court finds itself balancing two competing constitutional values. In this case, the Court upheld third-party searches by warrants of newsrooms against a Fourth Amendment challenge, provoking public criticism of heavy-handed police tactics and intrusions on privacy. The Court noted in its decision that the legislative and executive branches were free to "establish nonconstitutional protections against possible abuses of the search warrant procedure,"[53] and Congress answered the invitation two years later when it enacted limits on newsroom searches, requiring law enforcement officers to obtain a subpoena rather than a search warrant, thus, giving news publications an extra measure of protection. Fisher notes that both Congress and the Court engaged in the same balancing of constitutional values, but came out with very different solutions.[54]

Fisher uses the Court's decision in *Goldman v Weinberger* (1986) to illustrate a case with overlapping constitutional and statutory dimensions to it. At issue was an Air Force regulation prohibiting the wearing of headgear by service members while on duty indoors. As an Orthodox Jew whose religion prescribed the wearing of a yarmulke, Weinberger challenged the regulation as a violation of his First Amendment right of free exercise. The Court determined that the military's interest in discipline and order prevailed over any First Amendment values, but Congress responded by including a provision in a 1987 defense authorization bill that directly overturned this decision. It would now be permissible for religious service members to wear items of religious garb while on duty, unless doing so would interfere with military duties. The effect of this provision was, through Congress's effort, to overturn *Weinberger*, and to restore greater protection for free exercise than the Court was willing to acknowledge.[55]

2. SEPARATION OF POWERS
(OR, "RESOLUTION BY ACCOMMODATION AND INFORMAL AGREEMENT")

Fisher's professional career has been framed by his work on separation of powers. No other scholar can come close to matching the breadth and depth of not only his writing in this area but also his practical impact and guidance on the fluid, ongoing interactions between Congress and the president. Not surprisingly, his approach to separation of powers provides the foundation for his view of the governmental process as a whole, with the emphasis on moderation, reasonableness, accommodation, informal political resolution of disputes, and the exercise of institutional responsibility.

Characteristically, he looks not to the courts but to the political branches themselves as the locus for fleshing out the meaning of constitutional provisions and the scope of power of each of the branches:

> ... most of the principal disputes involving separation of powers are resolved outside the courts. The majority of these collisions never reach the courts or, if they do, are quickly pushed back to the executive and legislative branches for nonjudicial treatment.[56]

The reasons for this are both historical and pragmatic. For one, Fisher notes that the most crucial issues of the day were debated intensely in Congress (and were thoughtfully deliberated within the presidency) during the early years of the nation for the simple reason that there were no judicial decisions as precedents to guide the actions of the branches.

> The historical record, however, demonstrates that Congress deliberated for years on such constitutional issues as judicial review, the Bank of the United States, congressional investigative power, slavery, internal improvements, federalism, the war-making power, treaties and foreign relations, interstate commerce, the removal power, and the legislative veto long before those issues entered the courts. Congressional debate was intense, informed, and diligent. Indeed, it had to be, given the paucity of direction at that time from the Supreme Court and the lower courts.[57]

Secondly, more recent efforts by the Supreme Court to venture into separation of powers disputes have left a mixed legacy that Fisher calls "inconsistent and incoherent" in its search for a doctrinal approach, alternating between a functional, pragmatic, flexible approach of overlapping powers (e.g., *U.S. v Nixon* (1974), *Nixon v Administrator of General Services* (1977), *Commodity Futures Trading Commission v Schor* (1986), *Mistretta v U.S.* (1989), *Morrison v Olson* (1988)) and a rigid, strict, formalistic, unrealistic one of watertight compartments (e.g., *Nixon v Fitzgerald* (1982), *Northern Pipeline Construction Co. v Marathon Pipeline Co.* (1982), *INS v Chadha* (1983), *Bowsher v Synar* (1986)).[58] Thus, there is even greater pressure and incentive for the branches to decide these matters on their own, considering the uneven record of the Court, and, more pointedly, the inability of the Court to fully understand the "coping mechanisms," if you will, that Congress and the president have devised over the years to facilitate the real-life process of governing.

It was just this sort of judicial distance from the real world that Fisher attributes to the Court in its simplistic and shortsighted decision in *Chadha*. He faults the Court for its failure to recognize that the framers clearly understood the flexible nature of separation of powers, acknowledging an overlapping or sharing of powers. The Court showed its ignorance of history in its lack of knowledge about the origin of the legislative veto, and the fact that it was *not* coerced on an unreceptive president.[59] And finally, Fisher is most persuasive (and armed to the hilt with evidence) when he warns, with good reason, that decisions that are so out of step with reality only invite disregard and circumvention.[60] His running tally of legislative vetoes *since* their invalidation in *Chadha* currently numbers over four hundred and counting, but the larger point that he urges is instructive. Congress and the president had agreed to a mechanism (albeit, one outside of the Constitution) that smoothed the operations of government for both and that provided advantages to each. The removal of that device to bridge the separation between the branches will only result in the search for a newer version that will serve the same purpose. And, that is exactly what Fisher has found in the heightened use of committee and subcommittee controls via informal agreements, reprogramming, and other nonstatutory methods to monitor executive branch actions.[61]

Fisher's conclusion here is clear: many constitutional provisions and clauses owe their interpretation and definition not to the courts but to the compromises and accommodations reached by the legislative and executive branches. To illustrate, he catalogues a variety of constitutional questions that were answered by the customs, practices, and agreements that were developed over time by Congress and the executive branch. In some cases, courts entered this process, too, though often as a "junior partner," according to Fisher.[62] These matters included the investigatory power of Congress (i.e., did Congress have a right to demand information from a president? Did a president have an obligation to provide it?), the veto power (i.e., how soon after receiving a veto message must Congress schedule an override vote? What is the meaning of "2/3 of the House" for override purposes? Under what conditions may a president veto?), the pocket veto (i.e., can it be used intrasession, intersession, or only at *sine die* adjournment?), recess appointments (i.e., under what conditions are they appropriate? Does the timing of a vacancy matter?), incompatibility and ineligibility clauses, the legislative veto (agreed to by Congress and the president for fifty years before the courts entered the matter), and war powers and covert operations (left almost entirely to the political branches to arrive at their own workable solutions).[63]

For those cases that *do* reach the courts, many are sent back to the legislative and executive branches because of a failure to meet threshold requirements such as mootness, ripeness, standing, equitable discretion, or political question. The area of foreign affairs and questions of the division of power between the president and Congress over the use of military force are notorious for being turned aside by the courts, in most instances, on the basis of these threshold determinations or because "fact-finding" was required.

The refusal of the courts to rule on cases brought during the Vietnam War or in those cases that have asked for a ruling on the constitutionality or applicability of the War Powers Resolution are the most difficult ones to accept, when the nation cries out for an answer. Yet, Fisher is steadfast in his belief that the courts are correct to redirect these cases back to the branches that need to make the hard decisions in the political arena.

Moreover, he believes strongly that the courts should not be available to members of Congress who think they can run to the courts for another try every time they lose a vote on the floor of the House or Senate. In his view, if members have an institutional remedy available and where their appeal to the courts is simply for the purpose of trying to get another chance in a different forum, the courts are correct to deny them a hearing for lack of standing. In such matters where there is *no* institutional remedy available to members, and where a particular action by the president encroaches on an exclusive congressional power, then Fisher would support judicial intervention. He agreed with the recent Supreme Court decision on the line-item veto in *Raines v Byrd* (1997) to deny congressional standing as an example of the former; cases on the pocket veto, where the courts decided on the merits, illustrate the latter.

The area of war powers is one where the effort to achieve some level of agreement between Congress and the president over each one's respective powers has been ongoing for more than two hundred years. Fisher has explored this struggle for power from start to finish, but he has paid special attention to Truman's commitment of U.S. forces to Korea in June 1950 as the bellwether episode that set a precedent for presidential wars. Truman relied on United Nations Security Council Resolutions, but did not request authorization from Congress for U.S. participation in a full-scale war. Congress, for its part, "was largely passive in the face of Truman's usurpation of the war power," Fisher writes.[64] Senator Taft was one of the few, lonely voices to express opposition to Truman's action, and to jar the consciences of his fellow senators who had abdicated their institutional responsibility by standing idly by while Truman had expropriated their power.

Fisher notes that it took a year before the Senate roused itself to debate the legality of Truman's actions, denouncing them as violations of not only the U.S. Constitution but also the United Nations Charter and the United Nations Participation Act.[65]

The experience in Korea served to alert the Senate of the slippage of power it had permitted, so that when Truman proposed the sending of four U.S. divisions to Europe in January 1951, the Senate stepped up to its responsibility, and engaged in the "Great Debate" of 1951 over the conditions under which the president could make such a commitment.[66] It passed a modest, nonbinding resolution that did not restrain the president from the European commitment, but it did make clear that such a commitment should first get the approval of Congress, and that any future troop commitments to Europe must be approved by that body.[67] In this way, the Senate was provoked to respond to the president's actions, and, in the process, found itself forced to confront and assess its constitutional responsibility.

C. *Interpretation by States.* Constitutional interpretation occurs not only at the federal level but at the state level, as well. State courts and state legislatures are free to provide rights and to construe state constitutional protections more broadly than those recognized at the federal level. In this sense, the U.S. Constitution is a floor beneath which rights protection may not fall, but not a ceiling above which it may not rise.[68]

Fisher has identified certain issues and states which illustrate this pattern. California, New Jersey, Oregon, Washington and Wisconsin have been in the forefront of states that have interpreted their state constitutions and laws more expansively than the U.S. Supreme Court.[69] For example, Fisher notes that state supreme courts in Indiana and Wisconsin recognized the equivalent of a 6th Amendment right to counsel for indigent defendants almost a hundred years before *Gideon v Wainwright* (1963).[70] The exclusionary rule that was finally applied to criminal cases in state courts with the Supreme Court decision in *Mapp v Ohio* (1961) had already been adopted by about half of the states by then.[71] And, in the other direction, the "good-faith exception" to the exclusionary rule that the Supreme Court announced in *U.S. v Leon* (1984) has been rejected by a handful of states as too restrictive on defendants, and, thus, has been deemed inapplicable under state constitutional law in Michigan, Mississippi, New Jersey, New York, and Wisconsin.[72] Other issues reported by Fisher where state constitutional law has diverged from federal law are over church-state matters in education, property taxes for school financing, free speech on private property, public funding for abortions, and obscenity.[73] As of the 1983 Court decision in *Michigan v Long*, the Supreme Court has injected the standard that state courts that decide issues exclusively on the basis of state constitutions and state laws must show that their rulings are based on "separate, adequate and independent grounds."[74] Where those criteria are met, the Supreme Court will leave state court decisions undisturbed. Thus, the federal system of governance results in a federal system of constitutional protections, as well, allowing for the "balancing of competing political and social values" that is the essence, for Fisher, of constitutional law to be performed on both the state and federal levels.[75]

III. Protection of Judicial Independence

Consistent with Fisher's concern that each governmental institution exercise its power responsibly and protect its own prerogatives is his corresponding interest in insuring that the judiciary remains independent and free from undue political influence. Two recent issues underscore the potential for political interference with the judiciary, and Fisher's sensitivity to these matters brings them to the attention of scholars and political officials.

With the passage of the Line Item Veto Act of 1996 and under a proposed balanced budget constitutional amendment, Fisher cautioned that courts would be brought into the political mix in a troublesome way. The fear with the line item veto was that courts would be vulnerable to political maneuvers by a president who would have the power to excise "items" from the judicial branch's budget requests as retaliation for unfavorable court decisions. Courts, unlike Congress or executive agencies, are unable to engage in a bargaining process and, thus, would have no way to defend themselves. The executive branch, through the Department of Justice, litigates about half of the cases in the federal courts, so the potential for a conflict of interest would be real, when a court faced the prospect of ruling against the government, and leaving it then to wonder whether such action might provoke executive branch retribution.[76]

The Court removed that potential cause for concern when it held the line item veto unconstitutional in *Clinton v New York* (1998).[77] The larger point here, however, that underscores Fisher's thinking is that he believed that the Court needed to consider, even if the parties failed to present it, the possibility that the workings of the statute could lead to the compromising of judicial independence.[78] He notes two prior occasions where Congress had recognized the need to protect judicial independence by providing in the Budget and Accounting Act of 1921 that judicial branch appropriations requests could be changed only by Congress, not by the president, and by creating the Administrative Office of the U.S. Courts in 1939 to manage the finances of the judicial branch, thus, removing that function from the Department of Justice which, as a frequent player before the courts, had the potential for politicizing this task.[79] Fisher reminded Congress of these two examples in his testimony on the Line Item Veto Act before the Senate Committee on Governmental Affairs, although the bill passed both houses without any exemption for the judiciary.[80]

Repeated efforts to add a balanced budget amendment to the Constitution raise the issue of judicial independence in a different way. Here, Fisher suggests that the courts could get drawn into the mechanics of the budgetary process, where they could be asked to define the terms used in the amendment in cases brought to determine whether Congress and the president have complied with the amendment's requirements.[81] He points to experience with balanced budget requirements at the state level to demonstrate that courts in New Jersey, Missouri, Massachusetts, and Louisiana have ruled on whether specific actions taken by governors were justified under their state constitutions in order to satisfy the goal of achieving a balanced budget.[82] In this way, courts will need to pass judgment on the steps taken by presidents to balance the budget and will inevitably be expected to weigh complex political and fiscal factors in the process.[83]

Fisher's primary concern with both of these tools is that they would increase the president's power, bring courts into technical matters for which they are ill equipped and may well be ill served, and would substantially interfere with Congress's constitutionally delegated power of the purse.

Conclusions

Fisher's understanding of the role of the courts may seem paradoxical: he reduces or limits the judiciary's participation in the interpretive function by urging that this responsibility is shared with other branches, the states and the people; at the same time, he broadens the range of influences on the courts far beyond legal, technical ones to include the weighing of competing social and political values. Consonant with his belief that law and politics are inextricably intertwined is his characterization of the courts as the nexus where law and politics meet.

Yet, their rendezvous is much less for the lofty, philosophical reasons some might suggest than for the very pragmatic consideration that the legitimacy of the courts depends on public acceptance of their decisions.[84] For that reason, courts wander from the general contours of social and political forces at their peril.

> For their own institutional protection, courts must take account of social movements and political pressures.[85]

> Courts maintain their strength by steering a course that fits within the permissible limits of public opinion.[86]

This sensitivity to larger forces appears not only in the substance of court decisions but also in the process of reaching them.[87] Thus, the broad, sweeping decisions that revolutionize the legal and political landscape are few and infrequent. Much more common are the "half-steps" and "installments" that Fisher describes as the way the courts do their work, setting the foundation for future decisions that expand or contract with the times.[88]

Most of all, his model works. Fisher's vantage point at the crossroads of government and academia affords him a distinctive perspective from which to view the process and to inform the rest of us. He has seen it from all sides and has pronounced it "workable"—lumbering or fitful, at times, but at its best when its component parts exercise the careful, modest, reasoned, incremental judgments that the framers expected would fuel the system. And for chronicling the various paths that lead us to that conclusion, Fisher may be (though he may protest the designation) the "ultimate interpreter."

Notes

I wish to gratefully acknowledge the support of the New Paltz Foundation for providing me with a Research and Creative Projects Award for this project.

1. See Louis Fisher, *President and Congress: Power and Policy* (New York: The Free Press, 1972); Louis Fisher, *Presidential Spending Power* (Princeton, N.J.: Princeton University Press, 1975); Louis Fisher, *The Constitution Between Friends: Congress, The President and the Law* (New York: St. Martin's Press, 1978); Louis Fisher, *The Politics of Shared Power: Congress and the Executive* (Washington, D.C.: Congressional Quarterly Press, 1981).

2. See book of same title, Louis Fisher, *Constitutional Dialogues: Interpretation as Political Process* (Princeton, N.J.: Princeton University

Press, 1988), though he gives credit to Alexander Bickel for first charac-
terizing courts as involved in a "continuing colloquoy" with other political
bodies and the public (*Constitutional Dialogues*, p. 3).

3. *Id.* at 244.

4. *Id.* at 3–8.

5. *Roe v Wade* 410 US 113, 173 (1973); *Constitutional Dialogues,* 39.

6. *Constitutional Dialogues,* 8.

7. *Id.* at 10.

8. See Louis Fisher, "Does the Supreme Court Have the Last Word
on Constitutional Law?" in *E Pluribus Unum: Constitutional Principles
and the Institutions of Government* (Lanham: Md.: University Press of
Virginia, 1988), 166–190; Louis Fisher, "The Curious Belief in Judicial
Supremacy," *Suffolk University Law Review,* Vol. XXV, No. 1, Spring 1991,
86–116; Louis Fisher, "One of the Guardians, Some of the Time," in *Is the
Supreme Court the Guardian of the Constitution?* (Washington, D.C.:
American Enterprise Institute, 1993), 82–97; Louis Fisher, "How Supreme
is the Supreme Court?" in *Governance V: Institutions and Issues,* Kenneth
W. Thompson, ed. (Lanham, Md.: University Press of America, 1994), esp.
6–12; *Constitutional Dialogues,* Ch. 2.

9. "One of the Guardians, Some of the Time," 85.

10. *Constitutional Dialogues,* 243.

11. *Id.* at 243.

12. "The Curious Belief in Judicial Supremacy," 96–97; "One of the
Guardians, Some of the Time," 85–87; *Constitutional Dialogues,* 54–56;
"Does the Supreme Court Have the Last Word?" 175–177; "How Supreme
is the Supreme Court?" 6–7.

13. "The Curious Belief in Judicial Supremacy," 97; "One of the Guardians, Some of the Time," 86–87.

14. See "The Curious Belief in Judicial Supremacy;" "One of the Guardians, Some of the Time;" *Constitutional Dialogues,* Ch. 7.

15. "How Supreme is the Supreme Court?" 4–6; "The Curious Belief
in Judicial Supremacy," 85–87.

16. David Cole, "Conservatives Battle Themselves," *Legal Times,* July
14, 1997, S42.

17. *Id.* at S42.

18. *Id.* at S42.

19. *Id.* at S42.

20. *Id.* at S42.

21. *Constitutional Dialogues,* 247–251.

22. *Miranda v Arizona,* 384 US 436, 467 (1966).

23. Louis Fisher, "Protecting Religious Liberty: Guardians Outside the Supreme Court," (unpublished copy available from Fisher), 19–20; "How Supreme is the Supreme Court?" 11; "One of the Guardians, Some of the Time," 93; "The Curious Belief in Judicial Supremacy," 110.

24. *Employment Division v Smith,* 494 US 872, 890 (1990).

25. *Id.* at 890.

26. *City of Boerne v Flores,* (No. 95-2074 [1997], slip opinion, 27).

27. *Id.* at 27.

28. See T. R. Goldman, "Back in Congress' Court," *Legal Times,* July 14, 1997, 8–9.

29. See *Constitutional Dialogues,* 35–36.

30. "The Curious Belief in Judicial Supremacy," 94; *Constitutional Dialogues,* 238–239; "One of the Guardians, Some of the Time," 84–85.

31. "The Curious Belief in Judicial Supremacy," 94–95; *Constitutional Dialogues,* 239; "One of the Guardians, Some of the Time," 85.

32. 3 *Messages and Papers of the Presidents* 1145 (1897) as quoted in Fisher, *Constitutional Dialogues,* 240 and in "The Curious Belief in Judicial Supremacy," 98.

33. *Id.* at 1145.

34. *Constitutional Dialogues,* 241–242; "The Curious Belief in Judicial Supremacy," 98–100; "One of the Guardians, Some of the Time," 89; "Protecting Religious Liberty: Guardians Outside the Supreme Court," 4; "How Supreme is the Supreme Court?" 8.

35. See Harold M. Hyman, *A More Perfect Union: The Impact of the Civil War and Reconstruction of the Constitution* 6 (1975) quoted in *Constitutional Dialogues,* 242; "The Curious Belief in Judicial Supremacy," 98–99; and "Protecting Religious Liberty: Guardians Outside the Supreme Court," 4.

36. *Constitutional Dialogues,* 241; "The Curious Belief in Judicial Supremacy," 100; "One of the Guardians, Some of the Time," 89; "Protecting Religious Liberty: Guardians Outside the Supreme Court," 4; "How Supreme is the Supreme Court?" 8.

37. "The Curious Belief in Judicial Supremacy," 87.

38. "The Curious Belief in Judicial Supremacy," 100–101; "One of the Guardians, Some of the Time," 89–90; "Protecting Religious Liberty: Guardians Outside the Supreme Court," 5; "How Supreme is the Supreme Court?" 9.

39. "The Curious Belief in Judicial Supremacy," 100–101.

40. *Youngstown Sheet and Tube Co. v Sawyer,* 343 US 579 (1952); *U.S. v Nixon,* 418 US 683 (1974).

41. See *Ameron, Inc. v U.S. Army Corps of Engineers,* 610 F. Supp. 750 (D.N.J. 1985), aff'd as modified, 809 F. 2d 979 (3d Cir. 1986), cert. dismissed, 109 S. Ct. 297 (1988); *Lear Siegler, Inc. v Lehman* 842 F. 2d 1102, 1121–1126 (9th Cir. 1988), reh'g en banc ordered sub nom. *Lear Siegler, Inc. v Ball* 863 F. 2d 693 (9th Cir. 1988) (en banc).

42. See Robert J. Spitzer, "Presidential Prerogative Power: The Case of the Bush Administration and Legislative Power," *PS: Political Science and Politics,* Vol. XXIV, No. 1, March 1991, 38–42; Chuck Alston, "Bush Crusades on Many Fronts to Retake President's Turf," *CQ Weekly Report,* Vol. 48, No. 5, February 3, 1990, 294; Andrew Rosenthal, "Reaffirming Commitment, Bush Signs Civil Rights Bill: President Tries to Quell Furor on Intepreting Scope of New Law," *The New York Times,* 22 November 1991, 1, 20, as an example of the effect of signing statements.

43. "One of the Guardians, Some of the Time," 90–92; "Protecting Religious Liberty: Guardians Outside the Supreme Court," 6–7; *The Civil Rights Cases,* 109 US 3 (1883); *Bradwell v State of Illinois,* 16 Wall. (83 US) 130 (1873).

44. "The Curious Belief in Judicial Supremacy," 101–105; "One of the Guardians, Some of the Time," 91; "Protecting Religious Liberty: Guardians Outside the Supreme Court," 6–7.

45. *General Electric v Gilbert,* 429 US 125 (1976); Pregnancy Discrimination Act, 92 Stat. 2076 (1978).

46. *Hammer v Dagenhart,* 247 US 251 (1918); *Bailey v Drexel Furniture Co.,* 259 US 20 (1922).

47. See "The Curious Belief in Judicial Supremacy," 108–109; "How Supreme is the Supreme Court?" 9–10.

48. On the flag salute cases, see *Minersville School District v Gobitis,* 310 US 586 (1940); *Jones v Opelika,* 316 US 584 (1942); *West Virginia State Board of Education v Barnette,* 319 US 624 (1943). On the Japanese-American cases, see *Hirabayashi v U.S.,* 320 US 81 (1943); *Korematsu v U.S.,* 323 US 214 (1944).

49. "The Curious Belief in Judicial Supremacy," 109–110; "One of the Guardians, Some of the Time," 92–93; "Protecting Religious Liberty:

Guardians Outside the Supreme Court," 12–22; "How Supreme is the Supreme Court?" 10–11.

50. *Hirabayashi v U.S.,* 320 US 81 (1943); *Korematsu v U.S.,* 323 US 214 (1944).

51. *Korematsu v U.S.,* at 246 (Jackson, dissenting).

52. "The Curious Belief in Judicial Supremacy," 111–112; "One of the Guardians, Some of the Time," 94–95.

53. *Constitutional Dialogues,* 256; "One of the Guardians, Some of the Time," 95–96.

54. *Constitutional Dialogues,* 255–257; "One of the Guardians, Some of the Time," 95–96.

55. *Constitutional Dialogues,* 261–263; "One of the Guardians, Some of the Time," 96; "Protecting Religious Liberty: Guardians Outside the Supreme Court," 22–23.

56. Louis Fisher, "Separation of Powers: Interpretation Ouside the Courts," *Pepperdine Law Review,* Vol. 18, No. 1, 1990, 57.

57. Louis Fisher, "Constitutional Interpretation by Members of Congress," *North Carolina Law Review,* Vol. 63, No. 4, April 1985, 708–709.

58. "Separation of Powers: Interpretation Outside the Courts," 57–59; *U.S. v Nixon,* 418 US 683 (1974); *Nixon v Administrator of General Services,* 433 US 425 (1977); *Commodity Futures Trading Commission v Schor,* 478 US 833 (1986); *Morrison v Olson,* 487 US 654 (1988); *Mistretta v U.S.,* 488 US 361 (1989); *Nixon v Fitzgerald,* 457 US 731 (1982); *Northern Pipeline Construction Co. v Marathon Pipeline Co.,* 458 US 50 (1982); *INS v Chadha,* 462 US 919 (1983); *Bowsher v Synar,* 478 US 714 (1986).

59. "Separation of Powers: Interpretation Outside the Courts," 59; "Constitutional Interpretation by Members of Congress," 734–738.

60. "Separation of Powers: Interpretation Outside the Courts," 60.

61. *Id.* at 84–86.

62. "Separation of Powers: Interpretation Outside the Courts," 65.

63. See "Separation of Powers: Interpretation Outside the Courts," 57–93.

64. Louis Fisher, "The Korean War: On What Legal Basis Did Truman Act?' *The American Journal of International Law,* Vol. 89, No. 1, January 1995, 34.

65. *Id.* at 35; Louis Fisher, *Presidential War Power* (Lawrence, Kans.: University Press of Kansas, 1995), 88.

66. *Presidential War Power,* 98–100.

67. 97 *Congressional Record* 3283 (para. 6) (1951), cited in *Presidential War Power,* 100.

68. Louis Fisher, "How States Shape Constitutional Law," *State Legislatures,* Vol. 15, No. 7, August 1989, 37.

69. *Id.* at 37–39.

70. *Id.* at 37.

71. *Id.* at 37.

72. *Id.* at 37.

73. *Id.* at 38–39.

74. *Id.* at 39.

75. "Constitutional Interpretation by Members of Congress," 743.

76. Louis Fisher, "Judicial Independence and the Item Veto," in *The Judges' Journal,* Vol. 36, No. 1, Winter 1997, 19.

77. *Clinton v New York,* No. 97-1374 (1998) (slip opinion).

78. *Id.* at 53.

79. *Id.* at 20.

80. *Id.* at 20, 53.

81. Louis Fisher, "The Balanced Budget Amendment: Risks to Political Institutions," in *PRG Report,* Vol. XVI, No. 1, Spring 1994, 4.

82. *Id.* at 5.

83. *Id.* at 6.

84. See Louis Fisher, "The Law/Politics Dialogue: It's Not All Courts!" in *Handbook of Public Law and Public Administration,* Philip J. Cooper and Chester I. Newland, eds. (Jossey-Bass, 1997), 63–75.

85. *Id.* at 7.

86. *Id.* at 8.

87. *Id.* at 9.

88. *Id.* at 9.

5

Judicial Power, Coordinate Construction, and Presidential Warmaking

David Gray Adler

Louis Fisher's ascent to the front rank of constitutional scholars, a journey begun in the miasma of Vietnam and Watergate, marked by scholarly acclaim, characterized by a healthy suspicion of the mandarins, new or old, and guided by a dependable compass that signalled the importance of constitutional studies even when it was not fashionable, has soared into the seventh decade of his life with no apparent signs of cessation. The examination, analysis, and commemoration of the body of a scholar's work typically awaits passage to Mount Olympus,[1] or at least retirement, but in the case of Louis Fisher or, as we might say it, *In re Fisher,* time is not on the side of those who have undertaken this project in the shadow of Fisher's sixty-third birthday, not when those of us conducting the examination are forced to contend with a vitae that stretches some 20 pages and counts 14 books, 150 articles, and other works winding their way toward publication.[2] While our effort here is certainly not premature (indeed, it is overdue) we are, nonetheless, apt to overlook some of Fisher's significant contributions and writings. We simply cannot read everything—every book review, commentary essay, op-ed piece and letter to the editor—that he has written, and yet we cannot wait any longer lest, like Sisyphus, we'll fail to scale the mountain of Fisher's works.

My own task was a daunting one: "Fisher and the Constitution." It can't be done adequately, so I changed the focus to something a bit more manageable, "Judicial Power, Coordinate Construction, and Presidential Warmaking"—more manageable, to be sure, but even this topic requires a review of more than a thousand pages in print, not to mention references or discussions in related works, scattered across some twenty-five years. In this chapter I do briefly review Fisher's understanding of the issue of constitutional interpretation and the role of the judiciary in that process, among other subjects. But I'm particularly interested in discussing some angles and perspectives in his recent and prominent book, *Presidential War Power*,[3] a work that has placed him at the epicenter of discussion and debate about the constitutional repository of the war power, an issue of surpassing importance to the nation. In the spirit of his prize-winning book, *Constitutional Dialogues*,[4] I intend to review some of the more important reactions to his work on the war power and to offer responses to his critics.[5]

If it is true, as the title of Robert Spitzer's chapter implies, that Louis Fisher has rescued the Constitution from the lawyers, it is perhaps equally true that he has tried to save it from the courts.[6] For Fisher, the Constitution does not necessarily mean what the judges say it means.[7] He rejects the misreading and canonization of *Marbury v Madison*,[8] the result of which leaves students of constitutional law with the impression that constitutional interpretation is the exclusive province of the courts, that justices act while the rest of us wait passively for the impartation of truths.[9] That judicial conceit, which lies at the heart of the doctrine of judicial supremacy, has long been a favorite target of Fisher's. He has devoted himself to the cause of demonstrating that the Court does not enjoy exclusive jurisdiction in the enterprise of constitutional interpretation. Rather, the art of constitutional interpretation is a process or a dialogue among numerous actors, including the president, Congress, courts, states, and private citizens. In sum, as we shall see, Fisher is a proponent of departmentalism or coordinate construction.[10]

Judicial Finality

The widespread perception in America of the Supreme Court as the ultimate arbiter of the meaning of the Constitution is, in no small measure, attributable to the Court's own pronouncements.[11] The prevalence of that view, particularly in the legal community, also stems from the fact that most law school instructors preach the virtues of judicial supremacy.[12] Since Chief Justice John Marshall's declaration in *Marbury v Madison*, that "it is emphatically the province and duty of the judicial department to say what the law is,"[13] the Court has insisted that it alone delivers the "final word" on the meaning of the Constitution. In *Cooper v Aaron*, the Court stated that *Marbury* had "declared the basic principle that the federal judiciary is supreme in the exposition of the law of the Constitution. . . ."[14] The Court reaffirmed the principle in 1962:

> Deciding whether a matter has in measure been committed by the Constitution to another branch of government, or whether action of that branch exceeds whatever authority has been committed, is itself a delicate exercise in constitutional interpretation, and is a responsibility of this Court as ultimate interpreter of the Constitution.[15]

But as Fisher is fond of noting, being "ultimate interpreter" is not the same as being either the exclusive or final interpreter. He has exposed the careless characterization of the Court as final arbiter and has observed that such a description "does not grant the judiciary superiority in the sense that final judgments are unreviewable."[16] The Court has reviewed and overturned its "final" judgments, as the Flag Salute Cases, among others, have demonstrated.[17] As Fisher has noted, "the Court is especially prone to abandon the doctrine of stare decisis when the Court discovers errors of constitutional doctrine."[18] He cites, approvingly, a dissent written by Chief Justice Roger Taney, eight years before Dred Scott, in which Taney asserted that the Court's opinion "upon the construction of the Constitution is always open to discussion when it is supposed to have been founded in error, and that its judicial authority should hereafter depend altogether on the force of the reasoning by which it is supported."[19] And if judicial interpretations may be reviewed and reversed then they are, by definition, not final, in spite of Justice Jackson's elegant dictum that decisions of the Supreme Court "are not final because we are infallible, but we are infallible only because we are final."[20] Thus no decision by the Court is final. As Fisher has observed, "what is 'final' at one stage of our political development may be reopened at some later date, leading to fresh interpretation and overruling of past doctrines."[21] From Fisher's perspective, constitutional "truths" are not imposed by an all-powerful judicial authority. Constitutional authority is derived, in many cases, from conflicts left unfinished, which are reviewed,

renewed, and reappraised by contestants and subsequently fash-
ioned by an accommodationist politics between or among the various branches of government. Constitutional issues are rarely settled
in any way that resembles or suggests a finished product. Most
constitutional "solutions" tend to be contingent and unfinished, left
perhaps, in a state of tolerable reliability or tentative finality; in
short, they may be fairly-firmly settled, like a definite maybe.

Fisher is willing to concede an element of finality to judicial
decisions, but it is limited, as Lincoln said in his First Inaugural
Address, to those parties involved in the particular case before the
Court.[22] But he is equally clear that courts "are not the ultimate
interpreter . . . of the larger issue of which that case is a part."[23] For
Fisher, as for Lincoln, there is no sole or single interpreter of the
Constitution. The "meaning" of the Constitution may be said to
derive from a process of conversation, discussion, and debate which
involves Congress, the president, Courts, states, private citizens,
and public officials. This "discussion" will produce, not a final constitutional truth in the form of granitic certainty; it will yield,
rather, a Miltonesque truth like that envisioned in Aereopagitica.
That is not to say, however, that the process is a wholly unbuttoned
free-for-all in which all views, ideologies, opinions, and prejudices
are of equal value or command the same degree of respect. For
Fisher, the currency of a constitutional opinion, whether rendered
by the judicial, legislative, or executive branch "depends altogether
on the force of the reasoning by which it is supported."[24] The persuasive power of the reasoning, moreover, must be rooted in the
text of the Constitution, for Fisher has embraced Justice Felix
Frankfurter's view that "the ultimate touchstone of constitutionality is the Constitution itself and not what we have said about it."[25]
This approach establishes for Fisher a reference point for discussion about constitutional issues, and it serves to limit the judiciary
as well. Fisher is hardly an advocate of judicial activism, a point
he freely admits: "I am no more an admirer of judicial power than
of congressional or presidential power. Like any other branch of
government, the judiciary must operate within limits. Free wheel-
ing judicial activism should be indefensible from any quarter, liberal or conservative."[26]

Fisher recognizes, of course, that judges do legislate, for as he
has observed, "It is too late in the day to pretend that judges 'find'
the law rather than 'make it.'"[27] His preference for the exercise of
judicial review runs in harness with Benjamin Cardozo's 1921 classic study on the judicial process. In his famous work, *The Nature*

of the Judicial Process, Cardozo examined the issue of judicial legislation in a chapter on "The Judge as Legislator." Judges and
legislators share various qualities:

> The choice of methods, the appraisement of values, must
> in the end be guided by like considerations for the one as
> for the other. Each indeed is legislating within the limits
> of his competence. No doubt the limits for the judge are
> narrower. He legislates only between the gaps. He fills the
> open space in the law. . . . None the less, within the confines
> of those open spaces and those of precedent and tradi-
> tions, choice moves with a freedom which stamps its ac-
> tion as creative.[28]

At all events, as Cardozo later wrote, a judge "may not substitute
his own reading for one established by the legislature,"[29] an act
that represents the epitome of the judicial activism that Fisher
criticizes.[30] Perhaps Fisher would endorse Judge J. Skelly Wright's
observation: "the most important value choices have already been
made by the framers of the Constitution," and judicial value choices
"are to be made only within the parameters" of those choices.[31]
There are, indeed, some qualities of an interpretivist in Fisher's
view of the role of the judiciary in constitutional interpretation, but
this must be said with caution, for various reasons. First, it is true
that Fisher is critical of freewheeling judicial activism, as represented, for example, in either the Court's creation of the liberty of
contract doctrine or the role of the president as "sole organ" of
American foreign policy in *United States v Curtiss-Wright Export
Corporation.*[32] Second, as we shall discuss below, Fisher does believe that the framers' intentions or "choices," as Judge Wright
would put it, are discernible in some areas, as for example in the
area of warmaking. On that score, Fisher has justly stated: "It is
clear from the record of the Philadelphia Convention that the framers reserved the war power to Congress, with the single exception
of allowing the President to "repel sudden attacks."[33] The conclusion to be drawn here is not that Fisher is a devotee of original
intention jurisprudence but rather that while he recognizes the
influence, merit and value of the framers' purposes or choices, he
is not enslaved by them. As Fisher has observed, "the framers'
intent is an important but inadequate method of interpreting the
Constitution."[34] Standing by itself, original intention is rarely, if
ever, dispositive. The issues of the constitutional repository of the

power to initiate war may well constitute a unique issue, since the framers' purposes were so pellucidly clear, yet even here Fisher finds confirmatory evidence in the views expressed by early actions in the constitutional dialogue, including presidents, the courts, and Congress. Candor requires admission of the importance of the framers' intentions as a source of guidance on constitutional issues, but they are, as Fisher has stated, "an impractical remedy" for judicial activism.[35] A more adequate remedy, from Fisher's perspective, is the approach of coordinate construction, to which we now turn.

Coordinate Construction

As we have seen, Fisher adamantly believes that "constitutional law is not a monopoly of the judiciary."[36] Decisions by the courts rest "undisturbed only to the extent that Congress, the President, and the general public find the decisions convincing, reasonable, and acceptable. Otherwise, the debate on constitutional principles will continue."[37] The process of constitutional interpretation, then, is a fluid dialogue among many participants, a "constitutional colloquy," as Alexander Bickel described it.[38] According to the doctrine of coordinate construction, "the President and members of Congress have both the authority and the competence to engage in Constitutional interpretation, not only before the courts decide but afterwards as well. All these branches perform a valuable, broad, and ongoing function in helping to shape the meaning of the Constitution."[39] Thus, Fisher embraces Lincoln's view on the limited authority of the Dred Scott decision: "Congress and the President were free to reach their own constitutional judgments, even if at odds with past court rulings, and then let the Court decide again."[40] The interaction of the three branches in the process of constitutional interpretation reflects the doctrine of checks and balances in motion. There is nothing controversial here, because the courts expect the other branches of government to interpret the Constitution in their initial deliberations.[41] In fact, the Court said as much in *United States v Nixon*. "In the performance of assigned constitutional duties each branch of the Government must initially interpret the Constitution, and the interpretation of its powers by any branch is due great respect from the others."[42] Indeed, it is hard to believe that either Congress or the president could function responsibly without an initial determination of its authority or duty to act.

What rankles many judicial scholars about the doctrines of coordinate construction, of course, is not only the threat to judicial monopoly, but the potential mischief that can occur as a result of the claim made by Fisher that Congress and the president have the "authority and competence to engage in constitutional interpretation, not only before the courts decide but *afterwards* as well." Fisher quite clearly recognizes the potential for mischief in Thomas Jefferson's theory of coordinate construction, the specter of a Kentucky Feud—two branches unalterably opposed in their constitutional claims without the prospect of finality, judicial or otherwise. Jefferson believed that the three branches must be "co-ordinate and independent of each another." Decisions by one branch, including judicial interpretations of constitutional questions, were to be given "no control to another branch." Each branch has an equal right to decide for itself what is the meaning of the Constitution in the cases submitted to its action, and especially, where it is to act ultimately and without appeal."[43] Thus Jefferson seems to claim that each branch is supreme on certain constitutional issues. The difficulty with Jefferson's approach is that he does not identify those issues. Here is the potential for mischief. Fisher, himself, raises the question: "Without specifying the areas of supremacy, the country might face a multitude of conflicting and shifting interpretations, none with any greater significance or 'finality' than another. All would have equal weight. The risk of Jefferson's theory is substantial."[44] Fisher may have looked in the mirror and seen Jefferson, for he has raised one of the great questions surrounding Watergate: "What would have happened in 1974 had President Nixon, in the confrontation over the Watergate tapes, insisted that his interpretation of executive privilege had comparable merit and authority to that of the Supreme Court?"[45]

Fisher does not provide a direct answer to his hypothetical question, and critics of coordinate construction have found fault with him on this score. It has been fairly said, for example, that "Fisher does not attempt to specify the circumstances that he believes would justify the nonacquiescence in the Supreme Court's interpretations. He does not address how wrong the decision must be, how abhorrent its consequences, how likely overruling must be, how often the other branches can submit identical cases to the courts, or what other methods they should use to change the constitutional course."[46] The criticism is important and there remains the gnawing task of confronting it. One approach, apparently acceptable to Fisher, may be found in Alexander Bickel's "solution" to those southern officials who opposed desegregation and the Court's decision in *Cooper v Aaron*. The officials, Bickel wrote, could rightly "refuse to consider the issue settled and could relitigate it at every opportunity that the judicial process offered, and of course it offers a thousand and one."[47] Relitigation is often an alternative to unhappy contestants, but it is inconceivable that Fisher would have offered that advice to Nixon, for two reasons. First, as he has written, there "are certain moments in our constitutional history" where there is a "compelling need for an authoritative and binding decision by the Supreme Court."[48] He cites *Cooper v Aaron* as one example, and the Court's unanimous opinion in the *Nixon* case as another. Second, "court orders must be obeyed, but obedience here relates only to the orderly and expedious administrations of justice, not to the soundness or finality of a court order."[49] In *Nixon*, as the Court itself acknowledged, the "expeditious administration of justice" clearly required the president to surrender the tapes.

The issue of nonacquiescence to a judicial decision is an important one, to be sure, if for no other reason than that it raises the question of governmental compliance with constitutional norms, assuming, of course, that the Court has correctly identified the constitutional norm. Fisher's point is that the Court may fail in that task, and if it does, why should Congress, the president, or the American people for that matter, acquiesce in the Court's error? The Court, on occasion, will acknowledge its errors and reverse a previous decision. Justice Jackson, for example, wrote: "I see no reason why I should be consciously wrong today because I was unconsciously wrong yesterday."[50] When the Court errs, "it is particularly important," as Fisher has written, "that Congress, the President, the states, and the public have a duty to pursue other alternatives or prevail upon the Court to revisit and rethink anachronous holdings."[51] Constitutional errors are less likely to be perpetuated if they are subjected to a rigorous examination conducted by many participants in an ongoing dialogue.

Foreign Affairs, Executive Power, and Warmaking

Louis Fisher's most recent book, *Presidential War Power*, has, like his earlier books, drawn critical acclaim for its ability to provoke further inquiry, testing and challenge, and also boasts the distinction of having earned a very warm review in the *New York Times* from the distinguished observer, Theodore Draper.[52] *Presidential*

War Power is drawn from several articles and essays in various journals and books written in the past decade, and while it represents a culmination of a great deal of work, vast learning, and labor in the vineyards of original documents, it is hardly his last word on the subject of warmaking.[53]

Fisher's argument is crystal clear: a great gulf separates the constitutional blueprint for warmaking and governmental practice for most of the past half-century. As Fisher demonstrates in clear, lean, and lucid prose, the "constitutional framework adopted by the framers is clear in its basic principles."[54] The framers vested in Congress the authority to initiate war. The president, as commander in chief, was empowered to "repel sudden attacks" against the United States and to conduct a war authorized by Congress. The president was given no authority to initiate or commence hostilities. Throughout the nineteenth and into the twentieth century, the president and Congress largely adhered to this constitutional design. But since the end of World War II, unilateral presidential warmaking has become a commonplace, a breach, according to Fisher, of constitutional principles and democratic values.[55] Presidents and their defenders have addressed a variety of arguments as a defense, as we shall see, but Fisher dismisses them in a sure-footed and balanced manner.

The Constitution vests in Congress the sole and exclusive authority to initiate military hostilities, including full-blown, total war, as well as lesser acts of armed force. While the "original intent" of the framers toward some constitutional provisions may be unclear or beyond recovery, there is, remarkably, no doubt about their decision to establish Congress as the repository of the power to commence war on behalf of the American people.[56] A more impressive and even stunning feature of the framers' design, however, is the fact that it constituted a dramatic break from the existing models of government throughout Europe, which had placed the war power and foreign affairs firmly in the grasp of the monarch.

The framers' departure from prevailing schemes reflected their intellectual orientation, their understanding of history, and their own practical experiences.[57] In their aspiration to effectuate a republican government, the founders drafted a Constitution that "allowed only Congress to loose the military forces of the United States on other nations.[58] Deliberations at the Constitutional Convention demonstrate that the delegates embraced the principle of collective decision making, the concept of shared power in foreign affairs, and the cardinal tenet of republican ideology that the conjoined wisdom of many is superior to that of one.

The fact that the power of war and peace was historically associated with the monarchy was addressed repeatedly at the convention. On June 1, 1787, Charles Pinckney said he was for a vigorous president but was afraid that some of the proposals "would render the Executive a Monarchy, of the worst kind, to wit an elective one." John Rutledge wanted the executive power placed in a single person, "tho' he was not for giving him the power of war and peace." James Wilson sought to reassure the delegates. The prerogatives of the British monarchy were not "a proper guide in defining the executive powers. Some of these prerogatives were of a Legislative nature. Among others that of war & peace &c."[59] Edmund Randolph worried about executive power, calling it "the foetus of monarchy." The delegates at the convention, he said had "no motive to be governed by the British Governmt. as our proto- type." If the United States had no other choice he might adopt the British model, but the "fixt genius of the people of America re- quired a different form of Government." Wilson agreed that the British model "was inapplicable to the situation in this Country; the extent of which was so great, and the manners so republican, that nothing but a great confederated Republic would do for it.[60]

Alexander Hamilton, a favorite among extollers of a strong presidency, also rejected the British model of executive preroga- tives in the conduct of foreign affairs and the exercise of the war power. While he explained in a lengthy speech to the Convention on June 18 that in "his private opinion he had no scruple in declaring . . . that the British Govt. was the best in the world,"[61] he nevertheless agreed that the English scheme would have no appli- cation in the United States. He proposed that the Senate would have the "sole power of declaring war" and, in language that would anticipate the role of the president as commander in chief, the president would be authorized to have "the direction of war when authorized or begun."[62]

The framers' determination to preclude unilateral presidential authority to initiate military actions was demonstrated in the de- bates that surrounded the crafting of the war clause. On August 6, the Committee of Detail circulated a draft that provided that the legislature shall have the power "to make war."[63] This bore sharp resemblance to the Articles of Confederation, which vested the "sole and exclusive right and power of determining on peace and war" to the Continental Congress.

When the war clause was considered in debate on August 17, Charles Pinckney opposed placing the power in the full Congress.

"Its proceedings, he said, were too slow . . . The Senate would be the best depositary, being more acquainted with foreign affairs, and most capable of proper resolutions."[64] Pierce Butler "was for vesting the power in the President, who will have all the requisite qualities, and will not make war but when the Nation will support it." Butler's opinion shocked Elbridge Gerry, who said that he "never expected to hear in a republic a motion to empower the Executive alone to declare war." Butler stood alone in the Convention; there was no support for his opinion and no second to his motion.

The draft proposal to vest the legislature with the power to make war proved unsatisfactory to Madison and Gerry. As a consequence, they moved to substitute "declare" for "make," leaving the President "the power to repel sudden attacks." The meaning of the motion is unmistakable. Congress was granted the power to make, that is, initiate war; the president, for obvious reasons, could act immediately to repel sudden attacks without authorization from Congress. In genuine emergency situations, allowing no time for congressional deliberation, the president could order *defensive* actions. Roger Sherman spoke in support of the motion and thought it "stood very well. The Executive shd. be able to repel and not to commence war." George Mason "was agst giving the power of war to the Executive, because not <safely> to be trusted with it. . . . He was for clogging rather than facilitating war."[65]

The debates and vote on the war clause make it clear that Congress alone possesses the authority to initiate war. The warmaking power was specifically withheld from the president; he was given only the authority to repel sudden attacks. Confirmation of that understanding was provided by remarks of ratifiers in various state conventions, as well as by the early practice and contemporaneous statements of political actors.

In Pennsylvania, James Wilson expressed the prevailing sentiment that the system of checks and balances "will not hurry us into war; it is calculated to guard against it. It will not be in the power of a single man, or a single body of men, to involve us in such distress; for the important power of declaring war is vested in the legislature at large."[66] In North Carolina, James Iredell compared the limited powers of the president with those of the British monarch. The king of England was not only the commander in chief "but has power, in time of war, to raise fleets and armies. He has also the authority to declare war." By contrast, the president "has not the power of declaring war by his own authority, nor that of raising fleets and armies. These powers are vested in other hands."[67]

The meaning of the war clause was thus settled at the dawn of the republic. The word "declare" enjoyed a settled understanding and an established usage. As early as 1552, the verb "declare" had become synonymous with the verb "commence." They both meant the initiation of hostilities.[68] This was the established usage in international law as well as in England, where the terms declare war and make war were used interchangeably.

This practice was familiar to the framers. As Chancellor James Kent of New York, one of the leading jurists of the founding period, stated: "As war cannot lawfully be commenced on the part of the United States, without an act of Congress, such an act is, of course, a formal official notice to all the world, and equivalent to the most solemn declaration." While Kent interpreted "declare" to mean "commence," he did not assert that the Constitution requires a congressional declaration of war before hostilities could be lawfully commenced, but merely that it be initiated by Congress. What is "essential," according to Kent, is "that some formal public act, proceeding directly from the competent source, should announce to the people at home their new relations and duties growing out of a state of war, and which should equally apprize neutral nations of the fact."[69] Thus, Congress need not declare war. All that is required under American law is a joint resolution or an explicit congressional authorization of the use of military force against a named adversary.

The Constitution, then, grants to Congress the sum total of the nation's power to commence hostilities. There was, in the Convention, no doubt about the limited scope of the president's war power. The duty to repel sudden attacks represents an emergency measure that permits the president to take actions necessary to protect the United States. The president was never vested with a general power to deploy troops whenever and wherever he thought best, and the framers did not authorize him to take the country into full-scale war or to mount an offensive attack against another nation. John Bassett Moore, an eminent international law scholar, justly stated:

> There can hardly be room for doubt that the framers of the constitution, when they vested in Congress the power to declare war, never imagined that they were leaving it to the executive to use the military and naval forces of the United States all over the world for the purpose of actually coercing other nations, occupying their territory, and kill-

ing their soldiers and citizens, all according to his own notions of the fitness of things, as long as he refrained from calling his action war or persisted in calling it peace.[70]

The framers did not create the title of commander in chief, but adopted it in light of the 150-year-old English tradition of entitling the office at the apex of the military hierarchy as commander in chief and of subordinating the office to a political superior, such as a king or parliament. The office carried with it no warmaking power whatever. This practice was thoroughly familiar to the framers and perhaps this settled understanding and the consequent absence of concerns about the nature of the office account for the fact that there was no debate on the commander in chief clause at the Convention. Hamilton laid bare the dimensions of the office in Federalist No. 69:

> The President is to be commander-in-chief of the army and navy of the United States. In this respect his authority would be nominally the same with that of the king of Great Britain, but in substance much inferior to it. It would amount to nothing more than the supreme command and direction of the military and naval forces, as first General and admiral of the Confederacy; while that of the British King extends to the *declaring* of war and to the *raising* and *regulating* of fleets and armies—all which, by the constitution under consideration, would appertain to the legislature.[71]

This understanding of the constitutional allocation of the war power was reaffirmed by early practice, as Fisher demonstrates,[72] and by early Court decisions as old or older than *Marbury v Madison* (1803), the graybeard of all judicial precedents. At the dawn of the republic, the Supreme Court held, in several cases, that Congress enjoys exclusive authority to initiate military hostilities. No court in the intervening years has departed from that view.

In 1800, the Court held that it is for Congress alone to authorize either an "imperfect" (limited) war or a "perfect" (declared) war.[73] A year later, the Court stated with great clarity: "The whole powers of war, being by the constitution of the United States, vested in Congress, the acts of that body can alone be restored to as our guides in this enquiry."[74] The words are those of Chief Justice John Marshall, a member of the Virginia ratifying convention. In 1804, the Court held that President John Adams' instructions to seize ships were in conflict with an act of Congress and were therefore illegal.[75] Once again the opinion-writer was Chief Justice Marshall. In 1806, the question of whether the president may initiate hostilities was decided by Justice William Paterson, riding circuit, for himself and District Judge Tallmadge: "Does he [the President] possess the power of making war? that power is exclusively vested in congress. . . . it is the exclusive province of congress to change a state of peace into a state of war."[76] These decisions established the constitutional fact that it is for Congress alone to initiate hostilities, whether in the form of a general or a limited war. They remain the supreme law of the land.

Fisher's Critics

Presidential War Power is, indeed, a tour de force, but in spite of its power and lucidity, criticisms remain. In the spirit of promoting and continuing a constitutional dialogue, this section will examine two of the more important criticisms of Fisher's book.

Executive Power

It has been asserted that Fisher does not sufficiently appreciate the importance of the executive power clause as a source of presidential warmaking. This is a curious argument because it is not new, and it is without foundation. Article II, section 1 of the Constitution provides: "The executive power shall be vested in a President of the United States of America." In recent years, various presidents—Johnson, Nixon, Ford, and Carter—have sought to squeeze from the executive power clause a presidential authority to initiate hostilities.[77] But the very claim asserted by those presidents was considered and rejected in the Constitutional Convention; indeed, it caused the delegates much alarm. No member of the Convention ever suggested or even intimated that the executive power clause was a fountainhead of power to make war. Edmund Randolph, it will be recalled, introduced a plan that provided for a "national executive," which would have "authority to execute the national laws . . . and enjoy the executive rights vested in Congress by the Confederation." Charles Pinckney said he was "for a vigorous executive but was afraid the executive powers of the existing Congress might extend to peace and war which would render the executive a monarchy, of the worst kind, to wit an elective one."

John Rutledge shared his concern, saying "he was for vesting the Executive power in a single person, tho' he was not for giving him the power of war and peace." James Wilson sought to ease their fears; he "did not consider the Prerogatives of the British Monarch as a proper guide to defining the Executive powers. Some of these prerogatives were of a legislative nature. Among other that of war and peace. The only powers he conceived strictly Executive were those of executing the laws and appointing officers not appointed by the legislature. He added: "Making peace and war are generally determined by the writers on the Law of Nations to be legislative powers—executive powers . . . do not include the rights of war and peace."[78] Madison agreed with Wilson's definition of executive power. He thought it necessary "to fix the extent of Executive authority . . . as certain powers were in their nature Executive, and must be given to that department" and added that "a definition of their extent would assist the judgment in determining how far they might be safely entrusted to a single officer." The definition of the executives powers should be precise, thought Madison; the executive power "shd. be confined and defined."[79] And so it was. There was no challenge to the definition of executive power held by Wilson and Madison, nor was there even an alternative understanding advanced. No delegate asserted the clause as a source of warmaking.

Precedents and Presidential Warmaking

Presidents since World War II have resorted to an argument based on precedents; executive warmaking, if repeated often enough, acquires legal validity. Presidents and their supporters often invoke historical practice as a means of defending unilateral presidential warmaking. Former Secretary of Defense Richard Cheney advanced a historical argument on behalf of President George Bush on the eve of the Gulf War: "In the more than 200 times that U.S. military force has been committed over the history of the Nation, there are only five occasions in which the Congress of the United States voted a prior declaration of war.[80] Henry P. Monaghan has asserted that "history has legitimated the practice of presidential warmaking.[81] The argument rests in the premise that the president frequently has exercised the war power without congressional authorization. The actual number of these episodes varies among the several compilations, but defenders usually list between 100 and 200 unilateral acts, each of which constitutes a legitimizing precedent for future executive wars.[82] In detail and in conception the argument is flawed. In the first place, the lists are inaccurately compiled. Francis D. Wormuth deflated such claims with a microscopic analysis. Consider an error common to the lists: the claim that unilateral warmaking was initiated by undeclared war with France in 1798. That claim, as Wormuth justly observed, "is altogether false." Wormuth demonstrated that Congress had passed "a series of acts that amounted so the Supreme Court said, to a declaration of imperfect war; and Adams complied with these statutes."[83] In a more recent study of the quasi-war with France, the distinguished scholar, Dean Alfange, was able to confirm Wormuth's findings.[84] Moreover, many of the episodes involved initiation of hostilities by a military commander, not by authorization from the president. If practice establishes law, then the inescapable conclusion is that every military unit has the power to initiate war. Finally, it cannot be maintained that constitutional power, in this case the war power, can be acquired through practice. In *Powell v McCormack*, Chief Justice Earl Warren wrote: "That an unconstitutional action has been taken before surely does not render that action any less unconstitutional at a later date." Earlier, Justice Frankfurter, writing for a unanimous court, echoed a centuries-old principle of Anglo-American jurisprudence: "Illegality cannot attain legitimacy through practice."[85] The Court has repeatedly denied claims that the president can acquire power by a series of usurpations. If it were otherwise, the president might aggrandize all governmental power. Neither Congress nor the judiciary could lawfully restrain the exercise of the president's accumulated powers. Clearly, this practice would scuttle our entire constitutional jurisprudence. Thus, the most recent act of usurpation stands no better than the first.

As Louis Fisher has carefully explained, the postwar practice of unilateral presidential warmaking finds no support in either the text of the Constitution or in our constitutional architecture. There are other criticisms of his book on warmaking but they do not weaken or undermine his powerful examination of the relevant issues.

Notes

1. Holmes made reference to another, final, resting place in his criticism of judicial activism: "if my country wants to go to hell, I am here to help it." F. Biddle, *Justice Holmes, Natural Law, and The Supreme Court* 9 (1961).

2. Fisher continues to study war power issues, as demonstrated by a forthcoming article that he and I coauthored: Fisher and Adler, "The War Powers Resolution: Time to Say Goodbye," *Political Science Quarterly* 103 (Spring 1998) 1–20.

3. Fisher, *Presidential War Power* (1995).

4. Fisher, *Constitutional Dialogues: Interpretation as Political Process* (1988).

5. It is worth noting that Fisher's sternest critics have great respect for his work. See Turner, Book Review, *Strategic Review*, 66–71 (Winter 1996): "His research is sufficiently detailed and original that I can't recall reading one of his books that I didn't feel enhanced by my own knowledge of the subject. . . . In addition, he is a scholar of personal honor and intellectual integrity. . . ." *Id.,* at 66.

6. Robert Spitzer, "Saving the Constitution from the Lawyers."

7. Chief Justice Hughes's utterance concerning judicial supremacy created a misleading impression: "we are under a constitution, but the constitution is what the judges say it is." Quoted in Fisher, *Dialogues,* p. 245.

8. See the brilliant examination of recent interpretations of *Marbury* in Dean Alfange, "Marbury v. Madison and Original Understandings of Judicial Review: In Defense of Traditional Wisdom," *The Supreme Court Review,* pp. 329–446 (1993).

9. The impartation of judicial truths recalls the quaint notion of the law as a "brooding omnipresence in the skies," as reflected in Justice Owen Roberts's opinion for the Court in *United States v Butler,* in which he stated: "When an act of Congress is appropriately challenged in the courts as not conforming to the constitutional mandate the judicial branch of the government has only one duty,—to lay the article of the constitution which is invoked beside the statute which is challenged and to decide whether the latter squares with the former." 297 US 62–63 (1936).

10. Fisher acknowledges that the idea of coordinate construction is not new and credits Alexander Bickel's, *The Least Dangerous Branch* (1962), for charting the idea of a "constitutional colloquy." Fisher, *Dialogues,* p. 3.

11. In a survey over a decade ago, six out of ten people claimed they view the Supreme Court as the ultimate constitutional arbiter. *Washington Post,* 15 Feb. 1987.

12. Because most law schools promote the idea of judicial supremacy, there is, "no comprehensive course on constitutional law in any meaningful sense in American law school." W. Michael Riesman, "International Incidents: Introduction to a New Genre in the Study of International Law," 10 *Yale Journal of International Law,* 1, 8N.13 (1984).

13. 5 US (1 Cranch) 137, 177 (1803).

14. 358 US 1, 18 (1958).

15. *Baker v Carr,* 369 US 186, 211 (1962). The Court reiterated the doctrine of ultimate arbiter in 1968 in *Powell v McCormack,* 395 US 486, 549 (1969).

16. Fisher, "Constitutional Interpretation By Members of Congress," 63 *North Carolina Law Review* 707–747 (1985), at 716.

17. Compare, e.g., *Minersville v Gobitis,* 310 US 586 (1940) with *West Virginia Bd. of Education v Barnette,* 319 US 624 (1943); and *Plessy v Ferguson,* 163 US 537 (1986) with *Brown v Bd. of Education,* 347 US 483 (1954).

18. Fisher, "Constitutional Interpretation," at 717 n. 65, citing *Glidden Co. v Zdanok,* 370 US 530, 543 (1962).

19. Fisher, *Dialogues* at 244, quoting Taney's dissent in *The Passenger Cases,* 48 US (7 How.) 283, 470 (1849).

20. Jackson's statement that decisions by the Supreme Court "are not final because we are infallible, but we are infallible only because we are final," is spellbinding. *Brown v Allen,* 344 US 443, 540 (1953).

21. Fisher, *Constitutional Dialogues,* at 245.

22. See Fisher, "Constitutional Interpretation," at 714–715, 717.

23. *Id.,* at 717.

24. Quoting Taney's dissent in *The Passenger Cases,* 48 US (7 How.) 283, 470 (1849), Fisher, *Dialogues,* at 244. This view recalls Francis Wormuth's remark: "The republic of truth is an anarchy in which there is no authority but persuasion," in *Toward a Humanistic Science of Politics: Essays in Honor of Francis Dunham Wormuth,* Dalmas H. Nelson and Richard L. Sklar, eds. (1983) at xii.

25. Justice Frankfurter, in *Graves v New York* ex rel. O'Keefe, 306 US 466, 491–92 (1939).

26. Fisher, *Dialogues,* at 64.

27. Fisher, "Raoul Berger on Public Law," *Political Science Reviewer* 174–203 (1978), at 189.

28. Benjamin N. Cardozo, *The Nature of the Judicial Process,* 113–115 (1921).

29. Cardozo, *Paradoxes of Legal Science* 55 (1928).

30. Fisher, e.g., criticizes the Court's "discovery" of the Liberty of Contract Doctrine, in *Dialogues,* at 60.

31. J. Skelly Wright, "Professor Bickel, The Scholarly Tradition and the Supreme Courts," 84 *Harvard Law Review* 769, 777, 784 (1971).

32. 299 US 304 (1936).

33. Fisher, *Dialogues,* at 82.

34. *Id.* at 64. Fisher notes the hypocrisy of the Reagan administration's invocation of original intent as a rule of constitutional interpretation, but its violation of that rule in its embrace of unilateral presidential warmaking. *Id.* at 82.

35. *Id.* at 64.

36. *Id.* at 5.

37. *Id.* at 244.

38. *Id.* at 3.

39. *Id.* at 231–32.

40. *Id.* at 242.

41. Fisher, "Constitutional Interpretation," at 715.

42. 418 US 683, 703 (1974).

43. Quoted in Fisher, *Dialogues,* at 238–39.

44. *Id.* at 239.

45. *Id.*

46. Neuman, Book Review, "Variations for Mixed Voices," 137 *University of Pennsylvania Law Review.* 1851–1871 (1989) at 1856.

47. Bickel, *Least Dangerous,* at 264.

48. Fisher, *Dialogues,* at 276.

49. *Id.*

50. *Massachusetts v United States,* 333 US 611, 639–40 (1948).

51. Fisher, *Dialogues,* at 275.

52. See Theodore Draper, *New York Times,* 7 May 1995, at 1.

53. Fisher, *War Power,* at 11.

54. *Id.* at xi.

55. See generally, Louis Fisher, *Presidential War Power* (1995); John Hart Ely, *War and Responsibility* (1993); David Gray Adler, "The Constitution and Presidential Warmaking: The Enduring Debate," 103 *Political Science Quarterly* 1–35 (1988); Francis D. Wormuth and Edwin B. Firmage,

To Chain the Dog of War: The War Powers of Congress in History and Law (1986); Edward Keynes, *Undeclared War: Twilight Zone of Constitutional Power* (1982).

56. Fisher, *Presidential War Power,* pp. 1–6; *The Constitution and the Conduct of American Foreign Policy,* David Gray Adler and Larry N. George, eds., (University Press of Kansas, 1996), pp. 3–6.

57. See Adler, "Court, Constitution and Foreign Affairs," in *The Constitution and the Conduct of American Foreign Policy,* 10–56.

58. Edwin B. Firmage, "War, Declaration of," in 4 *Encyclopedia of the American Presidency* 1573 (Leonard W. Levy and Louis Fisher, eds., 1994).

59. *The Records of the Federal Convention of 1787* (Max Farrand ed.), Vol. I, p. 65–66, 73–74.

60. *Id.* at 66–67.

61. *Id.* at 288.

62. *Id.* at 292.

63. *Id.,* Vol. II, at 182.

64. *Id.,* Vol. II, at 318.

65. *Id.* at 318, 319.

66. *The Debates in the Several State Conventions* (Jonathan Elliot, ed.), Vol. II at 528.

67. *Id.* 4:107.

68. Huloet's dictionary provided this definition: "Declare warres. *Arma canere, Bellum indicere.*" We have here two meanings: to summon to arms; to announce war. Quoted in Wormuth & Firmage, *To Chain the Dog of War,* at 20.

69. James Kent, *Commentaries on American Law,* Vol. I, at 53 (Da Capo reprint, 1971).

70. *The Collected Papers of John Bassett Moore,* Vol. V, at 195–196 (1994).

71. Hamilton, *The Federalist,* No. 69, at 448.

72. See Fisher, *War Power,* at 13–44.

73. *Bass v Tingy,* 4 US 37 (1800).

74. *Talbot v Seeman,* 5 US 1, 28 (1801).

75. *Little v Barreme,* 6 US (2 Cr.) 169 (1804).

76. *United States v Smith,* 27 Fed Cas. 1192, 1230 (C.C. N.Y. 1806). (No. 16, 342).

77. See, e.g., Samuel B. Hoff, *Book Review, The Law and Politics Book Review,* 197–200 (July 1995): "other scholars such as John Norton Moore and Robert Turner give much credence to this provision as a rationale for presidential preeminence in military endeavors." *Id.,* at 200. Turner, likewise, accuses Fisher of ignoring the importance of the clause in his review of *Presidential War Power.* See Turner, *Book Review, Strategic Review,* (Winter 1996), pp. 66–71, at 67. See also, his article, "War and the Forgotten Executive Power Clause," 34 *Virginia Journal of International Law,* (1994), 903–979.

78. This discussion is drawn from David Gray Adler, "The Constitution and Presidential Warmaking," in Adler and George, eds., *The Constitution and the Conduct of American Foreign Policy,* at 195–198.

79. Farrand, *Records of the Federal Convention,* I: 62–70.

80. *Crisis in the Persian Gulf: Sanctions, Diplomacy and War: Hearings Before the House Comm. on Armed Services, 101 Cong. 589* (1990).

81. Monaghan, "Presidential War-Making," 50 *Boston University Law Review,* at 19.

82. For example, in 1967 the State Department published a study that listed 137 cases of unilateral presidential action (Dept. of State, Historical Studies Division, *Armed Actions Taken by the United States Without a Declaration of War, 1789–1967.*) J. Terry Emerson, legal assistant to Sen. Barry Goldwater, published a list of presidential acts of war without congressional authorization (119 *Cong. Rec.* S14174, daily ed., July 20, 1973).

83. See Wormuth, "The Nixon Theory of the War Power: A Critique," 60 *California Law Review* 623 (1972), at 652–664.

84. See Dean Alfange Jr., "The Quasi-War and Presidential Warmaking," in Adler and George, *Constitution and Conduct of American Foreign Policy,* at 274–291.

85. 395 US 486, 546 (1969); *Inland Waterways Corp. v Young,* 309 US 5187, 524 (1940).

6

The Supreme Court and Federalism: Yesterday and Today

Dean Alfange Jr.

On April 29, 1997, Louis Fisher, fulfilling a responsibility as Senior Specialist in Separation of Powers in the Government Division of the Congressional Research Service, submitted a report to Congress entitled "Congressional Checks on the Judiciary,"[1] in which he emphatically rejected, as he had done in the past,[2] the "conventional" view of "the judiciary—and especially the Supreme Court—as the ultimate and final arbiter of constitutional law," observing that even the Supreme Court "has recognized that it is not the only branch with authority and capacity to interpret the Constitution."[3] Nevertheless, whatever concessions the Court may previously have made to the competency of the other branches, within two months of the publication of this report, a majority of the justices made clear in no uncertain terms that they did not accept Fisher's view that the responsibility for interpreting the meaning of the Constitution was shared with the other branches of the federal government and insisted that the Court was the sole authoritative interpreter.

In *City of Boerne v Flores,*[4] the Court declared unconstitutional the Religious Freedom Restoration Act (RFRA) of 1993,[5] which sought, in Fisher's words, to "overrule the [C]ourt's interpretation of the Constitution,"[6] by nullifying the effect of the Court's 1990 decision in *Employment Division v Smith,*[7] where it was held that

107

religious beliefs did not create an exemption from the duty of obedience to a law of general applicability, so that members of the
Native American Church could constitutionally be punished for using
a controlled substance, peyote, in their religious rituals. The constitutional basis for the enactment of RFRA was § 5 of the Fourteenth Amendment, granting Congress power to enforce that
amendment, which has been held to make applicable against the
states the First Amendment's guarantee of the free exercise of
religion, but the Court in *Boerne* held that Congress may not "decree the substance of the Fourteenth Amendment's restrictions on
the States."[8] Congress's power to enforce the Fourteenth Amendment, the Court declared, was exclusively remedial, and RFRA was
not a remedial statute because it was not narrowly drawn to bar
only state laws that would be held unconstitutional by the Supreme Court.[9] The Court came very close to approving the ruling
in the *Civil Rights Cases*[10] of 1883, in which the Civil Rights Act
of 1875[11] was held to be an invalid exercise of Congress's power to
enforce the Fourteenth Amendment because it prohibited private
acts of racial discrimination, while § 5 only empowered Congress to
prohibit official state discrimination. While the Court in *Boerne*
conceded that the rulings in the *Civil Rights Cases* and similar
cases may "have been superseded or modified, . . . their treatment
of Congress's § 5 power as corrective or preventive, not definitional,
has not been questioned."[12]

    Justice Kennedy was the author of the *Boerne* opinion. Ironi-
cally, Louis Fisher had relied on his statements at his confirmation
hearing to the effect that legislators are not "immediately bound
by the full circumstances of a Supreme Court decree"[13] as evidence of judicial recognition that the responsibility for interpreting the Constitution is not the sole province of the courts.[14] But
the views expressed by Kennedy in *Boerne* were not the same as
those he expressed at his confirmation hearing. In *Boerne* he
declared that Congress must defer to the Court's interpretations
of the Constitution because, as John Marshall had stated in
Marbury v Madison, it is the Court's duty "to say what the law
is."[15] And he warned Congress not to attempt to alter or modify
judicial interpretations because "the Court will treat its precedents with the respect due them under settled principles, including *stare decisis,* and contrary expectations must be disappointed."[16]
So much for Louis Fisher's notion of interpretation as a process
of constitutional dialogue![17] In one of the more remarkable, not to
say hilarious, statements ever to be found in the United States

Reports, Justice Kennedy asserted that Congress could not be allowed a share of the responsibility for providing authoritative interpretations of the Constitution because, then, "[s]hifting legislative majorities could change the Constitution and effectively circumvent the difficult and detailed amendment process contained in Article V."[18] As if the recently shifted judicial majority was not busily engaged in changing the Constitution even as those words were being written![19]

Justice Kennedy's argument in *Boerne*, while assertedly based on the difference in the constitutional roles and responsibilities of the courts and Congress, appears ultimately to rest on a failure to appreciate the nature of that difference. For example, in *Katzenbauch v Morgan*[20] in 1966, the Supreme Court upheld § 4 (e) of the Voting Rights Act of 1965,[21] forbidding state denial of the right to vote for lack of English literacy to anyone who had completed the sixth grade in Puerto Rico, despite the fact that the Supreme Court had previously held that a literacy requirement was not an unconstitutional voting qualification.[22] In its earlier decision upholding the validity of literacy tests, the Court held that a state law requiring them could not be struck down because, in the absence of evidence of discriminatory application, it could not be said that it was unreasonable for a state to insist that its voters be literate.[23] In other words, given the fact that the judiciary is obligated, under standard equal protection principles, to accept a legislative classification that is rationally related to a permissible state goal, the Court could not declare the state literacy requirement to violate the Constitution. But Congress is a legislature, not a court, and thus is under no obligation to defer to any state policy judgment that is not unreasonable. Thus, to require Congress to defer to the Court's deference to the state legislative judgment would seem to put the cart before the horse. As the Court stated in *Katzenbach v Morgan*:

> A construction of § 5 that would require a judicial determination that the enforcement of the state law precluded by Congress violated the Amendment, as a condition of sustaining the congressional enactment, would depreciate both congressional resourcefulness and congressional responsibility for implementing the Amendment. It would confine the legislative power in this context to the insignificant role of abrogating only those state laws that the judicial branch was prepared to adjudge unconstitutional.[24]

The words are Justice Brennan's, but the sentiments are also those of Louis Fisher.

Boerne was not the only decision at the close of the Court's 1996 term that reflected what can be described, to borrow Senator Fulbright's title, as the arrogance of power—the arrogance that can be asserted solely by virtue of having five votes on the Supreme Court. In *Printz v United States,*[25] the Court held that Congress had not power to require a county sheriff, or any other state or local executive officer, to assist in the execution of federal law—in this case, to conduct the background checks necessary to ensure that the purchaser of a handgun is not ineligible to possess one because of a previous commission of a felony or other disqualifying factor, until such time as a federal system for conducting the checks can be made operative.[26] The five-justice majority of the Court reached this conclusion despite the fact that, from the very beginning of national experience with the Constitution, federal statutes assigned administrative duties to state courts,[27] the World War I draft law imposed a duty on state officials to aid in the administration of the draft,[28] acts of Congress requiring state courts to enforce federal laws have been upheld by the Supreme Court as unquestionably constitutional,[29] and, as Justice Stevens noted in his dissent: "There is not a clause, sentence, or paragraph in the entire text of the Constitution that supports the proposition that a local police officer can ignore a command contained in a statute enacted by Congress pursuant to an express delegation of power enumerated in Article I."[30] Presumably, Justice Kennedy did not see this as an instance of a shifting judicial majority changing the Constitution without resort to the amending process.

The principal value that the Court's five-justice majority seemed determined to defend in these decisions is the preservation of state sovereignty against acts of Congress that the majority sees as unjustifiably limiting the freedom of states to maintain their own policies. This value also appears predominant in several other decisions in recent terms. For example, in *New York v United States*[31] in 1992, the Court unprecedentedly invalidated a federal law that sought to implement a policy for the disposal of low-level radioactive waste that had been developed through negotiations among the states themselves by effectively requiring each state to enact legislation to provide for the disposal of the waste within its borders.[32] In 1996, in *Seminole Tribe of Florida v Florida,*[33] by the predictable margin of 5–4, it overruled *Pennsylvania v Union Gas Co.,*[34] and held that, unless it was acting through its powers to enforce the Civil War Amendments,[35] Congress could not abrogate a state's Eleventh Amendment immunity from suit in federal court as a means of ensuring their compliance with federal law. And, in *United States v Lopez*[36] in 1995, the Court, again by 5–4, invalidated a provision of the Gun-Free School Zones Act of 1990,[37] making possession of a gun in a school zone a federal crime, on the ground that the law exceeded Congress's power under the commerce clause and thus improperly intruded into an area of regulation reserved to the states by the Tenth Amendment—the first time in almost sixty years that the Court had invalidated an act of Congress regulating individual behavior as being in excess of the power to regulate interstate commerce.

It is in the area of federalism, then, that Louis Fisher's views of the respect due to congressional judgment in matters of constitutional interpretation are currently being put to their severest test. This is not without irony because Fisher's scholarly focus has not been on issues of federal-state relationships, but on the separation of powers, and he is best known for his brilliant analyses of how the three branches of the federal government arrive at an accommodation of their constitutional disputes and of how Congress can (and must) protect its prerogatives in the appropriation of funds and in deciding when the nation may use military force. But it is his insight that, at bottom, the constitutional issues of federalism are not different from, but are simply a subset of, separation of power issues. For the ultimate question in the constitutional law of federalism is not where the line between federal and state authority is to be drawn, but, rather, who is to draw it, and, putting aside the instances where the president vetoes or fails to implement an act of Congress that he believes to be in excess of federal authority,[38] the choices are Congress or the federal courts. The power to decide where the line between federal and state authority is to be located must, of course, rest definitively with a branch of the federal government if the United States is to be a true union rather than a confederation of independent states, and the current Supreme Court has claimed that power for itself, to the exclusion of Congress, citing, as the basis for its claim, John Marshall's assertion in *Marbury v Madison* that it is for courts "to say what the law is."[39] But Fisher tells us that the majority's claim is erroneous. "The meaning of federalism," he has written, "is not announced unilaterally by the Supreme Court," but is developed through a "process in which the Court, Congress, and the executive branch hammer out the sensitive and ever-changing relationships between the federal government and the states."[40] Moreover, he has noted that it is not the courts that fundamentally shape the nature of the federal system, but rather the actions of Congress, for the basic considerations that go into determining which issues are to be resolved at the federal level and which should be left to the states are inevitably questions of policy, not law.[41] Fisher's observations are eminently sound. Nevertheless, the Supreme Court, for a period of approximately fifty years prior to 1937, and, apparently, once again today, seems bent on denying Congress its appropriate authority in deciding the policy questions that are at the core of the constitutional law of federalism.

By any measure, the leading Supreme Court decision on the scope of federal legislative power is *McCulloch v Maryland*[42] in 1819, the opinion in which is generally recognized as John Marshall's greatest. Yet, as Louis Fisher points out, "*McCulloch* is a vivid example of Congress, the President, and executive officials contributing to three-branch interpretation. The political branches performed all the constitutional analysis, to be blessed [over a quarter of a century] later by the Court."[43] As is well known, the issue in the *McCulloch* case was whether Congress was constitutionally empowered to create a corporation, specifically a national bank, despite the absence of any express delegation of authority to do so in the Constitution. When Congress passed legislation to create the First Bank of the United States in 1791, President George Washington, in doubt as to its constitutionality, asked for the opinions of the officers of the principal executive departments (as he was specifically authorized to do in Article II, § 2, of the Constitution), as to whether creation of the bank was within Congress's constitutional power. Attorney General Edmund Randolph and Secretary of State Thomas Jefferson concluded that it was not; Secretary of the Treasury Alexander Hamilton argued that it was. It was Hamilton's reasoning that prevailed with President Washington, who signed the bank bill into law, and Hamilton's reasoning that was followed by Chief Justice Marshall in upholding the constitutionality of the Second Bank of the United States twenty-eight years later in *McCulloch*.

Even before the adoption of the Constitution and the passage of the bank bill, the basic argument for a broad reading of federal power was made by James Madison in *Federalist 44,* who there contended that Congress must be allowed to choose the means needed to carry out its responsibilities effectively: "No axiom is more clearly established in law, or in reason, than that wherever the end is required, the means are authorised; wherever a general power to do a thing is given, every particular power necessary for doing it is included."[44] But by 1791 Madison had had second thoughts on the matter and argued in the House of Representatives that creation of the bank by Congress would be unconstitutional.[45] In this regard, his views were now the same as those of his political ally, Thomas Jefferson, who forcefully argued the case against the bank in his opinion to President Washington. The bank, Jefferson contended, could not be constitutionally justified by the "necessary and proper" clause of Article I, § 8, because Congress's power to enact legislation "necessary and proper" for carrying its delegated powers into execution had to be limited to those powers that were absolutely necessary to the exercise of one of the expressly delegated powers—that is, "to those means without which the grant of the power would be nugatory."[46] It was Jefferson's fear that if Congress were allowed to exercise any nonenumerated power, it could then claim every nonenumerated power, "for there is no one which ingenuity may not torture into a *convenience in some way or other*, to *some one* of so long a list of enumerated powers."[47] The issue was thus squarely joined from the outset. If Congress is not permitted to choose the most effective means for executing its delegated powers, it will be crippled in its capacity to fulfill its constitutional responsibilities. On the other hand, if it were free to choose the means it believed appropriate to employ, it could displace state authority in a potentially unlimited range of activities, and thus eliminate local self-government.

For Marshall in *McCulloch*, the choice between these alternatives was inescapably clear. The controlling principle had to be the one articulated by Madison in *Federalist 44* (as opposed to the later Madison) and by Hamilton in his opinion in support of the bank.[48] The crucial consideration was the importance of the responsibilities assigned to Congress in the Constitution, "on the due execution of which the happiness and prosperity of the nation so vitally depends."[49] He insisted that the framers could hardly have wanted to hamper the execution of these responsibilities by denying Congress the means to carry them out effectively. "It must have been the intention of those who gave these powers, to insure, as far as human prudence could insure, their beneficial execution. This could not be done by confi[n]ing the choice of means to such narrow limits as not to leave it in the power of Congress to adopt any which might be appropriate, and which were conductive to the end."[50] From this principle, that Congress must be allowed to choose the means needed to carry out its responsibilities effectively, Marshall derived what is now recognized as the classic test for determining the constitutionality of acts of Congress under the "necessary and proper" clause: "Let the end be legitimate, let it be within the scope of the Constitution, and all means which are appropriate, which are plainly adapted to that end, which are not prohibited, but consist with the letter and spirit of the constitution, are constitutional."[51]

In applying this test to determine whether establishment of the bank was constitutional under the "necessary and proper" clause, Marshall made it crystal clear that it was not for courts to decide whether legislation passed by Congress was "necessary" to the attainment of an end within the scope of the Constitution: "But where the law is not prohibited, and is really calculated to effect any of the objects entrusted to the government, to undertake here to inquire into the degree of its necessity, would be to pass the line which circumscribes the judicial department, and to tread on legislative ground. This court disclaims all pretentions to such a power."[52] Therefore, the court's sole inquiry (apart from whether the law is prohibited by any provision of the Constitution) is whether the law is an appropriate means for the exercise of a delegated power. Since whether the law is a necessary means is to be excluded from the judicial calculus, the question before the courts as to whether the law is appropriate (or "really calculated" or "plainly adapted") to attain an end within the scope of the Constitution can involve no more than an inquiry into whether Congress could reasonably, or rationally, believe that the law is, as Marshall put it, "conductive to the [attainment of a constitutionally legitimate] end." Marshall thus lays down the rationality standard as the test that courts must employ to determine the constitutionality of an act of Congress that is challenged as impinging upon areas properly of state concern.[53]

But, since many means that can rationally be seen as appropriate to the execution of a delegated power would necessarily involve intrusion into areas of state authority, and thus the possible displacement of state policies in those areas, it must be conceded that Jefferson was absolutely right: if the "necessary and proper" clause were interpreted as broadly as this, the only limit on Congress's power would be its capacity for ingenuity in providing rational explanations of why whatever it wished to do was conducive to the exercise of one of its enumerated powers. Marshall's *McCulloch* test is thus thoroughly at odds with his reasoning in *Marbury v Madison*, where he not only declared that it was "emphatically the province and duty of the judicial department to say what the law is," but also asserted that the legislature cannot be allowed to define away those limits, and a written constitution becomes an "absurd attempt, on the part of the people, to limit a power in its own nature illimitable."[54]

Yet, in *McCulloch*, he was, in effect, stating that, with regard to the only limitation on congressional power that many people seriously cared about in 1819—the limitation on its capacity to legislate on matters reserved to the states—Congress was responsible for defining the constitutional limits on its authority. The checks on Congress in this area were not to be judicial because the question of whether a law was sufficiently necessary to the execution of a delegated power to be constitutionally warranted was not an issue of law, but an issue of policy, and to decide it would be "to tread on legislative ground." Obviously, as Jefferson in 1791 and Marshall in *Marbury* warned, this opens the door to legislative abuse, but, for Marshall in *McCulloch*, legislative abuse of legislative power was not to be corrected by judicial abuse of judicial power through judicial assumption of the authority to decide questions of legislative policy. Checks on legislative abuses would have to come through the political process. For Marshall in *McCulloch*, this was perfectly feasible, for, as he stated in *Gibbons v Ogden*, five years later: "The wisdom and discretion of Congress, their identity with the people, and the influence which their constituents possess at election, are, in . . . many . . . instances, the sole restraints on which [the people] have relied, to secure them from [legislative] abuse. They are the restraints on which the people must often rely solely, in all representative governments."[55]

Marshall's reasoning in *McCulloch* squares perfectly with Louis Fisher's insight that the issue of federal-state relations is an issue of the separation of powers. As Madison argued incontrovertibly in *Federalist 44* (albeit inconsistently with the Madison who drafted the Virginia Resolutions of 1798[56]), the power to determine the line between federal and state authority necessarily must rest with the federal government and not with the individual states, or else "the authority of the whole society [would be] every where subordinate to the authority of the parts."[57] But if that power must rest with the federal government, and if its exercise involves the decision of matters of policy, not law, then it is difficult to escape the logic of Marshall's conclusion that the power should be exercised by the branch of the federal government responsible for making decisions of policy, namely, Congress.

But power, not logic, would prove to be the controlling factor in determining, over the course of history, who was to draw the line between federal and state authority. And, right now, the Court is unequivocally claiming that power for itself. Doing so requires, of course, that *McCulloch* be explained away, and, in *Printz v United States,* Justice Scalia offered a novel and ingenious explanation of why *McCulloch* can be put aside. In holding that the law requiring state or local law enforcement officers to conduct background checks on persons seeking to purchase handguns was not sustainable under the "necessary and proper" clause despite the fact that it clearly met Marshall's test for constitutionality as an appropriate means of carrying out Congress's responsibilities under the commerce clause, Scalia asserted that, regardless of whether the law can be described as "necessary" under Marshall's approach, it must still be declared unconstitutional because, since it abridges state sovereignty, it is not "proper," and, to be constitutional, the law must be both "necessary" *and* "proper."[58] But that argument is patently specious, and the distinction Scalia advances is plainly a distinction without a difference. "Proper" has never been regarded as a constitutional standard separate from "necessary." It is merely another way of saying "appropriate" and "not prohibited by the Constitution." It is difficult to image Marshall saying that the Court could make the legislative determination of whether a law was "proper" even if it could not make the legislative determination of whether it was "necessary"—at least in the absence of a constitutional prohibition, and no constitutional prohibition was involved in either *McCulloch* or *Printz.* If an act of Congress satisfies Marshall's test for the purpose of determining whether it is "necessary," it must also satisfy it for the purpose of determining whether it is "proper." Since congressional statutes which are "necessary" under Marshall's criteria commonly abridge state sovereignty (as was the case in *McCulloch*), the mere fact that they do so cannot make them "improper."

For almost all of the nineteenth century, the question of defining the limits of Congress's constitutional capacity to intrude into areas within the police-power concerns of the states was largely academic. Congress did not undertake significant regulatory action in this period, and there was thus no occasion for the Court to rule on whether Congress had improperly infringed upon areas of state concern in the exercise of its commerce power or any other of its delegated powers. The commerce clause cases that arose in this period concerned questions of whether the states, in exercising their police powers, had improperly infringed upon the domain of Congress by imposing regulations on interstate commerce, not the reverse. In *Cooley v Board of Wardens*[59] in 1852, the Court ruled that states could regulate interstate commerce in the absence of conflicting congressional regulation, unless the aspect of commerce being regulated required regulation by a uniform rule throughout the nation. The *Cooley* doctrine, of course, required the Court to make the policy determination of which subjects of commerce had to be governed by a uniform national rule, and which did not, but, since these policy decisions were presumably subject to reversal by Congress, which had the last word on how interstate commerce was to be controlled, the separation of powers problems posed by disagreement between the Court and Congress over issues of policy were not implicated.

The Civil War and the adoption of the Fourteenth Amendment at the war's close drastically altered the preexisting relations between the federal government and the states. The amendment placed broad constitutional limitations on the states, which had theretofore faced only a few narrow and specific prohibitions, and granted Congress power to enforce these new limitations by appropriate legislation. It took the Supreme Court little more than twenty years, however, to convince itself that Congress's power to enforce the amendment was very narrow, while the Court's power to invalidate state legislation under it was vast. When the Reconstruction Congress sought to implement the equal protection clause through civil rights laws intended to protect blacks against brutality and discrimination, the Court greeted these laws with hostility, and its emasculation of them culminated in the *Civil Rights Cases*[60] of 1883, in which it struck down the Civil Rights Act of 1875, by which Congress sought to prohibit racial discrimination in places of public accommodation, on the ground that Congress's power to enforce the amendment was limited to prohibiting official state discrimination and did not extend to the prohibition of private discrimination. However, when the business and industrial community, which was then undergoing explosive growth in wealth and power, sought to persuade the Court to use the Fourteenth Amendment to provide it with federal constitutional protection against state regulation by giving the due process clause of the amendment a substantive reach, the Court, although initially reluctant to do so, soon succumbed.

The Court's initial reluctance was grounded in its adherence to the traditional distinction, so emphatically articulated by Marshall in *McCulloch,* between the legislature's responsibility to make policy and the judiciary's responsibility to apply the law. When the business community urged the Court to protect it against state regulation by embracing the notion of substantive due process, under which it could strike down legislation regarded as arbitrary or unreasonable, the Court saw that it was being asked to make policy determinations and, at least at first, sought to maintain the distinction between legislative and judicial functions. In *Munn v Illinois*[61] in 1877, faced with a claim that state regulation of grain elevators was unjustified by any public need, and was therefore a violation of due process, the Court responded that that was purely a legislative question. The only question for the Court was whether the law could reasonably be thought to meet a public need. Only "[i]f no state of circumstances could exist to justify such a statute" could it be declared unconstitutional.[62]

If such a state of circumstances could conceivably exist, then it was within the power of the legislature to enact the law, and the question of whether the law was necessary to meet the public need was entirely up to the legislature to decide. "For us," Chief Justice Waite declared for the Court in *Munn*, "the question is one of power, not of expediency."[63] The parallel between the reasoning of the Court in *Munn* and the reasoning of Marshall in *McCulloch* is exact. Under both, courts are only to decide if the law is within the power of the legislature to enact, and it is within the legislature's power if the law can reasonably or conceivably be seen as appropriate or plainly adapted to the execution of the legislature's constitutionally permissible responsibilities. For the courts to go beyond that, and to decide whether the law is necessary, or expedient, as a means of meeting those responsibilities would be "to tread on legislative ground."[64] As Waite put it in *Munn*: "Of the propriety of legislative interference within the scope of legislative power, the legislature is the exclusive judge."[65] Like Marshall, Waite recognized that unchecked legislative power could be abused, but, just as Marshall had declared in *Gibbons* that checks on legislative abuse in a democratic society must come through the political process,[66] Waite declared that protection against legislative abuse should be obtained by "resort to the polls, not to the courts."[67]

But Waite's careful distinction between the legislative and judicial functions was not maintained. By 1890, the composition of the Court had changed substantially, and the incoming justices, who were by then dominant, believed that judicial power should be used aggressively to protect the property rights of the business community against majoritarian legislatures. In *Chicago, Milwau-*

kee & St. Paul Railway Co. v Minnesota[68] in 1890, the new majority held, in direct contradiction of *Munn,* that the reasonableness of the content of legislative regulations was "eminently a question for judicial investigation," and that courts were responsible for checking legislative abuses.[69] And in 1905, in *Lochner v New York,*[70] the Court ruled that whether or not a state maximum-hour law was needed to serve a legitimate public purpose was a matter to be decided by judges.[71] Under the *Lochner* Court's approach, a law would be held to be within the power of the legislature only if the judges decided for themselves that it was expedient.[72] This was a Court that had no reluctance "to tread on legislative ground."

The legislative ground on which the Court trod in these cases was state legislative ground because Congress had left the regulation of business activity to the states until the increasingly urgent need to regulate interstate railroad transportation and the gigantic industrial monopolies that were emerging led to the passage of the first two major federal regulatory statutes—the Interstate Commerce Act of 1887[73] and the Sherman Anti-Trust Act of 1890.[74] Because Congress could regulate industrial activity far more effectively than the states, it was clear that a Court that was committed to the protection of business had to find the means to place constitutional restrictions on the delegated powers of Congress. The willingness to treat questions of legislative policy as matters of constitutional law that the Court was beginning to display obviously had to be utilized if Congress was to be kept within policy bounds that the Court approved, but, in order for the Court to be able to invalidate acts of Congress on policy grounds, it was absolutely essential for it to dismantle the constitutional jurisprudence established by John Marshall in cases like *McCulloch* and *Gibbons.* The task of dismantling it began in *United States v E. C. Knight Co.*[75] in 1895, when the Court was presented with a challenge to the use of Congress's power under the commerce clause to use the Sherman Act to break up a monopoly in the manufacture of refined sugar.

In *E. C. Knight,* the Court began its analysis by noting that the monopoly at issue was a monopoly of manufacturing, and that manufacturing was not commerce.[76] But, under Marshall's standard, that is not a controlling factor. Marshall's *McCulloch* test did not ask whether Congress was regulating a matter that it was expressly delegated the power to regulate, but whether its action could be regarded as an appropriate means of carrying out an expressly delegated responsibility. For Justice Harlan, the dissenter in *E. C. Knight,* if Marshall's test were employed, the answer was easy. He noted the underlying principle of Marshall's *McCulloch* opinion, that Congress must be able to choose the means that will enable it "to perform the high duties assigned to it in the manner most beneficial to the people,"[77] and then asked if it could be said that the end (removing obstructions to the free flow of interstate commerce) was not legitimate, or the means (controlling a monopoly that created such an obstruction) not appropriate, or prohibited by anything in the Constitution.[78] But Marshall's reasoning was not the reasoning of the Court in *E. C. Knight.* It ignored both his test for constitutionality and the fundamental principle on which it rested. Congress's ability to choose the means to carry out its responsibilities had to be sacrificed, it declared, in order to avoid improper interference with the autonomy of the states, and therefore the Court would have to decide whether the means Congress had chosen was constitutionally permissible.[79] The test put forward by the Court for determining the permissibility of congressional regulation of a matter (such as a monopoly of manufacturing) that was not itself interstate commerce, but that affected it, has been called the "direct/indirect effects" rule. If the activity affected interstate commerce only indirectly (as, in this case, the monopoly affected manufacturing directly and commerce only indirectly), Congress was without constitutional power to regulate it. Strikingly, this rule allows no account to be taken of the magnitude or extent of the effect on commerce of the activity being regulated. "[H]owever inevitable [the effect on commerce] and whatever its extent," the Court declared, Congress could not regulate it if its effect on commerce were indirect.[80]

It was more than a little remarkable that the Court could content that Congress could not protect interstate commerce from adverse effects so extreme that they might be catastrophic so long as those effects, however immense, could be described as indirect. The Court did not deny that this could lead to undesirable results, but it maintained that "acknowledged evils, however grave and urgent they may appear to be, had better be borne, than the risk be run, in the effort to suppress them, of more serious consequences."[81] The more serious consequences would be the loss of state autonomy, and the need to guard against that diminution of state power was so great that it was "vital" that the Court, and not Congress, be the body to define the boundary between federal and state authority.[82] This expression of the vital importance of preserving state autonomy was, of course, clearly reminiscent of Thomas Jefferson's similar expression of concern a century earlier.[83] But Jefferson's concern for state autonomy was sincere—a belief that the authority of the states must be diligently safeguarded in order to ensure that the people's right to govern themselves would not be lost by the transfer of power to a distant government likely to be insensitive to their needs and interests. In contrast, the concern for state autonomy expressed by the Court in *E. C. Knight* was plainly a sham. This was a Court that was ready to invoke the federal Constitution to overrule a state on the question of the reasonableness of the policies reflected in its laws,[84] and, within a decade, would tell the states that the judicial branch of the federal government would nullify its laws whenever federal judges decided that, in their opinion, those laws did not serve a legitimate public purpose.[85] State autonomy is no less sacrificed to federal power if the branch of the federal government overriding that autonomy is the judiciary rather than the legislature, and, to say the least, Thomas Jefferson would have been aghast at the idea that a state would only be able to implement its laws if the policies they embodied met the approval of federal judges—who purport to be their allies.

But the Court's concern was not for state autonomy, but for the protection of business from federal, as well as state, regulation. The "direct/indirect effects" rule was a useful vehicle for keeping Congress from using its commerce power to regulate matters that were not in themselves interstate commerce. However, more was needed to prevent Congress from interfering with business in ways the Court disapproved through the regulation of things that *were* interstate commerce. When Congress used its commerce power to regulate matters within the reach of the police powers of the states in ways the Court did not disapprove of, it was quite content to affirm the validity of those regulations. Thus, Congress had, with the Court's approval, restricted the interstate transportation of lottery tickets,[86] impure foods,[87] and prostitutes.[88] These were plainly regulations of interstate commerce, and the fact that their obvious purpose and effect was to regulate morals and health, matters that were squarely at the core of the police-power responsibilities of the states, was not troublesome for the Court. But allowance of this kind of regulation would appear to make possible sweeping congressional regulation of all manner of business activity, and so, when Congress undertook to use the same authority approved in the earlier cases to regulate labor conditions rather than immorality or illness, the Court took a dramatically different tack.

In *Hammer v Dagenhart*[89] in 1918, a bare majority of the Court voted to strike down the Keating-Owen Child Labor Act of 1916, which prohibited the shipment in commerce of articles produced under substandard labor conditions.[90] The power to regulate interstate commerce, the Court held, did not include the power to prohibit interstate commerce. It had, of course, been recognized as including that power in the case of lottery tickets, impure foods, and prostitutes, but the Court explained that that was because the transportation of those things would lead to evils, and there was nothing evil about the goods produced by child labor.[91] Moreover, said the Court, the Tenth Amendment is a prohibition on Congress, and prevents it from using its delegated powers to intrude in areas reserved for state regulation,[92] although, apparently, the prohibition only applied to congressional acts that regulated production, and not to laws that regulated health or morals even though those areas were equally reserved for state regulation. And, in any event, the Tenth Amendment, simply as a matter of language, cannot be a prohibition of congressional regulation of matters within the scope of its delegated powers. For the Tenth Amendment reserves to the states only the powers not delegated to Congress. The powers that *are* delegated to Congress, therefore, are not reserved to the states,[93] and, as Marshall stated in *Gibbons v Ogden,* each of Congress's delegated powers "is complete in itself, may be exercised to its utmost extent, and acknowledges no limitations, other than are prescribed in the constitution."[94]

Hammer v Dagenhart was directly at odds with Marshall's position. It rested on the view that Congress may not exercise its delegated powers to their utmost extent, and that those powers cease when their exercise brings about a regulation of a matter reserved to the states. That the doctrine of *Hammer* is an unjustified interference with the prerogatives of Congress is, if possible, made even more obvious by the fact that whether or not Congress may exercise its delegated powers to their utmost extent depends on whether the Court agrees with the policy it is seeking to implement. In the case of the regulation of gambling or vice, the Court was content with the policy of suppression and sustained it despite the fact that the purpose and effect of the laws was the regulation of matters within the police powers of the states. The only reason for a different outcome when the law's purpose was to control child labor was that the Court disagreed with the congressional policy of regulation of working conditions in production industries. To prevent the implementation of Congress's policy, the Court unabashedly chose to convert its own policy preferences into constitutional law, and, equally unabashedly, to repudiate Marshall's view that Congress must have the power to decide what laws are necessary for the fulfillment of its constitutional responsibilities, and that, for the Court to question Congress's judgment as to the necessity of a law, and thus to take away from Congress its effective authority to draw the line between federal and state power, would be "to tread on legislative ground." In no uncertain terms, the Court in *Hammer* declared that it was the body to draw the line between federal and state authority: "This court has no more important function than that which devolves upon it the obligation to preserve inviolate the constitutional limitations upon the exercise of authority, federal and state, to the end that each may continue to discharge, harmoniously with the other, the duties entrusted to it by the Constitution."[95]

Thus, when the Great Depression struck during the administration of Herbert Hoover, and Franklin Roosevelt was swept into office in the presidential election of 1932, the Supreme Court had already replaced the basic principles for interpreting the constitutional powers of Congress established by John Marshall with new rules under which it could invoke state autonomy as a reason for blocking congressional action when it disagreed with the policies that Congress was seeking to advance. Under these new rules, the efforts of Roosevelt and the new Democratic congressional majority to employ federal authority aggressively to alleviate the economic crisis were likely to be viewed with intense hostility by a Supreme Court committed to preserving the constitutional primacy of the economic philosophy of laissez faire. And, by 1935, this hostility had hardened into a firm resolve to thwart the programs and policies of the New Deal. In *Schechter Poultry Corp. v United States*[96] in 1935, the Court invalidated the National Industrial Recovery Act,[97] which was intended to help industries shattered by the Depression to revive themselves by bringing management and labor together to draw up "codes of fair competition," which would become federal law when promulgated by the president.

The Supreme Court invalidated the act in a case presenting a challenge to the code promulgated for the live poultry business of Brooklyn, New York, primarily on the ground that Congress had unconstitutionally delegated legislative power to the president because it had failed to provide adequate standards to limit the president's discretion as to the content of the codes.[98] But it also invoked the "direct/indirect effects" rule of the *E. C. Knight* case,[99] and held that the provisions of the code regulating sales practices and labor conditions in the poultry slaughterhouses in Brooklyn exceeded Congress's authority under the commerce clause and that these local practices affected interstate commerce only indirectly.[100] The decision was unanimous. Even the three Justices who might have been expected to vote to sustain New Deal legislation— Brandeis, Stone, and Cardozo—concurred, perhaps because of unease at the idea of delegating to individual industries essentially unlimited power to make the laws that would govern them, including "the planning of improvements as well as the extirpation of abuses."[101] But they also agreed with the majority that Congress had exceeded its commerce power. In his concurring opinion, Justice Cardozo declared that to uphold Congress's authority to regulate labor conditions in this tiny business would be to "obliterate the distinction between what is national and what is local in the activities of commerce."[102]

In his *Schechter* opinion, Justice Cardozo appeared to be proposing to the majority what can be called the "Cardozo compromise." As it had been applied, the "direct/indirect effects" rule gave no consideration to the magnitude of the effect on interstate commerce of the local activity that Congress sought to regulate, but, for Cardozo, that was not unacceptable. As he stated in *Schechter*, "[t]he law is not indifferent to considerations of degree."[103] What he seemed to be suggesting to the majority was a compromise in which the minority would concede that Congress may not regulate local activities having only a slight effect on commerce, while the majority would agree that activities with a significant effect on interstate commerce would be open to congressional regulation. But this apparent offer of compromise was of no interest to the majority. The following year, the constitutionality of the Guffey Bituminous Coal Conservation Act of 1935,[104] which sought to stabilize coal prices and avoid labor unrest in the mines in order to protect the coal-mining industry from economic collapse, came before the Court in *Carter v Carter Coal Co.*[105] Given the importance of coal as an energy source, the effect on interstate commerce of a protracted stoppage of coal production could have been incalculably large. But Justice Sutherland, writing for the majority, was nothing less than jubilantly explicit in rejecting any idea of compromise along the lines that Cardozo had suggested. The extent of a local activity's effect on commerce is entirely irrelevant to the question of Congress's constitutional authority, he declared. "The distinction between a direct and an indirect effect turns, not upon the magnitude of either the cause or the effect," for "the matter of degree has no bearing upon the question," and thus, "however extensive [the effect on commerce] may be, the local activity producing that effect may not be regulated by Congress if the effect is only indirect."[106] Since working conditions in the mining of coal affected production directly, and commerce only indirectly, Congress could not constitutionally regulate those conditions.

As in *E. C. Knight* and *Hammer*, the Court made clear in *Carter* that a heavy responsibility for protecting state autonomy rested with the judiciary, and it was "of vital moment" that it not shirk that responsibility in any way.[107] Ironically, the states, which were finding themselves in extremely difficult economic circumstances as a result of the Depression and were grateful for whatever relief from their difficulties the federal government could provide, were not at all anxious to have their autonomy defended. Seven states filed *amicus curiae* briefs in *Carter* arguing in support of the constitutionality of the Guffey Act, and no state filed an *amicus* brief in opposition. But the Court was determined to rescue them from themselves. Respect for the boundary line between federal and state authority, Justice Sutherland insisted, was "incumbent equally upon the federal government and the states. State powers can neither be appropriated on the one hand nor abdicated on the other."[108] But, as in *E. C. Knight,* the Court was only concerned with protecting state autonomy from federal legislative interference, not federal judicial interference. Only two weeks after the *Carter* decision was handed down, the Court, in *Morehead v New York ex rel. Tipaldo*,[109] declared that a state could not choose to have a minimum-wage law because five federal judges believed that such a law served no valid public purpose.

Dissenting in *Carter,* Justice Cardozo, joined by Brandeis and Stone, rejected the Court's rigid application of the "direct/indirect effects" rule. He repeated his admonition in *Schechter* that "the law is not indifferent to considerations of degree," and suggested replacing the words "direct" and "indirect" with "intimate" and "remote," to make clear that the magnitude of an activity's effect on commerce was critical in determining whether Congress should have constitutional power to regulate it.[110] Under some conditions, but not all, he argued, prices or wages in local businesses may affect commerce to such an extent that regulation of them by Congress may be not only appropriate, but essential. Thus, prices or wages should not be "considered in the abstract."[111] "The power [of Congress]," he concluded, "is as broad as the need that evokes it."[112]

Following the Court's assaults on New Deal programs, Franklin Roosevelt was returned to office in a landslide in the election of 1936, and, not surprisingly, set himself to the task of determining how to remove the Supreme Court as an obstacle to the achievement of the social and economic reforms that he saw as essential for national well-being. After considering other options, such as seeking to amend the Constitution, he settled on his notorious "court-packing" plan—to create additional federal judgeships, including up to six additional members of the Supreme Court, to supplement those judges who had reached the age of seventy but had not chosen to retire.[113] The plan was bitterly assailed as an attack on the independence of the judiciary and was ultimately defeated in Congress, but the ominousness of the threat doubtlessly led the Court to remove itself as the barrier to the achievement of the policies of the New Deal. Chief Justice Hughes and Justice Roberts suddenly switched sides in the spring of 1937 (the "switch in time that saved nine"), and joined Justices Brandeis, Stone, and Cardozo, to provide a five-justice majority that would sustain the constitutionality of congressional legislation against challenges that these laws regulated local matters in derogation of state autonomy, and would drastically curtail the authority of courts to decide constitutional questions on the basis of judicial agreement or disagreement with the policies embodied in legislation.

On March 29, 1937, this new majority, in *West Coast Hotel Co. v Parrish*,[114] upheld a Washington minimum-wage law for women, despite its holding in the *Morehead* case, less than a year earlier, that such laws were unconstitutional because they lacked a proper public purpose.[115] Two weeks later, the same majority, in *NLRB v Jones & Laughlin Steel Corp.*,[116] upheld the constitutionality of the Wagner National Labor Relations Act of 1935,[117] which sought to guarantee the right of workers in industry—including production industries—to bargain collectively with their employers, despite the rulings in the *Schechter* and *Carter* cases that Congress could not regulate working conditions or labor relations in production industries because they affected production directly and commerce only indirectly, regardless of the magnitude of the effect on commerce these activities might have. The Constitutional Revolution of 1937 had arrived!

Of these two decisions, *West Coast Hotel* was more sweeping in its concession of full legislative power to legislatures. Chief Justice Hughes, writing for the majority in that case, declared that if a law can reasonably be seen as an appropriate means to the attainment of a legitimate end, it is entirely up to the legislature to decide whether it is necessary or desirable—thus heeding Marshall's admonition in *McCulloch* that whether a law is necessary is solely a legislative question.[118] If the legislation "cannot be regarded as arbitrary or capricious," Hughes stated, "that is all we have to decide. Even if the wisdom of the policy be regarded as debatable and its effects uncertain, still the Legislature is entitled to its judgment."[119] Substantive due process, at least as applied to cases involving economic regulation, had come to the end of its run.

The Court's opinion in *Jones & Laughlin Steel*, however, while dramatically different from *Carter*, did not cede back to Congress the same total authority to decide policy questions under its commerce power that was returned to legislatures in economic substantive due process cases. What the Court did, instead, was to adopt the Cardozo compromise. Hughes, writing the majority opinion in this case, as in *West Coast Hotel*, explicitly embraced each of the points made in Cardozo's *Carter* dissent, affirming that the question of whether Congress can regulate a local activity because of its effect on commerce "is necessarily one of degree."[120] Throughout his opinion, he repeatedly used the adjectives "intimate" and "remote" that Cardozo had suggested in *Carter* as alternatives to "direct" and "indirect" in order to allow for consideration of the magnitude of the effect on commerce of the activity to be regulated.[121] And he insisted that the constitutionality of Congress's action was not to be decided by asking, in the abstract, whether Congress could regulate labor relations in production industries, but by asking whether labor relations in the particular industry involved in the challenge to the law had a potentially sufficient effect on commerce to warrant federal regulation. There was no question in the minds of the majority that labor relations in the steel industry, as well as in the industries in the companion cases decided together with *Jones & Laughlin Steel*, met this test.[122]

On the other hand, the Court also subscribed to the other half of Cardozo's compromise—articulated not only in his dissenting opinion in *Carter*, but also in his concurring opinion in *Schechter*. If a local activity, like Schechter's business, had only a slight effect on commerce—one that could be felt only through "distant repercussions," as Cardozo had put it in *Schechter*[123]—then Congress may not regulate it, for permitting federal regulation there would, in the words that Hughes borrowed from Cardozo, "obliterate the distinction between what is national and what is local and create a completely centralized government."[124] *Jones & Laughlin Steel*, therefore, did not strip the courts of policymaking authority with regard to determining the scope of congressional power, but it changed the question courts should ask. Instead of asking whether the activity to be regulated affected commerce directly or indirectly, they would now ask whether the magnitude of the effect on commerce of that activity was great enough to justify congressional regulation. The new question was certainly an improvement over the old, but the judiciary still retained the power to decide whether congressional regulation was necessary to the execution of Congress's constitutional responsibilities. But to decide whether an act of Congress was necessary is to do precisely what Marshall said should be beyond the province of the courts, for it would be "to tread on legislative ground."

The Cardozo compromise had initially been put forward as a plea for reason on the part of a majority committed to the limitation of federal regulatory power. It was undoubtedly a vital step in the creation of the 1937 majority, but compromise is only necessary if there are divergent views that need to be compromised. Within four years after *Jones & Laughlin Steel* there were no longer any divergent views on the Court with regard to Congress's constitutional powers. By 1941, the four dissenters in the historic decisions of 1937 had left the Court (as had Brandeis and Cardozo), all to be replaced by appointees of Franklin Roosevelt. In light of the new composition of the Court, the Cardozo compromise could be abandoned, as it was, and the jurisprudence of John Marshall could be fully restored. The vehicle for the achievement of this restoration was *United States v Darby*[125] in 1941, which upheld the constitutionality of the Fair Labor Standards Act of 1938,[126] which prohibited the shipment of goods in interstate commerce that were manufactured under working conditions with respect to wages and hours that were below the minimum standards that were spelled out in the act, and which further prohibited the employment of workers in the production of goods for interstate commerce under conditions that did not meet those specified standards. The Court unanimously sustained both of these key provisions of the law, and, in so doing, fully and unequivocally embraced the reasoning of John Marshall in both *Gibbons v Ogden* and *McCulloch v Maryland*.

The Court in *Darby* summarily overruled *Hammer v Dagenhart*, which had held that Congress was without power to prohibit the shipment of goods produced under substandard (child) labor conditions.[127] It rejected the argument of *Hammer* that Congress could not use its delegated powers to regulate matters reserved to the states, expressly reaffirming Marshall's statement in *Gibbons v Ogden* that each of Congress's powers "may be exercised to its utmost extent."[128] The notion that the Tenth Amendment was a limitation of Congress's capacity to fully exercise its delegated powers was dismissed out of hand, and the amendment itself described as "a truism."[129] Congress could thus prohibit whatever interstate shipments it wished, and its power to do so was not lessened in any way by the fact that the motive or purpose of the prohibition might have been to regulate a matter within the police-power concern of the states.[130]

The other principal provision of the act upheld in *Darby* was not a regulation of interstate transportation, but a regulation of working conditions in production industries. Under the "direct/indirect effects" rule of *E. C. Knight, Schechter,* and *Carter,* Congress could not impose labor standards on production industries because working conditions in those industries affected interstate commerce only indirectly. Under the rule of *Jones & Laughlin Steel,* Congress could impose such standards only if the effect on interstate commerce of working conditions in the industry involved was sufficiently great. But, under Marshall's test in *McCulloch,* the congressional regulation would be constitutional if it could reasonably be seen to be a means "plainly adapted" to carrying out Congress's responsibility to regulate and prohibit interstate commerce, and it was Marshall's test that the Court in *Darby* employed. It held that Congress "may choose the means reasonably adapted to the attainment of the permitted end, even though they involve control of intrastate activities,"[131] and, under this standard, the congressional action was clearly constitutional because it could reasonably be thought to be an appropriate means of attaining the legitimate end of protecting businesses engaged in interstate commerce from the damaging effects of a destructive competition based on the use of substandard working conditions.[132]

The *Darby* Court discarded the Cardozo compromise position, adopted in *Jones & Laughlin Steel,* that Congress could not constitutionally regulate local activities if those activities had only a "remote" or "distant" effect on interstate commerce, and thus affected it only slightly. Like the Court in *E. C. Knight* and *Carter,* it denied that the degree of the effect on commerce was relevant to whether the activity was subject to congressional regulation. But it did so for a wholly different purpose. Whereas, in the earlier cases, Congress was held to be without power to regulate local activities even if the magnitude of their effect on interstate commerce was immense, in *Darby,* Congress was recognized as having authority to regulate any matters that could reasonably be thought to affect commerce, either directly or indirectly, regardless of how small the effect on commerce of the precise activity being regulated. The Court acknowledged that, even if the particular activity being regulated had only a slight effect on commerce, there were likely to be many similar activities throughout the nation, and the cumulative effect on commerce of all of those activities, taken together, could be significant. Congress was entitled to act on that understanding.[133]

The effect of the restoration of John Marshall's constitutional jurisprudence in 1941 was to return to Congress the power to determine the location of the line between federal and state authority and responsibility. The recognition that that power properly belonged to Congress was an integral part of Marshall's jurisprudence, and was based on the understanding that location of that line was necessarily determined by considerations of policy, not law. Jefferson's perception that conceding that power to Congress would vest it with the capacity to take over whatever areas of state responsibility it wished[134] was perfectly accurate, but he offered no satisfactory solution to the problem he correctly identified. Clearly, as Marshall saw, the line between federal and state responsibility cannot be made so rigid that Congress would be rendered incapable of meeting its constitutional obligations.[135] Equally clearly, it is indispensable to national unity that the line be drawn by a branch of the federal government. Since the location of the boundary is a policy question, it would appear that the body to draw that line should be Congress. There must undoubtedly be greater room for judicial review of congressional policy judgments where the Constitution places prohibitions on congressional action, as in the Bill of Rights, but, in the absence of such prohibitions, the checks on the policy judgments of Congress should be political, as Marshall pointed out in *Gibbons.*[136] If these checks should prove inadequate, Congress may unquestionably be able to abuse its power. But shifting the authority to draw the federal-state boundary line from Congress to the federal judiciary, while providing an alternative remedy for congressional abuse, does not in any way resolve the problem of abuse, it merely shifts the potential for abuse from one place to another. Not only is policymaking not the appropriate function of courts, but granting the courts the unreviewable power to draw the federal-state boundary makes it possible for them to abuse that power by frustrating legitimate congressional efforts to meet federal constitutional responsibilities.[137] For a period of roughly fifty years, from 1887 to 1937, the Supreme Court claimed this authority for itself, and it was the resultant judicial abuse that led to the reembrace of Marshall's doctrines.

Darby's restoration to Congress of the breadth of authority inherent in Marshall's constitutional rulings cleared the way for the extension of congressional regulatory power into areas it has not previously been understood to reach. For a period of over fifty years following 1941, no act of Congress regulating private behavior under the commerce clause was ruled unconstitutional by the Supreme Court. Three examples, among others that might also be selected, illustrate how far Congress was allowed to go in the regulation of matters that, on the surface, would appear to be purely local. The year after *Darby*, the Court, in *Wickard v Filburn*,[138] unanimously affirmed an amendment to the Agricultural Adjustment Act of 1938,[139] that was intended to reduce the oversupply of wheat available for the market, and thus raise the price paid to farmers, by imposing a penalty on farmers who grew wheat in excess of an assigned quota. The challenge to the law in this case was brought by a farmer who objected to paying the penalty on excess wheat that he planned to consume on the farm, and not sell. The Court had no difficulty in upholding the law even as so applied. It was, in the Court's view, of no moment that this regulation fell on a purely local, noncommercial activity, or that this local activity had only an indirect effect on commerce. The question for the Court, it declared, was not whether it believed that the production of wheat for home consumption would have a substantial effect on the interstate commerce in that crop, but whether "Congress may properly have considered that wheat consumed on the farm where grown" would have such an effect. What the actual effects on commerce are, and whether they are of sufficient importance to warrant federal regulation, are matters to be determined solely by Congress as long as it has a reasonable basis for concluding that regulation is needed to carry out effectively its commerce power.[140]

A second post-*Darby* example of the breadth of Congress's commerce power under Marshall's doctrines is *Katzenbach v McClung*,[141] which, together with its companion, *Heart of Atlanta Motel v United States*,[142] provided the opportunity for the Court unanimously to uphold the public accommodations title (Title II) of the historic Civil Rights Act of 1964, prohibiting racial discrimination in privately owned places of public accommodation.[143] Because of the decision in the *Civil Rights Cases*[144] of 1883, (so fondly recalled by Justice Kennedy in *City of Boerne*), in which the very similar Civil

Rights Act of 1875 had been held unconstitutional on the ground that Congress had no power under § 5 of the Fourteenth Amendment to forbid private acts of racial discrimination[145]—a decision which had never been overruled—Congress concluded that it was risky to rely for the constitutional authority to enact legislation so vital to the cause of justice on its power to enforce the Fourteenth Amendment. Instead, it chose to rely on a much more secure source of authority—its power to regulate interstate commerce.

Katzenbach v McClung involved the application of Title II to prohibit racial discrimination in a neighborhood restaurant that rarely, if ever, served interstate travelers, but which was covered by the law because "a substantial portion of the food which it serve[d]" had moved in interstate commerce.[146] Had Congress been required to prove that racial discrimination in such restaurants diminished interstate shipments of food, it would have faced a difficult task, but that was not necessary. The Court took cognizance of testimony before Congress that indicated a reduction in consumer spending where racial discrimination was prevalent (even when income differences were taken into account), that widespread discrimination discouraged interstate travel by blacks, and that businesses were frequently reluctant to relocate in areas where discrimination was practiced.[147] On the basis of this testimony, it concluded that Congress "had a rational basis for finding that racial discrimination in restaurants had a direct and adverse effect on the free flow of interstate commerce."[148] For the Court, that was enough to answer the question of the constitutionality of Title II, as applied in this case, because "where we find that the legislators, in light of the facts and testimony before them, have a rational basis for finding a chosen regulatory scheme necessary to the protection of commerce, our investigation is at an end."[149] The Court made no inquiry into the necessity of the law or the degree of the effect on interstate commerce caused by racial discrimination. Those were matters for the exclusive consideration of Congress.

A third example is *Perez v United States*[150] in 1971, in which the Court, this time with one Justice dissenting, sustained the constitutionality of a conviction for engaging in an "extortionate credit transaction" in violation of Title II of the Consumer Credit Protection Act of 1968.[151] An "extortionate credit transaction," as defined in the statute, is the lending of money under the threat that, if repayment is not made on the lender's terms, violence or other criminal means of causing harm will be used as a means of collection.[152] The government proved in this case that the defendant had made a loan in violation of the statute, but it offered no proof that the loan was in any way related to interstate commerce. Justice Stewart dissented on the ground that this was simply a local crime, and while local crime is a national problem that adversely affects interstate commerce, Congress cannot take responsibility for criminal law enforcement.[153] But an eight-justice majority upheld the conviction.

The Court reviewed the factors that led Congress to pass the act, and noted that there was evidence showing that the employment of extortion to collect loans—i.e., "loan sharking"—was an important tool of organized crime.[154] Relying on *Darby, Wickard v Filburn,* and *Katzenbach v McClung,* among other decisions, it held that because of the interstate character of organized crime, Congress could identify loan sharking as a "class of activities" to be made unlawful.[155] Once Congress has properly identified and prohibited a "class of activities" that affect interstate commerce, its prohibition may apply to all activities that fall within that class, without regard to whether the specific act to which the law is being applied can be shown to have an adverse effect on interstate commerce. Where Congress may constitutionally regulate the entire class, "the courts have no power 'to excise, as trivial, individual instances' of the class."[156]

A crack in the uniform understanding of the breadth and scope of Congress's commerce power appeared in 1976, in a Court which then included four appointees of Richard Nixon. In that year, in an effort to protect the states, as governmental entities, from federal regulation, the Court held, 5–4, in *National League of Cities v Usery,*[157] that, despite the fact that the wages and hours of state and local governmental employees affected commerce to the same extent as the wages and hours of the employees of private businesses, Congress could not, without unconstitutionally interfering with state sovereignty, extend the Fair Labor Standards Act to require states and local governments to meet federal wage, hour, and overtime standards with regard to those of their employees performing "traditional governmental functions."[158] The Court made clear that its ruling did not affect Congress's recognized power under the commerce clause to require private employers to meet federal labor standards.[159] But in 1985, in *Garcia v San Antonio Metropolitan Transit Authority,*[160] Justice Blackmun, who had provided, with some misgivings, the fifth vote to create the *National League of Cities* majority, shifted sides, and the decision in *National League of Cities* was overruled. Critical to the reasoning of the Court in *Garcia* was the conclusion that, while state sovereignty was an essential element of the American constitutional system, that sovereignty was necessarily limited by the grants of power in the Constitution to the federal government, whose valid legislative acts had supremacy over state law. Thus, state sovereignty was to be safeguarded, not by the imposition of judicial restrictions on Congress, but by the influence that states possessed in the political process and by the role given to the states "in the selection both of the Executive and the Legislative Branches of the Federal Government."[161]

Events in Congress following *Garcia* tended to bear out both the Court's assessment of the states' capacity to protect themselves politically at the federal level, and Louis Fisher's observation that the meaning of federalism is developed through a process of political negotiation by which the relevant actors "hammer out the sensitive and ever-changing relationships between the federal government and the states."[162] As Fisher himself has noted, after *Garcia* effectively reapplied federal wage, hour, and overtime requirements to the states, Congress was persuaded by the states that these requirements "threatened [them] with massive costs," especially for overtime pay for police and firefighters, and, consequently, enacted legislation to postpone the application of the federal standards to state and local governments, and to allow compensatory time off to be given as a substitute for overtime pay.[163] Fisher has underscored his point by quoting the remarks on the floor of the Senate by Senator Howard Metzebaum of Ohio, a sponsor of this legislation, in which he noted that states and cities had been instrumental in drafting the law and had enthusiastically endorsed it, and then applauded the faith of the Court's *Garcia* majority in "the role of Congress as a cornerstone of our Federal system of government," and the majority's recognition that the "Constitution contemplates that the proper protection for the sovereign interests of States and their political subdivisions lies not in directives issued by the Federal Judiciary but rather in the give-and-take of our federal system—especially the role of the States and cities in the political process."[164]

As late as 1985, therefore, a majority of the Supreme Court, but by then only a precarious one, still held to the views of John Marshall that Congress was free to exercise its delegated power "to its utmost extent," as long as it had a reasonable basis for believing that its laws were appropriate for the attainment of a legitimate end, and that restrictions on Congress's power should come from the political process. Indeed, even two years later, the Court, with only two justices dissenting (one of them being Brennan!) upheld Congress's exercise of the spending power to require states to raise their legal drinking age to twenty-one as a condition of eligibility to receive their full share of federal funds for highway construction.[165] Chief Justice Rehnquist, the author of the Court's opinion in this case as well as the Court's opinion in *National League of Cities*, explained his greater tolerance for this type of federal intrusion into state autonomy by declaring that Congress has greater freedom from constitutional restrictions when exercising its spending power than when exercising its regulatory powers,[166] and noting that states may always preserve their autonomy by declining to accept federal funding.[167]

By the early 1990s, however, a new majority had emerged on the Supreme Court as a result of the appointment of Presidents Reagan and Bush, and, in 1992, a six-justice majority made up of the appointees of these two presidents, plus Chief Justice Rehnquist, who had been appointed to the Court by Richard Nixon and elevated to chief justice by Ronald Reagan, struck down a provision of a 1985 federal statute requiring a state that had not taken adequate action to provide for the disposal of low-level radioactive waste generated within its territory to take title to the waste, and thus assume direct responsibility for it.[168] Since taking title to the waste was obviously an unpalatable option, the effect of the federal law, in the view of the majority, was to force recalcitrant states to enact legislation providing for its disposal, and thus to " 'commandeer' state governments into the service of federal regulatory purposes," a tactic which the Court held to be unconstitutional because it was "inconsistent with the federal system of our Government."[169] The ironic aspect of this decision was that, as Justice White noted in dissent, Congress had specifically refrained from imposing on the states a federal solution to the problem of disposal, which it had undoubted constitutional authority to do, but, instead, had allowed the states to work out a resolution among themselves (a process in which New York took part) through the good offices of the National Governors' Association, and then had enacted legislation to enforce this resolution.[170] Solicitor General Kenneth Starr, on behalf of the Bush administration, strongly defended Congress's action before the Court, arguing in his brief for the United States that Congress had deliberately adopted a "state-oriented solution" to an interstate dispute, and that, "[i]n light of . . . assiduous care Congress displayed in attending to the interests and concerns of the several States, the Act is a constitutionally permissible example of cooperative federalism designed to preserve, rather than preempt, state authority."[171] But the Reagan/Bush majority, determined to curtail federal authority as against the states, chose to constrict Congress's power, even to the extent of forbidding Congress from using its legislative authority in support of policies worked out by the states themselves to resolve multistate problems.

The idea that the federal government has no power to force state governments to take action they do not wish to take, and thus to "commandeer" them for the purpose of implementing federal policy, had been urged by Justice O'Connor in a dissenting opinion in 1982,[172] and later became the basis for the Court's 1997 ruling in *Printz v United States*,[173] holding unconstitutional the provision of federal gun-control legislation requiring local officials to conduct background checks on persons seeking to purchase handguns, because Congress was thereby "commandeering" those officials for the purpose of enforcing federal law. But *New York* and *Printz*, like *National League of Cities,* which, for a time, limited the capacity of Congress to require states and municipalities, as employers, to comply with federal labor standards, were decisions that only restricted the capacity of the federal government to impose duties or obligations on state and local governments or their officials. It was *United States v Lopez*[174] in 1995 that, for the first time since 1936, invalidated congressional regulation of private behavior as in excess of the power of Congress under the commerce clause, and thus suddenly altered what had been settled understandings of almost sixty years regarding the scope and breadth of the delegated powers of Congress, and how the limits on those powers were to be identified and enforced.

In *Lopez*, a bare 5–4 majority brought about this counterrevolution in constitutional adjudication by declaring invalid, as in excess of the commerce power, the prohibition against knowing possession of a firearm in a school zone contained in the Gun-Free School Zones Act of 1990.[175] Under the test for the constitutionality of federal legislation established by John Marshall in *McCulloch*, which had been restored in 1941 in *United States v Darby* and applied consistently for the next fifty-four years, this law was clearly within the power of Congress to enact, for that test recognizes Congress's power to "choose the means reasonably adapted" for carrying out its delegated powers.[176] Dissenting in *Lopez*, Justice Breyer, joined by Justices Stevens, Souter, and Ginsburg, amply demonstrated that the congressional prohibition on guns in schools meets this test. Guns in schools seriously interfere with education, and the quality of education is vital to a healthy and competitive economy, and thus to interstate and foreign commerce.[177] "At the very least," in Breyer's view, "Congress could rationally have concluded that the links [between guns in schools and commerce] are 'substantial.' "[178] While he conceded that courts were obligated to examine "independently" Congress's claim that the activity to be regulated has a substantial or significant effect on commerce,[179] the independent judicial examination would not be for the purpose of ascertaining whether the effect was, in fact, substantial, but whether Congress had a rational (or reasonable) basis for concluding that it was. That was a straightforward application of Marshall's *McCulloch* approach: courts should only look to determine whether the means chosen by Congress could reasonably be regarded as "appropriate," not whether they were "necessary," for to decide the latter question would be "to tread on legislative ground."[180]

The majority, however, was quite willing to tread on legislative ground. It declined to apply the *McCulloch/Darby* standard because it found the implications of doing so to be unacceptable. If Congress could regulate any local activity whenever it could demonstrate a rational basis for believing that that activity had a significant effect on commerce, its power would be unlimited. If violent crime affects commerce, then Congress would be able to regulate any activity that may lead to violent crime. Given that it is important to interstate and foreign commerce that the United States have a productive citizenry, Congress could regulate all activities, including family relationships, that could affect individual productivity. Thus, Chief Justice Rehnquist wrote for the Court, "if we were to accept the government's arguments, we are hard pressed to posit any activity by an individual that Congress is without power to regulate."[181]

Although Rehnquist's examples have something of a "parade of horribles" quality, his point is incontrovertible. It is identical to Jefferson—give to Congress the power to do whatever it deems necessary to the exercise of a delegated power, and it may do anything, for there is nothing "which ingenuity may not torture into a *convenience in some way or other,* to *some one* of so long a list of enumerated powers."[182] If that is undesirable, as it is, and if it is inconsistent with the federal system underlying the Constitution, as it is, the question is how to ensure that Congress will not act in a way that would destroy the independence of the states. For Rehnquist and the *Lopez* majority, it was clearly the responsibility of the judiciary to prevent congressional abuse of authority. The limits on the enumerated powers of Congress, Rehnquist asserted, are "judicially enforceable," and, he added, quoting *Marbury v Madison*, it is "the Judiciary's duty 'to say what the law is.' "[183] The problem with this claim of judicial authority is that it is only the judiciary's duty to say what the *law* is, and the question of whether a local activity threatens sufficient injury to commerce to justify a decision that it should be federally regulated is entirely a question of policy, not law. For Marshall in *Gibbons*, unlike Rehnquist in *Lopez,* checks on Congress's choices regarding the exercise of its powers properly come through the political process,[184] and it was that understanding that provided the basis for the deference accorded to Congress in *Darby* and the cases that followed it.

To be sure, as Justice Stone, the author of *Darby*, noted three years earlier, in his celebrated footnote in *United States v Carolene Products Co.,*[185] there may be circumstances where the courts should not extend deference to Congress (or state legislatures), and there is now broad agreement that heightened judicial scrutiny should replace deference where laws abridge fundamental human rights or classify individuals invidiously on the basis of factors such a race, religious belief, ethnicity, or gender. But whether a matter should be regulated by Congress or the states does not generally raise concerns about individual freedom and dignity, and, where it does, these concerns are more likely than not to militate in favor of federal regulation.[186] In *Garcia,* Justice Blackmun suggested that states could safely rely, for the protection of their rightful authority, on the political strengths that they can wield within the branches of the federal government,[187] and while it has been argued that these checks are not really effective,[188] it is much harder to defend that argument after the election of 1994, where the Republican Party won control of Congress through a campaign based largely on the claim that Congress had taken too much power away from the states. One of the first enactments of that new Congress was the Unfunded Mandates Reform Act, which made it procedurally more difficult for Congress to impose mandates on the states without providing federal funds to meet the cost of compliance,[189] which prompted Justice Stevens to comment in his dissent in *Printz v United States* that the passage of such a law by Congress "demonstrates that unelected judges are better off leaving the protection of federalism to the political process in all but the most extraordinary circumstances."[190] The "extraordinary circumstances" that Justice Stevens referred to presumably would be actions by Congress that would threaten the states' "separate and independent existence,"[191] at which extremity judicial intervention would be appropriate. Needless to say, the Gun-Free School Zones Act did not approach such an extremity.

The majority in *Lopez* faced the task of explaining why it was not following the unbroken line of precedents that, since 1936, had upheld every congressional regulation of individual behavior based on the commerce power. It did not overrule any of those precedents or suggest that they were wrongly decided. Instead, it distinguished them on the ground that they involved "commercial activities that substantially affect[ed] interstate commerce,"[192] whereas the mere possession of a gun in a school zone is not a commercial activity. But it should not be relevant, for the purpose of determining the scope of Congress's commerce power, whether the activity being regulated is itself economic in character or is part of a commercial transaction, and, as Justice Breyer pointed out, the Court did not treat it as relevant in any of the commerce clause precedents from *Darby* on.[193] The only question asked by the Court in *Darby* was whether the activity could reasonably be thought to have a substantial effect on interstate commerce.[194] In *Wickard v Filburn,* Congress was conceded to have power to regulate an activity "even if [it] be local and though it may not be regarded as commerce, . . . if it exerts a substantial effect on interstate commerce."[195] And, as the Court noted in *Jones & Laughlin Steel,* in the course of discarding the "direct/indirect effects" rule as it had been previously understood, "[i]t is the effect upon commerce, not the source of the injury, which is the criterion."[196] The artificiality of the Court's new "commercial/noncommercial" distinction seemed to the dissenters distressingly reminiscent of the artificiality of the "direct/indirect effects" rule as it had been employed prior to *Jones & Laughlin Steel,* where the actual effect upon commerce was treated as irrelevant to the question of whether the activity causing that effect was open to regulation by Congress.[197] If the activity can rationally be seen as having an effect on commerce sufficient to warrant regulation, it is of no greater moment whether the activity is commercial than whether the effect on commerce that it brings about is direct or indirect.

But the *Lopez* majority chose to arrogate to itself the authority to determine whether an activity was or was not sufficiently commercial and whether its effect on commerce was substantial, and to make those judicial determinations critical to the decision of whether the activity is subject to congressional regulation under the commerce clause. Although the Court conceded that judicial resolution of such questions could "result in legal uncertainty," it dismissed that concern because legal uncertainty was an inevitable by-product of the exercise of judicial review, and judicial review was inevitably necessary here because Congress's "enumerate powers are interpreted as having judicially enforceable outer limits."[198] The Court's self-justification is a gigantic truism and properly represents the beginning, rather than the end, of the analysis. John Marshall in *McCulloch* certainly did not deny that the enumerated powers of Congress had judicially enforceable outer limits, as Chief Justice Rehnquist pointedly noted in *Lopez*,[199] but that does not even pose, let alone answer, the critical questions, which are how do the courts go about the task of identifying the limits to be enforced, and what matters should a court consider before proclaiming that those limits have been passed.

In *McCulloch,* Marshall famously declared that "should Congress, under the pretext of executing its powers, pass laws for the accomplishment of objects not entrusted to the government, it would become the painful duty of this tribunal . . . to say that such an act was not the law of the land."[200] But when can an act be described as having been passed "for the accomplishment of objects not entrusted to the government"? Marshall cannot have meant that it is passed for an improper purpose when its subject is not identified within the enumerated powers because, in *McCulloch* itself, he upheld Congress's power to create a bank, and that is not in the list of enumerated powers. His answer to the question comes in his next sentence. A law is *not* passed for an illegitimate purpose when it is really calculated to effect any of the objects entrusted to the government," and the determination of whether the law "is really calculated" to do so, Marshall emphasized, is to be made by the courts without "inquir[ing] into the degree of its necessity," for engaging in that inquiry would be "to pass the line which circumstances the judicial department, and to tread on legislative ground." He immediately added: "This court disclaims all pretentions to such a power."[201]

But that is precisely the power that the Court in *Lopez* claimed pretentions to. The question of whether the activity to be regulated has a sufficiently substantial effect on interstate commerce to warrant congressional regulation is nothing but an inquiry into the degree of the law's necessity. And the question of whether the activity has a sufficiently commercial character to be subject to regulation is not only a question of policy, but the wrong question at that, because, to reiterate the Court's statement in *Jones & Laughlin Steel*, "[i]t is the effect upon commerce, not the source of the injury, which is the criterion."[202] Therefore, in deciding whether a law "is really calculated to effect any of the objects entrusted to the government," courts must be limited to asking whether the law can reasonably be thought to be an appropriate means, "plainly adapted" to achieving an end within the scope of Congress's delegated powers. As the dissenters in *Lopez* stressed, by that standard, Congress's prohibition of guns in schools is undoubtedly "really calculated" to attain a constitutionally permissible end. Consequently, to strike the law down, the court had to abandon the Marshall standard, and to claim the power to decide the question of constitutionality on the basis of its assessment of the law's necessity. In so doing, it not only repudiated the core of the reasoning of so venerable a decision as *McCulloch v Maryland*, but it also rejected the reasoning on which the Court's commerce clause precedents for the previous fifty-four years had rested. This was nothing less than an alteration of the settled understandings of the meaning of the Constitution brought about by a new majority of the Court put in place by the appointments of two presidents. This happens, of course—as it did when a new majority of the Court put in place after 1937 by the appointments of a single president, Franklin Roosevelt, scrapped the constitutional understandings of the half-century prior to 1937. But it does underscore the ironic nature of the concern expressed by Justice Kennedy in 1997 that courts must have the final word in defining the limits of Congress's powers, or else "[s]hifting legislative majorities could change the Constitution" without recourse to the process of constitutional amendment.[203] Perhaps *Lopez* should be seen as a preemptive strike by a shifting judicial majority to change the Constitution before "[s]hifting legislative majorities" could do so.

It was no accident that, in seeking to find respectable precedent for its decision in *Lopez*, the Court relied on the majority opinion in *Jones & Laughlin Steel*, and on Cardozo's concurring opinion in *Schechter*,[204] for the latter opinion put forward Cardozo's suggestion for a compromise with the pre-1937 majority of the Court, while the former reflected the adoption of that compromise by the shift of the two transigent members of the old majority. And the Cardozo compromise, which briefly became constitutional law in *Jones & Laughlin Steel*, rested on the assumption that courts would, as they had consistently been doing for many years, be ruling on the constitutionality of acts of Congress on the basis of the judges' views of the necessity or desirability of the policies they embodied. In that context, all it asked was that courts not decide on the necessity of congressional regulation of an activity that affected interstate commerce without considering the magnitude of the effect that that activity could have on commerce.[205] With the departure after 1937 of the justices committed to using their power to protect laissez faire, the newly unanimous Court could put aside the Cardozo compromise, as it did, because the assumption on which it rested—that courts would decide constitutional questions on the basis of policy considerations—was no longer valid. The *Jones & Laughlin Steel* decision, therefore, turned on the Court's assessment of the seriousness of the potential effect on commerce of work stoppages in the steel industry, whereas the Court, beginning with *Darby,* returned to Marshall's principles, and no longer sought to assess the necessity or desirability of legislation in deciding on its constitutionality.

What the Court in *Lopez* did was to turn the clock back to before *Darby,* and reset it in 1937, when the Cardozo compromise was momentarily the law of the Constitution. In *Jones & Laughlin Steel,* the Court assumed that it was the body to decide whether the effect on interstate commerce of the local activity being regulated was sufficient to permit congressional regulation. It expressly reasserted the holding in *Schechter* that the effect on commerce of the practices in that small business was too slight to be within the reach of Congress's commerce power, but it readily conceded that the potential effect on commerce of labor unrest in the steel industry was certainly great enough to justify congressional legislation aimed at avoiding it.[206] In *Lopez,* the Court employed the same assumption that underlay the Cardozo compromise—that it could treat questions of policy as questions of constitutional law, and decide whether the nature of the activity to be regulated or the magnitude of the effect on commerce of that activity was such as to render it open to congressional control. It was thus *Jones & Laughlin Steel* that set the standard for the Court's review, not *Darby,* which had provided the standard from 1941 until the *Lopez* decision.

Justice Souter, dissenting in *Lopez,* noted that that "decision may be seen only as a misstep" in the Court's jurisprudence, "but hardly an epochal case," but also expressed concern that it could prove to be epochal.[207] That is, of course, the fear that *Lopez* generates. The precise issue in the case is not of paramount importance, and Congress promptly reenacted the law invalidated by the Court in a slightly modified form,[208] which may prove acceptable to the Court. The decision might even have the beneficial effect of causing Congress to think twice before jumping in to deal with local problems where federal concerns are only marginally implicated and where federal involvement is not essential. But if *Lopez* is a harbinger of a pattern of future invalidations of congressional legislation under the commerce power based on judicial disagreement with the necessity or desirability of the laws, it is cause for serious concern. It is a legislature's responsibility to decide whether laws are needed. For courts to do so is a misuse of judicial power. That was the lesson that Marshall taught, and it is to be hoped that the current majority on the Court will not choose to ignore it.

Finally, a word should be said about the concurring opinion of Justice Clarence Thomas in *Lopez,* with which, it may be noted with relief, no other justice expressed agreement. Based on his eccentric and highly dubious reading of constitutional history and precedent, he maintained that it was not intended for Congress to have any police power, and therefore it should have no authority under the commerce clause to regulate any matter except interstate commerce itself.[209] The concession to Congress of any power to regulate local activities is unsound, in Thomas' view, because "it appears to grant Congress a police power over the Nation."[210] Justice Thomas is, of course, correct that allowing Congress to regulate matters that affect commerce gives it potentially very broad power. However, denying Congress such power would be far more troublesome. If the power to regulate commerce includes the power to protect commerce against major obstructions, then Congress must have power to regulate matters that are neither interstate nor commerce if they can create such obstructions. As Chief Justice Marshall stated in *McCulloch,* it makes little sense to vest Congress with "such ample powers, on the due execution of which the happiness and prosperity of the nation so vitally depends" without granting them the authority needed to exercise those powers effectively in the interest of the nation as a whole.[211] If Congress could not regulate local activities that have a substantial effect on interstate commerce, then it could not control monopolies of manufacturing, or maintain safety standards in production industries, or enact fair labor standards legislation, or impose national air and water quality requirements, or impose regulations to combat drug use, or do a myriad of other things to protect the people of the United States against nationwide evils or difficulties. One reads with disbelief Justice Thomas's rejection of Justice Breyer's observation—which one would have thought to be absolutely unexceptionable—that the commerce power of Congress must be interpreted in light of economic realities, so as to ensure that Congress can effectively meet national needs, and so that the nation is not rendered "powerless to defend itself against economic forces that Congress decrees inimical or destructive of the national economy."[212] But, in the most explicit terms, Thomas rejects national need as a criterion for interpreting the commerce clause and would deny Congress ability to regulate a local matter under its commerce power merely because, if not federally regulated, it could be "destructive of the national economy.' "[213] To be sure, Thomas does express recognition of the fact that it may be "too late in the day to undertake a fundamental reexamination of the past 60 years . . . [and] wipe the slate clean,"[214] but it was surely thinking like his that Marshall had in mind when he wrote in *Gibbons v Ogden* of those who would content "that the powers expressly granted to the government of the Union, are to be contracted by construction, into the narrowest possible compass, and that the original powers of the states are retained, if any possible construction will retain them, . . . [and thereby] explain away the constitution of our country, and leave it a magnificent structure indeed, to look at, but totally unfit for use."[215]

The current Supreme Court majority is clearly unpersuaded by Louis Fisher's claim that "[t]he meaning of federalism is not announced unilaterally by the Supreme Court."[216] To the contrary, it would appear that the Court is insisting on the power unilaterally to define the nature of the federal system. The current majority seems willing to give only lip service to the idea that Fisher ardently believes—that Congress shares with the Court the responsibility for interpreting the Constitution. It clearly believes otherwise. Justice O'Connor has perhaps stated the Court's view of its own supremacy in this area most sharply and succinctly in her statement that, because it has the "obligation to draw its own conclusions regarding the Constitution's meaning[,] Congress, no less than this Court, is called upon to consider the requirements of the Constitution and to act in accordance with its dictates. But when it enacts legislation in furtherance of its delegated powers, Congress must make its judgments consistent with this Court's exposition of the Constitution."[217] The Court claims that it is its duty to enforce the "outer limits" of congressional power,[218] and it seems determined to constrict those "outer limits" to whatever degree is needed to protect state sovereignty. It has forbidden Congress (except under the enforcement clauses of the Civil War Amendments—as if that should make a difference) to allow suits against states to ensure prospective compliance with federal law.[219] It will not allow Congress, under its power to enforce the Fourteenth Amendment, to use its legislative authority to prohibit acts of states or municipalities that it, but not the Court, deems to be violative of constitutional rights.[220] It will not allow the federal government to require executive branch officials in the states or their subdivisions to cooperate in the enforcement of federal law,[221] even, as Justice Stevens despairingly noted, on an interim basis until federal enforcement machinery can be put in place, and even, presumably, in a national emergency.[222] It will not allow Congress to require legislative action of the states, even where the states have requested it to enact such a requirement as a means of resolving multistate problems.[223] And it will not allow Congress to pass legislation that can reasonably be thought to be appropriate for carrying into execution its commerce power if the Court does not agree that it is an appropriate measure.[224]

Federalism, one would suppose, while surely recognizing the desirability of preserving state autonomy in matters of purely local concern, was not designed to frustrate Congress's ability to ensure the effectiveness of its execution of its constitutional responsibilities, or its capacity to exercise its delegated powers to their "utmost extent."[225] Louis Fisher has seen, more clearly than the Court, that the judges must not insist on their own answers to the constitutional questions of federalism, but must be prepared to accept the constitutional responsibility of Congress in the "process in which the Court, Congress, and the executive branch hammer out the sensitive and ever-changing relationships between the federal government and the states."[226] But, since today's Court majority seems adamantly disinclined to accept the constitutional responsibility of Congress to decide the policy questions that must be answered in establishing the boundary line between federal and state authority, and seems determined to maintain its expansive view of its own authority to decide such questions of policy for itself, a change in the Court's position is likely to occur only if there is a change in the Court's membership. A shifting judicial majority could then, as in 1937, remedy a problem caused by judicial intransigence. But the shifting judicial majority of 1937, and the New Deal consensus that made the new majority position so long lasting, came into being only in the wake of a national economic calamity. It is distressing to contemplate that the nation may need to await the occurrence of another calamity before the federal authority needed to avert such an event may again be accepted as an unquestioned aspect of the American constitutional system.

Notes

1. Louis Fisher, "Congressional Checks on the Judiciary" (Congressional Research Service, April 29, 1997).

2. See, *e.g.,* Louis Fisher, "The Curious Belief in Judicial Supremacy," 25 *Suffolk University Law Review* 85 (1991).

3. Fisher, *supra* note 1, p. 1.

4. 117 S.Ct. 2157 (1997).

5. 107 Stat. 1488 (1993).

6. Fisher, *supra* note 1, p. 10.

7. 494 US 872 (1990).

8. 117 S.Ct. at 2164.

9. *Id.* at 2170.

10. 109 US 3 (1883).

11. 18 Stat., Part 2, 335 (1875).

12. 117 S.Ct. at 2166.

13. "Nomination of Anthony M. Kennedy to be Associate Justice of the Supreme Court of the United States," *Hearings Before the Committee on the Judiciary, United States Senate* (100th Cong., 1st Sess.), p. 222.

14. Fisher, *supra* note 1, pp. 11–12.

15. 1 Cranch 137, 177 (1803), cited 117 S.Ct. at 2172.

16. 117 S.Ct. at 2172.

17. See Louis Fisher, *Constitutional Dialogues* (Princeton, N.J.: Princeton University Press, 1988).

18. 117 S.Ct. at 2168.

19. It is apparently Justice Kennedy's belief that there is no need to be concerned about shifting judicial majorities because "the Court will treat its precedents with the respect due them under settled principles, including *stare decisis.*" *Id.* at 2172. Quoted in text *supra,* at note 16. It seems that this statement was made with a straight face, but Justice Kennedy cannot be so naive as to believe it. After all, it was put forward at a time when the Court majority, voting 5–4 on important constitutional issues with remarkable consistency (although the Court in *Boerne* was split differently), was deciding those issues in ways that seemed to disregard settled constitutional law. To cite just two examples, in *Adarand Contractors v Pena,* 515 US 200 (1995), the Court invalidated a federal

affirmative action program that was clearly constitutional under *Fullilove v Klutznick*, 448 US 448 (1980). And in *Rosenberger v University of Virginia*, 515 US 819 (1995), it held that a state agency was constitutionally obliged to use public funds to support the publication of religious messages—contrary to, *e.g.*, *Everson v Board of Education*, 330 US 1 (1947)— if it supported other types of publications. Can it be doubted that the replacement of a single justice of the current majority could result in the Constitution being changed back, thus "effectively circumventing the difficult and detailed amendment process contained in Article V" (117 S.Ct. at 2168). Perhaps Justice Kennedy's remark will find its place in history alongside Justice Roberts's infamous observation that, in deciding on the constitutionality of legislation, the Court "has only one duty,—to lay the article of the Constitution which is invoked beside the statute which is challenged, and to decide whether the latter squares with the former. . . . The only power [the Court] has, if such it may be called, is the power of judgment. This court neither approves nor condemns any legislative policy." *United States v Butler*, 297 US 1, 62–63 (1936).

20. 384 US 641 (1966).

21. 79 Stat. 437, 439 (1965).

22. *Lassiter v Northhampton County Board of Elections*, 360 US 45 (1959).

23. *Id.* at 52–53.

24. 384 US at 648–49.

25. 117 S.Ct. 2365 (1997).

26. 107 Stat. 1536, 1537–38 (1993), § 102 (a) (2).

27. See 117 S.Ct. at 2370.

28. See *id.* at 2375.

29. See *Second Employers' Liability Cases*, 223 US 1, 55–59 (1912); *Testa v Katt*, 330 US 386, 389–94 (1947).

30. 117 S.Ct. at 2389 (Stevens, J., dissenting).

31. 505 US 144 (1992).

32. *Low-Level Radioactive Waste Policy Amendments Act*, 99 Stat. 1842, 1850–51, Title I, § 102 (1985).

33. 517 US 44 (1996).

34. 491 US 1 (1989).

35. Congress's power to abrogate a state's Eleventh Amendment immunity as a means of enforcing the Civil War Amendments was affirmed

in *Fitzpatrick v Bitzer,* 427 US 445 (1976), which, as of today, is still good law.

36. 514 US 549 (1995).

37. 104 Stat. 4844 (1990).

38. The classic instance of this is Andrew Jackson's veto of the bill to recharter the Bank of the United States in 1832. In his veto message, he declared that he regarded the bank as unconstitutional and that he was not bound by the judgment of the Supreme Court affirming its constitutionality. See James D. Richardson, ed., 2 *A Compilation of the Messages and Papers of the Presidents* (Washington, D.C.: Government Printing Office, 1896), pp. 581–91. In 1833, Jackson sealed the doom of the bank by appointing Roger Brooke Taney secretary of the treasury for the express purpose of withdrawing the federal funds on deposit there. See Arthur M. Schlesinger Jr., *The Age of Jackson* (Boston: Little, Brown & Co., 1945), pp. 97–102.

39. 1 Cranch at 177. See text *supra,* at note 15. See also *United States v Lopez,* 514 US at 566.

40. Louis Fisher & Neal Devins, *Political Dynamics of Constitutional Law* (2nd Ed., St. Paul, Minn.: West Publishing Co., 1996), p. 94.

41. Louis Fisher, *American Constitutional Law* (2nd Ed., New York: McGraw-Hill, 1995), p. 494. It is ironic that Fisher uses, as a principal basis for this observation, statements by Antonin Scalia at his confirmation hearing before the Senate Judiciary Committee expressing the view that Congress, through its policymaking authority, is "the primary defender of the constitutional balance, the Federal Government versus the States . . . the primary institution to strike the right balance is the Congress." *Ibid.,* quoting from "Nomination of Judge Antonin Scalia," *Hearings Before the Committee on the Judiciary, United States Senate* (99th Cong., 2nd Sess.), p. 81. As it turned out, Justice Scalia was the author of the Supreme Court's opinion in *Printz v United States, supra* note 25, which emphatically rejected the proposition that Congress was the "primary institution to strike the right balance" between the federal government and the states. See text *supra,* at notes 25–30.

42. 4 Wheaton 316 (1819).

43. Fisher & Devins, *supra* note 40, p. 35.

44. *Id.,* p. 38, quoting from *Federalist 44* (J. Madison), in *The Federalist,* Jacob E. Cooke, ed. (Middletown, Conn.: Wesleyan University Press, 1961), pp. 304–05.

45. 2 *Annals of Congress* (1st Cong., 3rd Sess.), cc. 1894–1902, 1956–60. On the House floor, Madison expressed vigorous opposition to any interpretation of the "necessary and proper" clause that would provide

Congress with authority to incorporate a bank, arguing that no interpretation of the clause "can be admitted, that would give an unlimited discretion to Congress." *Id.*, c. 1898. In his remarks six days later, just before the House vote on the bank bill, he went to the heart of the matter with regard to judicial enforcement of the limits on congressional powers. These limits, he saw, must be maintained by congressional sensitivity to the boundary between federal and state authority because courts would have no basis in law for identifying those limits, but only a basis in "the rules of expediency." *Id.*, c. 1958. Thus, Madison recognized, judicial efforts to police the federal-state boundary, to keep Congress from crossing it, would require the courts to decide questions of policy, not law.

46. Thomas Jefferson, "Opinion on the Constitutionality of the Bill for Establishing a National Bank," in 19 *The Papers of Thomas Jefferson,* Julian P. Boyd, ed. (Princeton, N.J.: Princeton University Press, 1974), p. 278.

47. *Ibid.* (Emphasis is in original.)

48. Alexander Hamilton, "Opinion on the Constitutionality of an Act to Establish a Bank," in 8 *The Papers of Alexander Hamilton,* Harold C. Syrett, ed. (New York: Columbia University Press, 1965), pp. 97–134.

49. *McCulloch v Maryland,* 4 Wheaton at 408.

50. *Id.* at 415.

51. *Id.* at 421.

52. *Id.* at 423.

53. The view that Marshall's opinion in *McCulloch* established the deferential rationality standard for adjudging the constitutionality of acts of Congress challenged as intruding into areas of state responsibility has not been without distinguished critics. For example, Gerald Gunther, who brought together the attacks on Marshall's *McCulloch* opinion that were published pseudonymously by Virginia judges Spencer Roane and (it is believed) William Brockenbrough in the Richmond *Enquirer,* accusing Marshall of granting Congress total freedom to expand its powers at the expense of the autonomy of the states, and Marshall's responses to those attacks, also published pseudonymously in newspapers more sympathetic to his position, express the belief in his introduction to that volume that Marshall was sincere when, in his responses, he maintained that *McCulloch*, as Gunther described it, "did not give Congress carte blanche, that [it] did preserve a true federal system in which the central government was limited in its powers—and that the limits were capable of judicial enforcement." Introduction, *John Marshall's Defense of* McCulloch v Maryland, Gerald Gunther, ed. (Stanford, Calif.: Stanford University Press, 1969), p. 10. Based on Marshall's responses to his critics, William Van Alstyne has also contended that the view that the *McCulloch* opinion stands for

the proposition that is for Congress to draw the constitutional boundary line between federal and state authority, and that there is no room for judicial review of its judgments, "purports to be the tone of John Marshall, but it is not." Marshall made clear in his defense of *McCulloch*, he argues, that it was for the judiciary to prevent Congress from abridging state autonomy. William W. Van Alstyne, "The Second Death of Federalism," 83 *Michigan Law Review* 1709, 1733 (1985).

But I find nothing in Marshall's essays in defense of *McCulloch* that contradicts the argument that that opinion holds that the line between federal and state authority, being a line based on considerations of policy, is, in almost all cases, to be drawn by Congress. What he said in his defense was that Congress, having been delegated certain powers in the Constitution, has the "right" and the "duty" to choose the means for the execution of those powers

> which are most advantageous to the people, provided that they be within the limits of the constitution. Their constitutionality depends on their being the natural, direct, and appropriate means, or the known and usual means, for the execution of the given power.
>
> In no single instance does the court admit the unlimited power of Congress to adopt any means whatever, and thus to pass the limits prescribed by the Constitution. . . . [T]he discretion claimed for the legislature in the selection of its means, [is] always limited in terms, to such as are appropriate. . . .

Gunther, ed., *supra*, pp. 186–87.

However, Marshall had already made clear in *McCulloch* that courts could strike down acts of Congress that were not appropriate—or "plainly adapted" or "really calculated"—to carry out a delegated power, and thus he had not said in that opinion that the discretion of Congress was unlimited. And nothing in the defense suggests that any more searching judicial inquiry into the validity of acts of Congress is required than the inquiry whether Congress could reasonably have believed that the means it had chosen was "plainly adapted" or "really calculated" to attain an end within the scope of the delegated powers. Nowhere is his defense does he in any way qualify his statement in *McCulloch* that if a law is an appropriate means to a legitimate end, courts cannot examine the necessity of the law because that is a legislative question. He does not allude in his defense to that aspect of the *McCulloch* opinion, presumably because it was there that he was most vulnerable to his critics' accusations, and certainly nothing in his defense can be said to contradict it.

Professor Van Alstyne, *supra*, p. 1725 n. 66, notes that, in his defense, Marshall treated one of Brockenbrough's arguments—that some of the justices in the *McCulloch* case might have been of the opinion that the establishment of the bank should be upheld simply on the ground that

Congress had decided that creation of the bank was within its powers, and that the courts ought not to question its judgment—as a suggestion that that approach would have been preferable to deciding on the merits that the bank was constitutional, and that he then "heaped scorn on" that suggestion. That part of Marshall's defense is in Gunther, ed., *supra*, pp. 104–05. But it seems clear that, here, Marshall was simply creating a straw man to demolish. Brockenbrough could hardly have preferred complete judicial abnegation, and demolishing the straw man was an effective way of denying the soundness of his critics' principal argument—that the Court had held in *McCulloch* that there were no enforceable limits on Congress's powers. In any case, to reject the suggestion that there should be no judicial review at all is not to reject the view that the standard of review should be highly deferential. If, as *McCulloch* ruled, courts are not to examine the necessity of legislation, but only its appropriateness, it would be difficult to employ any test for constitutionality other than the rationality standard because any higher level of scrutiny would unavoidably involve an inquiry into the law's necessity. As a practical matter, of course, there is little discernible difference between holding that there are no judicially enforceable limits on Congress's powers and holding that those limits can be judicially enforced only if it cannot reasonably be believed that the law passed by Congress is appropriate for the execution of a delegated power. Marshall suggested no different standard of review in his defense of *McCulloch* than in *McCulloch* itself, and that standard was faithfully employed by a unanimous Court in *Katzenbach v McClung,* upholding Title II of the Civil Rights Act of 1964:

> Of course, the mere fact that Congress has said when particular activity shall be deemed to affect commerce does not preclude further examination by this Court. But where we find that the legislators, in light of the facts and testimony before them, have a rational basis for finding a chosen regulatory scheme necessary to the protection of commerce, our investigation is at an end.

379 US 294, 303–04 (1964). See text *infra,* at notes 146–149.

54. 1 Cranch 137, 177 (1803). See text *supra,* at note 15.

55. *Gibbons v. Ogden,* 9 Wheaton 1, 197 (1824).

56. See 4 *Debates in the Several State Conventions on the Adoption of the Federal Constitution,* Jonathan Elliot, ed. (2nd Ed., Philadelphia: J. B. Lippincott Co., 1836), pp. 528–29. In his Report to the 1799–1800 Session of the Virginia House of Delegates on the Virginia Resolutions, Madison wrote: "The states, then, being the parties to the constitutional compact, and in their sovereign capacity, it follows of necessity that there can be no tribunal, above their authority, to decide, in the last resort, whether the

compact made by them be violated; and consequently, that, as the parties to it, they must themselves decide, in the last resort, such questions as may be of sufficient magnitude to require their interposition." James Madison, "Report on the Virginia Resolutions," *id.,* pp. 546, 548.

57. *Federalist 44,* in Cooke, ed., *supra* note 44, p. 306.

58. 117 S.Ct. at 2379. In support of this proposition, Justice Scalia cited *Federalist 33,* in which Hamilton stated that acts of Congress "which are *not pursuant* to its constitutional powers" are "merely acts of usurpation and will deserve to be treated as such." Cooke, ed., *supra* note 44, p. 207 (emphasis is in original). But, for Hamilton, federal laws which are appropriate to the execution of a delegated power cannot be described as being "not pursuant to [Congress's] constitutional powers." Nowhere in *Federalist 33,* or, as far as I know, anywhere else, does Hamilton draw any distinction between the words "necessary" and "proper," or suggest that a law "necessary" to the execution of a delegated power might be regarded as not "proper," and, therefore, outside the scope of Congress's constitutional authority, if it were in some way to impinge on state sovereignty. In fact, what Hamilton does say in *Federalist 33* about the question of whether a federal law is "necessary and proper" is that that question is to be decided by Congress, and that the checks on Congress must come from the people. He wrote that

> the national government, like every other, must judge in the first instance of the proper exercise of its powers; and its constituents in the last. If the Federal Government should overpass the just bounds of its authority, and make a tyrannical use of its powers; the people whose creature it is must appeal to the standard they have formed, and take such measures to redress the injury done to the constitution, as the exigency may suggest and prudence justify. *The propriety of a law in a constitutional light, must always be determined by the nature of the powers upon which it is founded.*

Cooke, ed., *supra* note 44, p. 206. (Emphasis added.)

The idea of a distinction between "necessary" and "proper" that Justice Scalia put forward was apparently suggested to him by the article he cites in support of such a distinction. Gary Lawson and Patricia B. Granger, "The 'Proper' Scope of Federal Power: A Jurisdictional Interpretation of the Sweeping Clause," 43 *Duke Law Journal* 267 (1993). In that article, it is contended, on the basis of an historical analysis, that the word "proper" serves the same limiting function in the Constitution as the Tenth Amendment does in the Bill of Rights, commanding that state sovereignty remain inviolate, thus circumscribing Congress and allowing it only to enact laws "belonging to" or "peculiar to" its delegated responsibilities. *Id.,* pp. 272–74. It remains unclear how "proper" in this sense is different from "necessary," or how it raises questions of law, rather than policy, that would be appropriate for judicial determination. To interpret "proper" in this way would turn the "necessary and proper" clause into a *limitation* on Congress, and, above all else, that was what Marshall insisted it was not. See *McCulloch,* 4 Wheaton at 419–21; Gunther, ed., *supra* note 53, pp. 178–81. In *McCulloch,* Marshall contended that inclusion of the word "proper" merely weakened the argument that "necessary" must be read to mean "absolutely necessary," for, if "necessary" were so strictly interpreted, addition of the word "proper" would have been useless. The only possible effect of the word "proper," Marshall argued, "is to qualify that strict and rigorous meaning; to present to the mind the idea of some choice of means of legislation not straightened and compressed within the narrow limits for which gentlemen contend." *McCulloch v Maryland,* 4 Wheaton at 419.

59. 12 Howard 299 (1852).

60. 109 US 3 (1883).

61. 94 US 113 (1877).

62. *Id.* at 132.

63. *Ibid.*

64. See text *supra,* at note 52.

65. 94 US at 134.

66. See text *supra*, at note 55.

67. 94 US at 134.

68. 134 US 418 (1890).

69. *Id.* at 458.

70. 198 US 45 (1905).

71. *Id.* at 56.

72. See *id.* at 57.

73. 24 Stat. 379 (1887).

74. 26 Stat. 209 (1890).

75. 156 US 1 (1895).

76. *Id.* at 12.

77. *Id.* at 39 (Harlan, J., dissenting), quoting 4 Wheaton at 421.

78. 156 US at 39–40 (Harlan, J., dissenting).

79. 156 US at 13.

80. *Id.* at 16.

81. *Id.* at 13.

82. *Ibid.*

83. See text *supra,* at note 46.

84. See *Smyth v Ames,* 169 US 466 (1898).

85. *Lochner v New York,* 198 US 45 (1905). See text *supra,* at notes 70–72.

86. *Champion v Ames,* 188 US 321 (1903).

87. *Hipolite Egg Co. v United States,* 220 US 45 (1911).

88. *Hoke v United States,* 227 US 308 (1913).

89. 247 US 251 (1918).

90. 39 Stat. 675 (1916).

91. *Id.* at 269–72.

92. *Id.* at 274–75.

93. This point was expressly made by Justice Stevens, dissenting, in *Printz v United States,* 117 S.Ct. at 2387–88.

94. 9 Wheaton at 196.

95. 247 US at 276.

96. 295 US 495 (1935).

97. 48 Stat. 195 (1933).

98. 295 US at 529–42.

99. See text *supra,* at note 80.

100. 295 US at 546–50.

101. *Id.* at 553 (Cardozo, J., concurring).

102. *Id.* at 554.

103. *Ibid.*

104. 49 Stat. 991 (1935).

105. 298 US 238 (1936).

106. *Id.* at 308–09.

107. *Id.* at 294.

108. *Id.* at 295.

109. 298 US 587 (1936).

110. *Id.* at 327–28 (Cardozo, J., dissenting).

111. *Ibid.*

112. *Id.* at 328.

113. See William E. Leuchtenburg, *The Supreme Court Reborn* (New York: Oxford University Press, 1995), pp. 82–162.

114. 300 US 379 (1937).

115. *Morehead v New York ex rel. Tipaldo,* 298 US 587 (1936). See *supra* note 109, and the text thereat.

116. 301 US 1 (1937).

117. 49 Stat. 449 (1935).

118. See text *supra,* at note 52.

119. 300 US at 399.

120. 301 US at 37.

121. See, *e.g., id.* at 42 and *passim.*

122. *Id.* at 41. In the companion cases to *Jones & Laughlin Steel* that dealt with labor relations in production industries, *NLRB v Fruehauf Trailer Co.,* 301 US 49 (1937), and *NLRB v Friedman-Harry Marks Clothing Co.,* 301 US 58 (1937), the Court relied on the findings of the NLRB demonstrating the significance of the interstate activities of those companies. It noted that Freuhauf was "the largest concern of its kind in the United States," with over three million dollars in sales—mostly interstate—in 1934, 301 US at 53, and that "[t]he men's clothing industry is among the twenty most important manufacturing industries in this country," 301 US at 72, and that Friedman-Harry Marks did about two million dollars in business in the first ten months of 1935. *Ibid.* It accepted the clothing industry's own statement that it "is conducted as an interstate business and is entirely dependent on interstate commerce." *Id.* at 73.

123. 295 US at 554 (Cardozo, J., concurring).

124. 301 US at 37, paraphrasing 295 US at 554 (Cardozo, J., concurring). See text *supra,* at note 102.

125. 312 US 100 (1941).

126. 52 Stat. 1060 (1938).

127. See text *supra,* at notes 90–92.

128. 312 US at 114, quoting 9 Wheaton at 196.

129. 312 US at 124.

130. *Id.* at 115.

131. *Id.* at 121.

132. *Id.* at 122.

133. *Id.* at 123.

134. See text *supra,* at note 47.

135. See text *supra,* at note 50.

136. See text *supra,* at note 55. Perhaps the strongest argument for judicial abnegation in cases where acts of Congress are challenged as abridging state sovereignty is in Jesse H. Choper, *Judicial Review and the National Political Process* (Chicago: University of Chicago Press, 1980), pp. 171–259. Professor Choper does not merely argue that courts should employ a deferential rationality standard, such as Marshall claimed to employ, to decide such challenges, but should simply treat them as entirely nonjusticiable. *Id.,* p. 175. He contends that state and local governments have ample political power to protect themselves against truly damaging federal action, *id.*, pp. 176–81, and that, therefore, judicial review is largely unneeded, and likely to be ineffective, as a protector of the vital interests of the states. If a question of the scope of federal power "is a close one," he argues, "as virtually all real world ones are, then, irrespective of its 'correct' answer, the political branches should be trusted to produce a reasonable and fair judgment." *Id.,* p. 222.

137. For this reason, the Supreme Court, in *McCray v United States,* 195 US 27 (1904), categorically rejected the notion that the judiciary could legitimately "restrain the exercise of a lawful power wherever it seems to the judicial mind that such lawful power has been abused" because such an idea rests on the erroneous "contention that, under our constitutional system, the abuse by one department of the government of its lawful powers is to be corrected by the abuse of its powers by another department," and, "if sustained, would destroy all distinction between the powers of the respective departments of the government." *Id.* at 54–55.

138. 317 US 111 (1942).

139. 55 Stat. 203 (1941), amending 52 Stat. 31 (1938).

140. 317 US at 128–29.

141. 379 US 294 (1964).

142. 379 US 241 (1964).

143. Pub. L. 88–352, July 2, 1964 (Title II). 78 Stat. 241, 243–46 (1964).

144. 109 US 3 (1883).

145. See text *supra,* at notes 10–12.

146. Pub. L. 88–352, July 2, 1964 (Title II), § 201 (c). 78 Stat. 241, 243 (1964).

147. 379 US at 299–300.

148. *Id.* at 304.

149. *Ibid.*

150. 402 US 146 (1971).

151. 82 Stat. 146, 159–62 (1968).

152. 82 Stat. 146, 159 (Title II), § 201 (a) (2).

153. 402 US at 157–58 (Stewart, J., dissenting).

154. 402 US at 156.

155. *Id.* at 152–54.

156. *Id.* at 154, quoting *Katzenbach v McClung,* 379 US at 301, and *Maryland v Wirtz,* 392 US 183, 193 (1968).

157. 426 US 833 (1976).

158. *Id.* at 852.

159. *Id.* at 841.

160. 469 US 528 (1985).

161. *Id.,* at 551. The seminal article describing the protections for the states built into the structure of the constitutional system, which was clearly influential in shaping the opinion of the Court in *Garcia,* is Herbert Wechsler, "The Political Safeguards of Federalism: The Role of the States in the Composition and Selection of the National Government," 54 *Columbia Law Review* 543 (1954). See also Choper, *supra* note 136, pp. 176–90. For vigorous rejections of the relevance of these putative safeguards as a justification for restricting the role of the courts in employing constitutional criteria to protect state autonomy against federal intrusion, see, *e.g.,* Van Alstyne, *supra* note 53, pp. 1722–27; Larry Kramer, "Understanding Federalism," 47 *Vanderbilt Law Review* 1485, 1503–14 (1994).

162. See Fisher & Devins, *supra* note 40, p. 94.

163. *Id.,* p. 99. The bill was the Fair Labor Standards Public Employees Overtime Compensation Act of 1985. 99 Stat. 787 (1985).

164. Fisher & Devins, *supra* note 40, p. 103, quoting 131 *Congressional Record* (99th Cong., 1st Sess.), p. 28984. For a general study of the

effectiveness of states' efforts to protect themselves against congressional legislation adverse to their interests, in which it is suggested that when state and local governments make the effort to use their political influence in Congress, these efforts are generally, if not always, successful, see Carol F. Lee, "The Political Safeguards of Federalism? Congressional Responses to Supreme Court Decisions on State and Local Liability," 20 *Urban Lawyer* 301, 333–35 (1988).

165. *South Dakota v Dole,* 483 US 203 (1987). Justice Brennan dissented because he believed the Twenty-first Amendment reserved to the states full power to regulate the use of liquor, and "Congress cannot condition a federal grant in a manner that abridges this right." *Id.* at 212 (Brennan, J., dissenting).

166. 483 US at 209.

167. *Id.* at 210–12.

168. Low-Level Radioactive Waste Policy Amendments Act, 99 Stat. 1842 (1985), § 2021e (d) (2) (C).

169. *New York v United States,* 505 US 144, 175 (1992). For a careful analysis, demonstrating persuasively that the reasoning of the Court in this case was "without a firm basis in the founding-era discussion or the subsequent history of constitutional debate," see H. Jefferson Powell, "The Oldest Question of Constitutional Law," 79 *Virginia Law Review* 633, 635 (1993). See also Richard E. Levy, *"New York v United States:* An Essay on the Uses and Misuses of Precedent, History, and Policy in Determining the Scope of Federal Power," 41 *University of Kansas Law Review* 493 (1993).

170. 505 US 189–94 (White, J., dissenting).

171. Brief for the United States, *New York v United States,* in 213 *Landmark Briefs and Arguments of the Supreme Court of the United States* (1991 Term Supplement), Philip Kurland & Gerhard Casper, eds. (Bethesda, Md.: University Publications of America, 1993), pp. 314–15.

172. *FERC v Mississippi,* 456 US 742, 776–96 (O'Connor, J., concurring and dissenting). Justice O'Connor's views on federalism are summarized in Powell, *supra* note 169, pp. 639–52.

173. See text *supra,* at notes 25–28.

174. 514 US 549 (1995).

175. 104 Stat. 4844 (1990).

176. *United States v Darby,* 312 US at 121.

177. 514 US 618–25 (Breyer, J., dissenting).

178. *Id.* at 623.

179. *Id.* at 617.

180. 4 Wheaton at 423.

181. 514 US at 564. Much of the reasoning in Chief Justice Rehnquist's opinion in this case is drawn from his opinion in *Hodel v Virginia Surface Mining and Reclamation Assn.,* 452 US 264, 307–13 (1981) (Rehnquist, J., concurring in judgment).

182. See text *supra,* at note 47.

183. 514 US at 566, quoting 1 Cranch at 177.

184. 9 Wheaton at 197. See text *supra,* at note 55.

185. 304 US 144, 152–53 n. 4 (1938).

186. For a summary of the arguments that recognizing the constitutional power of the federal government to displace state policies is more likely than not to protect individual freedom and dignity, see David L. Shapiro, *Federalism: A Dialogue* (Evanston, Ill. Northwestern University Press, 1995), pp. 52–56.

187. See *supra* note 161, and the text thereat.

188. See, *e.g.,* Kramer, *supra* note 161, pp. 1503–14.

189. 109 Stat. 48 (1994). It is certainly correct, however, as Louis Fisher has noted, that this law does not in any way forbid unfunded mandates. It merely erects procedural barriers that have to be overcome before such mandates can be enacted. See Fisher & Devins, *supra* note 40, p. 106.

190. 117 S.Ct. at 2396 (Stevens, J., dissenting).

191. In *Lane County v Oregon,* 7 Wallace 71, 76 (1869), the Court unanimously declared that "the people of each state compose a State, having its own government and endowed with all the functions essential to separate and independent existence." In that case, the Court held, as a matter of statutory interpretation, that the legal tender acts passed by Congress in 1862, which provided that United States notes were "legal tender in payment of all debts, public and private," 12 Stat. 345 (1862), did not include state taxes within the meaning of the word "debts," and thus did not prohibit the states from requiring that all taxes owed them be paid in gold or silver coin. Perhaps the least controversial constitutional decision invalidating an act of Congress as an improper abridgement of state sovereignty was *Coyle v Smith,* 221 US 559 (1911), in which Congress was held to be without power to require Oklahoma to maintain its state capital in the city of Guthrie until 1913, as had been provided in the 1906 Enabling Act, 34 Stat. 267, 269 (1906), authorizing the admission of Oklahoma as a state.

192. 514 US at 566.

193. *Id.* at 628 (Breyer, J., dissenting).

194. 312 US at 122.

195. 317 US at 125.

196. 301 US at 32, citing Second Employers' Liability Cases, 223 US 1, 51 (1912).

197. See 514 US at 608 (Souter, J., dissenting).

198. 514 US at 566.

199. *Ibid.,* citing 4 Wheaton at 405.

200. 4 Wheaton at 423. Marshall also stated that the courts could declare an act of Congress unconstitutional if it violated a constitutional prohibition, *ibid.,* but that has no bearing where, as in *Lopez,* the issue is merely whether Congress has exceeded its powers.

201. *Ibid.* Writing in 1985, Martha Field noted that, in deciding commerce clause challenges to acts of Congress, "the Court would almost inevitably be compelled to engage in close judgments about the important of the challenged federal legislation." Martha A. Field, *"Garcia v San Antonio Metropolitan Transit Authority:* The Demise of a Misguided Doctrine," 99 *Harvard Law Review* 84, 106 (1985). She added that, in doing so, "the Court would face the choice between symbolic and ambitious application. It is clear which course presents the least hazard for the Court and the country. That lesson, at least, *Lochner* has taught." *Ibid.*

202. See text *supra,* at note 196.

203. See *supra* notes 18–19, and the text thereat.

204. See 514 US at 557, 566–67.

205. See text *supra,* at notes 102–103, 120–124.

206. 301 US at 40–42.

207. 514 US at 614–15 (Souter, J., dissenting).

208. 110 Stat. 3009, 3369–70 (1996). 18 U.S.C. § 922 (q) (2) (A).

209. 514 US at 584–99 (Thomas, J., concurring).

210. *Id.* at 600.

211. 4 Wheaton at 408.

212. 514 US at 625 (Breyer, J., dissenting), quoting *North American Co. v SEC,* 327 US 686, 705 (1946).

213. 514 US at 602 (Thomas, J., concurring).

214. *Id.* at 601 n. 8.

215. 9 Wheaton at 222.

216. Fisher & Devins, *supra* note 40, p. 94. See text *supra*, at note 40.

217. *City of Boerne v Flores,* 117 S.Ct. at 2176 (O'Connor, J., dissenting).

218. *United States v Lopez,* 514 US at 566.

219. *Seminole Tribe of Florida v Florida,* 116 S.Ct. 1114 (1996).

220. *City of Boerne v Flores,* 117 S.Ct. 2157 (1997).

221. *Printz v United States,* 117 S.Ct. 2365 (1997).

222. *Id.* at 2386–87 (Stevens, J., dissenting).

223. *New York v United States,* 505 US 144 (1992).

224. *United States v Lopez,* 514 US 549 (1995).

225. *Gibbons v Ogden,* 9 Wheaton at 196.

226. Fisher & Devins, *supra* note 40, p. 94.

7

Probing Government Secrecy:
Louis Fisher and the
Hidden Side of Government

Loch K. Johnson

Introduction

In the spring of 1969, I opened an envelope from the American Political Science Association (APSA) and, to my delight, found I had been awarded a Congressional Fellowship. Having just finished my doctorate, I could now spend a year at the heart of American politics comparing my book learning with firsthand observations of Congress at work. I arrived in Washington in the fall, newly married and thrilled at the prospect of being in the nation's capital.

Walter Beach of the APSA served as our Fellowship mentor for the year. His first directive to us was to fan out across the Hill and find legislators with whom we would enjoy working and, the other half of the equation, who would give us office space and a set of duties. We were to spend six months in the Senate and six months in the House.

Following these instructions, my first destination was the office of Senator Frank Church, who in 1956 had been elected to the Senate from Idaho at the tender age of thirty-two. He was a staunch critic of the war in Vietnam and a rising star on the Foreign Relations Committee. I admired his intellect (Phi Beta Kappa, Stanford

University) and his forensic skills (winner of the Joffee Medal for debate at Stanford and the 1960 keynote speaker at the Democratic Nominating Convention). Further, he had a noninterventionist—though certainly not an isolationist—view of foreign policy that appealed to me. The Senator's administrative assistant (AA, in Hill vernacular), a gracious middle-aged woman who knew practically everybody in Idaho, invited me to come for an interview the next week.

Nervously, I arrived at the designated hour, and the AA ushered me into the Senator's stately Russell Building office. It featured an oil painting of William Borah, another Idaho senator who had risen to the august chairmanship of the Foreign Relations Committee before the outbreak of the Second World War. Senator Church, a tall, handsome man with thick black hair and a ready smile, greeted me warmly, settled us on a spacious leather couch beneath Borah's fixed gaze, and asked a series of questions about my background and about my opinions on U.S. foreign policy.

A half hour later he concluded the interview, shook my hand, and asked me to start work on Monday. My assignments would include research, speechwriting, and assisting him with foreign policy legislation. The first item of business would be to help him write an essay "on some constitutional issue of interest" (according to a letter he showed me from the editor of the *Stanford Law Review*, who had invited him to submit an article).

Thus began a memorable year of close interaction with one of the premier members of the Senate and, along with J. William Fulbright of Arkansas, its most forceful spokesman on foreign policy. At midyear, I asked and received permission from the APSA to remain in the Senate with Church for the second half of the fellowship. President Richard M. Nixon had dispatched troops into Cambodia in the spring of 1970, and Frank Church became the chief organizer of the Senate's effort to halt the spread of the Vietnam War into Cambodia and Laos. Suddenly his office, like many others on the Hill, had became a maelstrom of antiwar activities, and he desperately needed all the staff assistance he could acquire.

Before the Cambodian invasion and the subsequent tragedy at Kent State University threw the nation and the Congress into turmoil, Senator Church and I spent a few hours each week discussing speech drafts and various legislative initiatives, as well as early versions of the law review article. He had decided to write on the emerging constitutional issue of impoundment, the practice whereby presidents refused to spend money that had been duly appropriated by law.[1] Even though every president since George Washington had impounded funds at one time or another, Senator Church and a handful of his colleagues had grown wary of President Nixon's excessive use of this extraconstitutional device. This president, unlike his predecessors, had found impoundment a useful method to scuttle major social and environmental programs, not just minor pork-barrel legislation.

I had never heard of impoundment, outside of what happened to student automobiles parked illegally at the University of California; so, starting from scratch, I began to assemble a bibliography on the subject. Sitting in the cozy, hideaway staff library just off the Capitol Rotunda, I studied the few articles written on the subject. The work I found most useful had been published by a staff person in the Legislative Research Service (or LRS in Washington's alphabet soup of acronyms, and now called the Congressional Research Service or CRS), a unit of the Library of Congress (LC) meant to serve legislators as a research arm. The author's name was Louis Fisher, who according to the brief biographies in the articles had recently earned a Ph.D. (1967) from the New School for Social Research in New York City.

Given his close proximity just across the grassy knoll that separates the Capitol from LC's magnificent gray sandstone building, I telephoned him and asked if I could drop by for a visit. A cordial voice replied, "Come on over," and I set off for the LRS offices, which proved to be a labyrinth of dimly lit, musty corridors and endless shelves of books and periodicals in an annex building behind the main Library. After a few wrong turns, I finally arrived at the proper nook and found—surrounded by law journals, political science quarterlies, and row after row of books—a young, friendly looking man, of medium build and wavy brown hair, and wearing glasses that accentuated a guileless, open face suggesting intelligence and strength of character. He seemed too young to be one of the nation's top experts on impoundment, but I knew from my bibliographic searches that indeed he was.

Fisher removed a stack of newspapers from a chair and offered me a seat. I explained my interest in impoundment and his eyes lit up, as if I had just freshly arrived in Amherst, Massachusetts, and asked a local about Emily Dickinson. He told me about President Nixon's recent impoundment of funds for various environmental measures. He drew from a file several additional papers he had recently prepared on the topic, yet unpublished, and proceeded to tell me about the more technical features of impoundment, with special attention to the incumbent president's flagrant excesses, extending to impoundment use unprecedented both for its prolific use, and unvarnished partisan motives. I began to take notes furiously. I, Balboa, had just found the Pacific.

Upon completing my research on impoundment, I began to explore more of Fisher's work, particularly on questions of the proper constitutional balance among the branches of government. I found in his writing a rich mine of information and insight on the spending power, the war power, and the treaty power.

Especially attractive to me were his efforts to grapple with the issue of government secrecy. Impoundments have often been carried out in secret; the presidential use of the war power has its obvious hidden dimensions, most controversially (in recent times) with the secret escalation of the war in Vietnam by Lyndon Johnson in 1965–66 and the surprise invasion of Cambodia ordered by Nixon in 1970 ("incursion," in the President's euphemism); executive agreements have secretly supplanted the place of treaties on important occasions; and, spending in the executive branch has often taken on the characteristics of a shell game designed to fool the public and its surrogates in Congress.

The Question of Secrecy

Since my first meeting with Lou Fisher thirty years ago, the CRS has moved into a new suite of offices in the sleek, modern James Madison Memorial Building—the largest library building in the world, covering an entire city block across Pennsylvania Avenue from the old, more charming original LC (now named the Thomas Jefferson Building). On a marble wall in the foyer of the Madison Building is chiseled a remark from its famous eponym that could easily serve as an introduction to Fisher's work. In Madison's words: ". . . power, lodged as it must be in human hands, will ever be liable to abuse."

A Less Than Perfect World

As Madison reminded us in *Federalist Paper No. 51*, human beings must govern themselves for, unfortunately, this is a world without angels. With respect to the Watergate and Iran-contra scandals, Fisher once noted: "People in power regularly exhibited ignorance and contempt for popular control and representative government."[2] The genius of James Madison and the other founders lies in their recognition of this ever present potential for the misuse of power and their inclusion of safeguards into the Constitution to protect liberty. In the modern era, Louis Fisher has stood in the vanguard of a group of political scientists devoted to the study of how well these safeguards have worked—especially with respect to the powers for spending, war-making, and treaties.

The Spending Power

Beyond the power of impeachment—a heavy, unwieldy piece of artillery rarely used by legislators—the power of the purse remains the greatest strength of Congress (as Senator Church understood when he sought to cut off funds for the continuation of President Nixon's war in Cambodia). Yet, the executive branch has tried time and again to steal this power away from the legislative branch. Impoundment has been but one example, albeit an important one that Congress has dealt with through the Congressional Budget and Impoundment Control Act of 1974—a law that has put into place reporting requirements and restrictions on the practice. At the time of its passage, retiring Speaker of the House, Carl Albert, referred to this law as one of the two most important statutes passed in his long career in Congress.[3]

Impoundment. During the Nixon years, the executive branch would refuse to spend appropriated funds, without a single word of discussion with Congress—or even the courtesy of informing legislators. The monies would simply lay at rest in the federal treasury, despite constitutionally based expectations among the nation's law makers, governors, and mayors that "the check was in the mail." Finally, the affected parties would have to mount a further lobbying effort—after lobbying extensively in the first place for passage—to seek release of the funds from the federal treasury. Sometimes they would be successful, often not. Little wonder that Nixon's excesses in this domain stirred strong political opposition and led to the impoundment-control law enacted in the same year as the impeachment proceedings against him.

Other Secret Spending. The "executive shell game"[4] that takes place with respect to the nation's spending power extends beyond impoundment. The Constitution's Statement and Account Clause, for instance, has suffered extensive erosion from its original intent.

According to the wording of this clause, "A regular Statement and Account of the Receipts and Expenditures of all public Money shall be published from time to time." (Art. I, sec. 9)

As Fisher has noted with respect to this provision:

> In a democratic society, budgeting is expected to satisfy such fundamental standards as visibility, clarity, explicitness, and comprehensiveness. Without adherence to those standards the public is unable to judge and hold accountable the actions of governmental officials.[5]

Yet, in place of the visibility required by the clause has evolved the practice of confidential funding, where the appropriation is public but the expenditure and auditing remain secret; and, more slippery still, secret funding, where all stages of the budgeting—from appropriation through auditing—are kept concealed from the public.

Among the many examples of secret funding is one that involved Senator Clifford Case (R, New Jersey), a distinguished member of the Appropriations Committee and the Foreign Relations Committee during the Vietnam War era. The senator had to find out from a newspaper story that the Nixon administration had agreed to finance Thai troops in Laos. In another instance, Senator Stuart Symington (D, Missouri, and a senior member of the Armed Services Committee) never knew about the CIA's secret war in Laos during its formative stages.[6]

The elusive spending practices of the executive branch during the Vietnam War

> emphasized the fact that, although Congress still retains the power to appropriate money, it is fast losing control over how it is spent. The executive branch—through its ability to transfer funds, impound money, create unauthorized commitments, and engage in covert financing—now holds a substantial portion of the spending power.[7]

Impoundments, contingency funds, transfer authority, and reprogramming, along with the secret manipulation of monies originally appropriated for refugee programs, public health, economic and technical projects, and agricultural assistance (even the use of "Food for Peace" funding for military purposes)—all have been part of the long list of cryptic spending procedures that outside researchers have found difficult to uncover. Considerable danger to the republic lies in such hidden spending practices. With no debate over spending, there is no opportunity for the public to understand how funds are being spent; and, absent an informed public, the United States will have "traveled far from that basic underpinning of democratic government."[8]

Spending for Spies.   In more recent years, the issue of whether to reveal the nation's aggregate intelligence budget—held top secret since the end of World War II—came to be a critical (if chiefly symbolic) test of the Statement and Account Clause. Some claim that revelation of this figure would advantage America's enemies or lead ineluctably to demands for yet more budgetary details about intelligence spending. Others have countered that the aggregate amount would tell our enemies nothing they haven't read repeatedly in this nation's newspapers; that Congress is responsible and can easily hold fast on the revelation of further details; and that publication of the aggregate figure would pay homage to the Statement and Account Clause, while at the same time provide the U.S. public with an accurate, official disclosure of how much is spent each year on intelligence activities.[9]

Several directors of Central Intelligence (DCIs) have endorsed disclosure of the aggregate figure, joined by panel after panel that have looked into the subject—most recently the Aspin-Brown Commission on Intelligence in 1996.[10] In a succession of close votes, though, a majority of Congress chose to keep this "secret" bottled up.[11] Finally, in October of 1997, a lawsuit by the Federation of American Scientists forced the incumbent DCI to officially release the current aggregate figure: $26.6 billion.[12]

Despite Fisher's long-term study of budgetary legerdemain by the executive branch, the brazen claims expressed by Reagan administration officials over spending power came as a shock even to him. The most startling constitutional claim to emerge from this administration during the Iran-contra investigations was the assertion that Congress could not control foreign affairs by withholding appropriations. If Congress refused to appropriate monies for executive programs (in this case, aid for the contra faction in Nicaragua), the administration would simply raise the funds from friendly foreign governments and sympathetic private U.S. citizens.

For many observers, this imperial view of executive spending authority amounted to a sounding of the death knell for legislative control over the nation's purse strings. While foreign and private funds had been used in the past for federal operations, this had occurred infrequently and only when authorized by Congress. This blatant attack on the Constitution represented a peril to the nation more far reaching than even Watergate.[13]

The War and Treaty Powers

Executive secrecy has played a disquieting role in the exercise of the nation's war and treaty powers, too. It has often undermined the notion of power sharing and consensus building between Congress and the president that is so vital to the establishment of legitimacy for any major policy.

War-Making. With respect to the war power, secrecy has been most damaging in the early stages of preparation for combat. The War Powers Resolution, passed over a presidential veto in 1973, extolled the desirability of "collective judgment" by the executive and legislative branches before the nation enters into military hostilities—a principle "foursquare" with the intent of the founders.[14] The resolution requires the executive to consult with Congress "in every possible instance" on "pending" war-related decisions.

Instead, however, the history of war consultation since 1973 has been one of evasion and duplicity by the executive branch (abetted in part by some ambiguous and contradictory language in the law itself).[15] Presidents have intervened militarily in Cyprus (1974), South Vietnam (1975), Cambodia (1975), Iran (1980), Libya (1981, 1986), Lebanon (1982), Grenada (1983), El Salvador (1984), Persian Gulf (1987), Panama (1989), Kuwait (1990), Somalia (1992), and Haiti (1994) without any meaningful consultation with Congress—not with even a small group of its leaders. These operations remained veiled in secrecy until it was, practically speaking, too late for Congress to do much other than support U.S. troops already bivouacked in zones of hostility.

While secrecy obviously has its place in military operations, in a democracy so does debate—especially on such an important matter as invading another country and sending young Americans to their possible deaths. There will be times when the president must act with great secrecy and dispatch, if the vital interests of the United States are imminently threatened; but in almost all instances, there will be time enough for open deliberation about the fate of this nation and its soldiers. As columnist Anthony Lewis has put it (in reference to President Bill Clinton's deliberations in 1994 over whether to invade Haiti without congressional authority): "A unilateral Presidential decision to invade would offend the Constitution in a most profound sense. It would deprive the military operation of essential public legitimacy."[16]

Yet, in almost every case since passage of the War Powers Resolution, secrecy has trumped over consultation between the branches. Properly, President George Bush sought congressional authorization for Operation Desert Storm in Iraq (1991); but even then he stated that he also had independent authority to enter into war, based on his status as Commander in Chief as well as on a United Nations authorization—as if the U.N. could determine when the United States should go to war, but not the Congress! President Clinton has also embraced this doctrine of executive supremacy over the war power, despite his sharp criticism during his first presidential campaign of Lyndon Johnson's excessive secrecy and arrogance during the Vietnam War era. War-making by executive fiat, clothed in secrecy, appears to remain the dominant philosophy in the current White House.

Nevertheless, some observers hold out hope that the War Powers Resolution, regardless of its many inadequacies, will encourage presidents (as it did Bush, despite all of his rhetoric on "inherent powers") to seek out congressional authorization at least for major military operations. To overcome the tendency toward secrecy and the exclusion of Congress, Fisher encourages legislators to strengthen the consultation provisions of the resolution by making this requirement more explicit; and by relying on a reasonably sized delegation from Congress (eighteen or so legislators, including the top leaders) for purposes of meeting with the president in a preliminary dialogue over the wisdom of military action in any given circumstance.[17]

Treaties. The other great foreign policy power in the Constitution deals with treaties. As a Congressional Fellow in Senator Church's office, I heard much grousing from him and his colleagues about presidential usurpation of the treaty powers. Senators Case and Fulbright waxed livid on the subject, and Church (as was often the case) followed Fulbright's lead with eloquent speeches in support of restoring Congress's authority over treaties. These influential legislators were convinced that, through secret means, presidents were set on robbing the Congress of its important check on the ability of the executive branch to make binding commitments for the United States abroad—a concern as old as the founders's fear of "entangling alliances" in Europe.

The unilateral executive agreement—sometimes consummated in secret—has taken the place of the treaty on some significant occasions and warrants the close attention of those who would defend the Constitution.[18] This abandonment of the treaty as an instrument for solemn commitments to other nations represents yet another example of an erosion in the sharing of powers between the branches, as so brilliantly advocated by the founders. To their astonishment, legislators learned in 1969—four years after the fact— that a secret executive agreement between the United States and Thailand promised the commitment of U.S. troops to that country in case of external attack. "Congress was not consulted in the formulation and signing of the agreement," Fisher wrote at the time, "and could look forward only to a possible advisory role in the event the agreement were placed in operation."[19]

Fisher's research on this topic foreshadowed and contributed to important initiatives by Congress to restore its authority in this domain. His data on the rise of executive agreements and his warnings about the implications of diminishing legislative control over U.S. commitments abroad helped to inform the drafting of legislation to require systematic reporting to Congress by the executive branch on the use of executive agreements (the Case-Zablocki Act of 1972[20]).

Just as he has been concerned about America's entry into foreign commitments without the participation of Congress, so has Fisher helped to sound the alarm about the misuse of presidential authority to end commitments abroad without the participation of Congress. A central example is President Jimmy Carter's termination of a defense treaty with Taiwan, "without ever consulting with legislators."[21] If presidents are expected to join solemnly with the Senate in the consummation of treaties, why should presidents be permitted to abrogate them without the same sense of seriousness and full participation by both branches? Once again, the proper model of governance is shared powers, for the alternative—policy by executive fiat—is anathema to the principles of democracy.

Intelligence Activities

The leitmotiv in Fisher's writings on secrecy and intelligence activities resonates with the central theme of his collective works: the executive has often misled the Congress and sometimes ignored it altogether, often resulting in the failure of policy and the lasting regret of presidents who have subsequently found themselves embarrassed and unpopular. The classic illustration from the field of intelligence is the Iran-contra affair of 1986–87.[22]

The Iran-contra Affair. "Executive officials, called upon by Congress to explain their activities, repeatedly responded with evasion and deceit," recalls Fisher from his service as a staff aide on the U.S. House Iran-contra investigative committee.[23] For officials in the Reagan administration—some on the staff of the National Security Council (NSC), others in the intelligence agencies—the preservation of secrecy was more important than telling the truth to congressional investigators, even in closed session. It was a sad spectacle that others have witnessed first-hand as congressional aides investigating intelligence activities.[24]

The findings of the Iran-contra committees point to a succession of shell games similar to those played in the budgetary domain, this time with the intent of fooling not only the Congress but also other executive branch officials about intelligence operations. Testimony before the committees reveals, for example, that not even the Secretary of State at the time, George P. Shultz, was aware of a key "finding" (the term for a president's official approval of a covert action) related to the Iran-contra operations—just one of several instances where the secretary of state (and his Department of Defense counterpart, Caspar W. Weinberger) were left in the dark.

As for keeping Congress's intelligence overseers informed, they may as well have been in residence on the dark side of the moon as far as the Iran-contra perpetrators were concerned. By law (the Intelligence Accountability Act of 1980[25]), members of the two Intelligence Committees on Capitol Hill were supposed to be briefed on covert actions—or at a minimum, in times of extraordinary emergency, the top congressional leaders; instead, Congress found out about the Iran-contra activities through Lebanese newspaper accounts, as reported by U.S. newspapers ten months after the fact.

One of President Ronald Reagan's national security advisers innovatively suggested in testimony before Iran-contra investigators that a formal, explicit presidential finding for the secret operations in Iran and Nicaragua was really unnecessary, since the president had made a "mental finding."[26] This is precisely the kind of executive branch arrogance and gobbledygook that lies behind Fisher's scholarly insistence on proper legal and constitutional procedures. He sums up the scandal with this searing indictment: "Iran-contra is what one would expect to happen when activists within the White House have contempt for Congress, for responsible cabinet officials, for constitutional principles, and for the rule of law."[27]

The operative word is "contempt." High-ranking executive officials "become contemptuous of government and make government contemptible by their actions."[28] Observers of Washington politics have often heard this contempt expressed by high executive officials, before and after Iran-contra. (By no means all officials; fortunately, most of the government's cabinet members and top aides have displayed a strong respect for the law and for interbranch cooperation, or else by now the government would have frozen up like an engine without oil.) Even as recently as 1995, officials in the Central Intelligence Agency (CIA) tried to conceal from Congress and the Department of Justice their agency's ties with a murderous colonel in the Guatemalan military. This kind of questionable circumstance, when discovered, is meant (by law) to be reported to congressional and Justice Department overseers as soon as possible.[29]

Sometimes those who refuse to honor the concept of power sharing resort to the argument that Congress is simply untrustworthy when it comes to the nation's highest secrets. Yet everyone who has looked seriously at this question understands that almost all of the leaks of sensitive government information have come from the executive branch itself (not to mention the traitors inside the intelligence agencies who have sold secrets to America's adversaries, including the CIA's Aldrich H. Ames).

Occasionally, classified information has seeped from the Hill, although almost always inadvertently and without serious consequence. As Senator William S. Cohen (R, Maine, and subsequently Secretary of Defense) has said, "Congress has demonstrated that it can keep secrets at least as well as those in the executive branch and outside the government who are planning and executing covert actions."[30] This is a conclusion that most former DCIs would endorse as well, according to my interviews with them.[31]

It is not the Congress that brought us Iran-contra, or for that matter Watergate, Vietnam, or CIA domestic spying. Instead, it is the secrecy system that has bred an antidemocratic impulse inside the executive branch. The fundamental deficiencies of this system were evident during the Iran-contra affair:

- a belief in presidential supremacy
- distrust among administration officials
- the exclusion of advice and information

- a pattern of lying and deception
- the destruction of official documents, and
- an inability to hold the president and vice president accountable.[32]

Secrecy Pledges. Another of the troubling features of this secrecy system is the secrecy pledge, whereby government officials are required to sign nondisclosure forms as a prerequisite of their employment in the national security domain. Fisher has asked the important question, "Will nondisclosure agreements inhibit the ability of Congress to obtain the information it needs from the executive branch to legislate and to oversee the agencies?"[33] And he might ask as well: Will the American people have the information they need to judge their government's activities? Fisher encourages Congress to seek "full access to information in the executive branch," not accepting the excuse of secrecy pledges as an answer for keeping vital facts from the representatives of the American people.[34]

Balancing Executive Secrecy with Public Accountability. What are the appropriate remedies for overcoming excessive secrecy in government? The central answer to this malady, and most others that have disrupted the proper functioning of the American political system from time to time, is for the branches of government to honor their original constitutional boundaries. In what could be taken as the central thesis of his entire oeuvre, Fisher writes: "Executive domination of foreign policy would not be good for Congress, the country, or even for the executive branch."[35] No funding shell games by the executive, because Congress has constitutionally based powers over spending; no more secret military interventions by the president, because no one person should commit the United States to war; no more secret executive agreements, because important foreign "entanglements" should also rest on the judgment of more elected officials than the president alone; no more covert actions without timely reporting to Congress; no more overly broad nondisclosure agreements that shift control over information to the executive branch.

With respect to secrecy and the resort to nondisclosure pledges binding officials (and former officials) from discussing policy with legislators, Fisher acknowledges that "the President has important duties and prerogatives in protecting confidential information," but he further suggests that "Congress must share in those duties and prerogatives . . ."[36] The president's proper remedy to protect information that legitimately must be held within a small circle of executive policy officials is "to invoke executive privilege selectively rather than depend on overly broad nondisclosure agreements."[37]

It is appropriate to argue in foreign affairs generally that "the *conduct* is purely executive but the *policy* is executive-legislative."[38] Yet, since the branches are sometimes tempted to transgress this bright line (notably the executive department in the modern era), simply evoking the shibboleth of "constitutional boundaries" is an insufficient guard against abuse—especially since the Constitution is filled with silences and ambiguities in the drawing of some boundary lines. Ever necessary is an alert watchfulness by members of Congress, executive officials, and private citizens with an appreciation for the philosophy of sharing power across the departments of government to prevent its dangerous aggrandizement in any one department.

Among the most appropriate guidelines for both successful policy and the maintenance of a proper constitutional balance with respect to secrecy and related matters are these:

Policy Based on a Consensus

If the president fails to persuade Congress on a course of action through open discourse (with no secret agenda kept hidden from legislators), he or she should withdraw the proposal.[39] "To be successful," Fisher observes, "foreign policy must be based on the collective efforts of both the President and the Congress."[40] Instead of secretly bypassing Congress to raise funding for the contras from foreign powers and home-grown conservatives when the Congress progressively shut down covert action in Nicaragua with a series of amendments, the executive should have realized the policy lacked sufficient public support to continue.

Legislative, not Judicial, Remedies

If Congress seeks to discipline a president who overreaches constitutional authority, its members should resort to legislative remedies rather than rely on the judicial branch, which is typically wary of political disputes and apt to side reflexively with the president—especially on issues of secrecy and national security.[41] Commenting on the chilling effect of secrecy pledges required of federal employees in the national security establishment, Fisher notes that "remedies announced by federal courts are likely to be too rigid and cumbersome."[42] Congress will have to take on the question of excessive secrecy by clarifying the classification rules by law, ensuring that only the most highly sensitive information remains hidden from the American people (such as weapon blueprints and the names of foreign agents).

The Need for Comity

Superior still to formal legal remedies, the legislative and executive branches must endeavor to seek a compromise between themselves over disputes involving secrecy and public policy. "No statute can force cooperation between the branches," Fisher has commented with respect to the failures of the War Powers Resolution.[43] Rather, in matters of secrecy just as in matters of spending, war, and international agreement making, the branches must respect each other and be willing to consult and discuss issues together in a spirit of comity.[44] Fisher cites approvingly a law case that deals with secrecy, in which the presiding judge concluded: "A compromise worked out between the branches is most likely to meet their essential needs and the country's constitutional balance."[45]

How can the branches arrive at the desired comity? No magic formula exists; rather it is a matter of daily dialogue among officials in the executive and legislative branches—an ongoing constitutional debate, ideally conducted with an air of civility (often absent in recent political discourse, to the nation's detriment). Speaking specifically to the question of secret intelligence spending, Fisher advises how the branches must arbitrate constitutional differences of opinion: ". . . this is how it is done . . . through the hearing process, the Floor process, the individual negotiations."[46]

Political Checks and Balances

If a president fails to share information with Congress related to national security or any other topic on the public policy agenda, legislators can retaliate politically with the many tools at their disposal. These tools include the refusal to confirm a nominee, the cancellation of funds for presidential priorities, the rejection of a treaty, and "any number of other effective sanctions and penalties."[47] All too often the tools available to Congress for the protection of its constitutional prerogatives are left untouched, as legislators whine about their declining powers without doing much about it.

The "powers of Congress under the Constitution and the practicalities of government are immense, in domestic affairs as well as in foreign affairs, but those powers must be exercised," Fisher emphasizes.[48] Even if presidents refuse to comply fully, legislators should exercise their powers as a means of expressing the Congress's sense of prerogatives and constitutional duties. "Otherwise, executive officials are likely to interpret congressional inaction as evidence of uncertainty or acquiescence in the executive's unilateral assertion of power [as occurred] during the Iran-contra affair."[49] What is likely to be the end result of a docile acceptance by Congress of presidential omnipotence in foreign affairs? Fisher has no doubt: ". . . we can expect variations of Iran/contra to recur."[50]

Impeachment

Ultimately, the Congress can impeach a president who flagrantly abuses power. Had it been certain to investigators that President Reagan himself had explicitly violated the restrictive legislation (the Boland amendments) and ordered the raising of foreign monies to fight the covert war in Nicaragua—turning the NSC staff into his own in-house secret agency—the President would have invited, and deserved, impeachment proceedings.[51] President Reagan's role in this affair has proved impossible to confirm, because of the evasiveness of witnesses and the lack of a clear paper trail; if a president were willing to go this far in defiance of Congress, however, Fisher concludes that he or she would fail in the "constitutional duty to see that the laws are faithfully executed, and [the President] would precipitate a constitutional crisis by merging the power of the sword with the power of the purse."[52]

Conclusion

Those who study government have an obligation to alert the American people—and the government itself—to the dangers of eroding democratic principles and practices. As best they can, at least some serious scholars must try to cast the light of learning into the darkest crevices of government, where secrecy reigns, where the spending, war, international agreement, and intelligence powers are often exercised without the benefit of public discourse.

Toward this end, Louis Fisher has provided important guidance. He has been a foe of Constitutional abuse by any of the branches of government, including the legislature. In this age of concentrated executive power, though, he is hopeful that Congress—the people's branch—will lead the nation toward an understanding, restoration, and preservation of the balance between liberty and security, between the public's right to know and the need for some legitimate concealment, between openness and the veils of secrecy.

Fisher's optimism that legislators can and will rise to this challenge is tempered with a realization that sometimes they have displayed an unwillingness to protect the delicate balance among the branches.[53] Much of his work (and mine) implores them to try harder to defend the theory of constitutional power sharing. Above all, he realizes with Justice Robert H. Jackson (in a quote from the 1952 steel seizure case that has guided Fisher throughout his career) that ". . . only Congress itself can prevent power from slipping through its fingers."[54]

Notes

The author would like to thank Leena S. Johnson and Robert J. Spitzer for editing an earlier draft of this paper.

1. Frank Church, "Impoundment of Appropriated Funds: The Decline of Congressional Control Over Executive Discretion," *Stanford Law Review* 22 (June 1970), pp. 1240–53.

2. Louis Fisher, book review of Louis Henkin's *Constitutionalism, Democracy, and Foreign Affairs* (New York: Columbia University Press, 1990), in *Political Science Quarterly* 106 (1991), p. 129.

3. Carl Albert, interview by the author, Washington, D.C., 21 February 1974, Washington, D.C. Fisher's first scholarly article was entitled "Impoundment of Funds by the President: The Constitutional Issue," *George Washington Law Review* 38 (October 1969), pp. 124–37, followed by "The Politics of Impounded Funds," *Administrative Science Quarterly* 15 (September 1970), pp. 361–77, both of which informed the Frank Church essay in the *Stanford Law Review* and were centerpieces in the congressional hearings on impoundment in 1971 and 1973 that preceded passage of this Budget and Impoundment Control legislation. According to Speaker Albert, the other vital law (also influenced by Fisher's research at CRS) was the War Powers Resolution of 1973.

4. Fisher (or, more likely, an editor) uses this phrase as a heading to his "Hiding Billions from Congress," *The Nation* (November 15, 1997), p. 486.

5. Louis Fisher, *Presidential Spending Power* (Princeton, N.J.: Princeton University Press, 1975), p. 202. For a brief summary of Fisher's perspectives on the spending power, see Louis Fisher, "Spending Power," in *Encyclopedia of the American Presidency,* Leonard W. Levy and Louis Fisher, eds., 4 (New York: Simon & Schuster, 1994), pp. 1392–93.

6. Fisher, *Presidential Spending Power*, p. 217.

7. Fisher, "Hiding Billions," p. 490.

8. Fisher, *Presidential Spending Power*, p. 228.

9. See Louis Fisher, statement and responses, "Public Disclosure of the Aggregate Intelligence Budget Figure," *Hearings*, Permanent Select Committee on Intelligence, U.S. House of Representatives, 103rd Cong., 2d Sess. (February 23, 1994), pp. 109–219; and, more generally, "Whether Disclosure of Funds Authorized for Intelligence Activities Is in the Public Interest," *Hearings*, Select Committee on Intelligence, U.S. Senate, 95 Cong., 1st Sess. (1977). See also, Loch K. Johnson, "Statement and Account Clause," in *Encyclopedia of the American Presidency*, Leonard W. Levy and Louis Fisher, eds., Vol. 4 (New York: Simon & Schuster, 1994), pp. 1401–02.

10. Commission on the Roles and Capabilities of the United States Intelligence Community (the Aspin-Brown Commission), *Preparing for the 21st Century: An Appraisal of U.S. Intelligence* (March 1, 1996), p. 142.

11. The most recent vote against disclosure of the aggregate intelligence budget was 56-to-43 in the Senate on June 19, 1997. This figure, estimated at some thirty billion by the *New York Times*, has been referred to by its chief intelligence reporter as "one of the worst-kept secrets in Washington" (Tim Weiner, "Secret Budget for Intelligence Is Approved by Senate, 98-1," *New York Times*, 20 June 1997, p. A10).

12. See Tim Weiner, "For First Time, U.S. Discloses Budget on Spying: $26.6 Billion," *New York Times* (16 October 1997), p. A17.

13. The Committee's official designation was the Select Committee to Investigate Covert Arms Transactions with Iran, chaired by Representative Lee H. Hamilton (D, Indiana). This Committee issued a joint report (with its Senate counterpart) entitled *Report of the Congressional Committees Investigating the Iran-Contra Affair*, H. Rept. 100–433, S. Rept. 100–216, 100th Cong., 1st Sess., Washington, D.C., U.S. Government Printing Office, November 1987. Fisher wrote the portions of this report that dealt "with constitutional and institutional issues" (Louis Fisher, letter to the author, dated May 1, 1997).

14. Louis Fisher, *Presidential War Power* (Lawrence, Kans.: University Press of Kansas, 1995), p. 131.

15. See David P. Auerswald and Peter F. Cowhey, "Ballotbox Diplomacy: The War Powers Resolution and the Use of Force," *International Studies Quarterly* 41 (September 1997), pp. 505–528.

16. Anthony Lewis, "'Not in a Single Man,'" *New York Times*, 12 September 1994, p. A15. Despite such good advice, President Clinton decided to use his supposed unilateral "authority" for the use of military force in Haiti, a decision receiving widespread criticism on Capitol Hill (though no penalties).

17. Fisher, *Presidential War Power*, pp. 133, 193–94.

18. My study of this subject (*The Making of International Agreements: Congress Confronts the Executive*, New York: New York University Press, 1984) stemmed from discussions with Frank Church and the reading of Fisher's early research on U.S. commitments abroad.

19. Louis Fisher, *President and Congress: Power and Policy* (New York: Free Press, 1972), p. 47.

20. 1 U.S.C., 1126 (1972).

21. Louis Fisher, "Understanding the Role of Congress in Foreign Policy," *George Mason University Law Review* 11 (Fall 1988), p. 168.

22. Fisher served as research director for the majority on the House investigative committee that probed this scandal, which allowed him a close inside look at the events of the affair. One of the hallmarks of his scholarship is not only original research, but service as an aide in congressional deliberations who is subsequently able to report to the public through his writings on the outcome of these deliberations—the classic scholar-public servant in the tradition of Archibald Cox, the Harvard University law professor and independent counsel during the Watergate inquiry.

23. Louis Fisher, book review of Edmund S. Muskie, Kenneth Rush, and Kenneth W. Thompson, *The President, the Congress and Foreign Policy* (Lanham, Md.: University Press of America, 1986), in *California Law Review* 76 (July 1988), p. 942.

24. See Michael J. Glennon, "Investigating Intelligence Affairs: The Process of Getting Information for Congress," in *The Tethered Presidency*, ed. by Thomas Franck (New York: New York University Press, 1981), pp. 141–52; and, Loch K. Johnson, *A Season of Inquiry: The Senate Intelligence Investigation* (Lexington, Ky.: University Press of Kentucky, 1985).

25. 50 U.S.C. 401 (1980).

26. Fisher, *California Law Review*, *op.cit.*, p. 955, note 67; this quote from Robert C. McFarlane is in the final report of the investigative committees, *op.cit.*, p. 423. The Hughes-Ryan Act is at 22 U.S.C. 2422 (1974).

27. Fisher, *California Law Review, ibid.*, p. 950.

28. Louis Fisher, "Congressional Access to Executive Branch Information: Lessons from Iran-Contra," *Government Information Quarterly* 6 (1989), p. 393.

29. As stipulated in the 1980 Intelligence Accountability Act, *op.cit.*, and reiterated in the 1991 Intelligence Authorization Act (Pub. L. No. 102–88); on the Guatamala case, see Loch K. Johnson, *Secret Agencies: U.S. Intelligence in a Hostile World* (New Haven, Conn.: Yale University Press, 1996), p. 111.

30. Fisher, *California Law Review, op.cit.*, p. 958; for additional views by Fisher on the superiority of Congress over the executive for preserving legitimate secrets, see Fisher, *Government Information Quarterly, op.cit.*, p. 390.

31. See Johnson, *Secret Agencies, op.cit.*

32. For this listing, see Louis Fisher, "The Foundations of a Scandal," *Corruption and Reform* 3 (1988), p. 157.

33. Louis Fisher, "Congressional-Executive Struggles over Information: Secrecy Pledges," *Administrative Law Review* 42 (Winter 1990), p. 89.

34. *Ibid.*, p. 107.

35. Fisher, *California Law Review, op.cit.*, p. 959.

36. Fisher, "Secrecy Pledges," *op.cit.*, p. 103.

37. *Ibid.*, p. 107.

38. *Ibid.*, p. 103 (emphasis added).

39. This point is made by Louis Henkin in his *Constitutionalism, Democracy, and Foreign Affairs*, p. 33) and cited by Fisher approvingly as "sound judgment" in his view of the book (Fisher, *Political Science Quarterly, op.cit.*, p. 129).

40. Fisher, *California Law Review, op.cit.*, p. 940.

41. See Louis Fisher, book review of Barbara Hinckley, *Less Than Meets the Eye: Foreign Policy Making and the Myth of the Assertive Congress* (Chicago: University of Chicago Press, 1994), in *American Political Science Review* 89 (1995), p. 207, in which he approvingly cites a comment to this effect by Hinckley (p. 89). On the tendency of the Supreme Court to side with the presidency, see Gordon Silverstein, *Imbalance of Powers: Constitutional Interpretation and the Making of American Foreign Policy* (New York: Oxford University Press, 1997).

42. Fisher, "Secrecy Pledges," *op.cit.*, p. 107.

43. Fisher, *California Law Review*, *op.cit.*, p. 941.

44. The final report of the Iran-contra investigative committees concluded that "the intelligence agencies must deal in a spirit of good faith with Congress. Both new and ongoing covert action operations must be fully reported, not cloaked in broad Findings. Answers that are technically true, but misleading, are unacceptable" (*op.cit.*, pp. 383–84).

45. Fisher, "Secrecy Pledges," *op.cit.*, p. 106.

46. Fisher, "Public Disclosure of the Aggregate Intelligence Budget Figure," *op.cit.*, 1994, p. 109.

47. Fisher, "Secrecy Pledges," *op.cit.*, p. 106.

48. Fisher, "Understanding the Role of Congress," *op.cit.*, p. 168.

49. Fisher, 1988, *California Law Review*, *op.cit.*, p. 959.

50. Fisher, "Understanding the Role of Congress," *op.cit.*, p. 153.

51. Louis Fisher, "How Tightly Can Congress Draw the Purse Strings?" *American Journal of International Law* 83 (1989), p. 765.

52. *Ibid.*

53. "For all that is written about the Imperial Congress with its penchant for micromanagement," Fisher writes, "there is too great a temptation on the part of Congress to let down its guard and fail to defend its prerogatives" ("Congressional Checks on Military Initiatives," *Political Science Quarterly* 109 [Winter 1994–95], p. 761).

54. Louis Fisher, "Hiding Billions from Congress," (1971) *op.cit.*, p. 490, and *Presidential War Power* (1995), *op.cit.*, p. 199, citing *Youngstown Co. v Sawyer*, 343 U.S.C. 654.

8

Saving the Constitution from Lawyers

Robert J. Spitzer

The legal profession is often credited as the profession most capable, or most well situated, to offer judgments on the meaning and consequences of constitutional doctrine. The Constitution is, after all, a legally binding document, and from that document is spun the array of legal challenges and doctrinal disputes that in turn generates the corpus of court cases that formulates modern constitutional meaning. By much conventional wisdom, then, the Constitution was written by lawyers, is interpreted by lawyers and judges, and even implemented by lawyers.

One example of this the-Constitution-belongs-to-the-lawyers perspective was seen in the nation's commemoration of the Constitution's Bicentennial, where lawyers were given center stage in most important aspects of the organization and implementation of the commemoration. To pick but one modest if illustrative example, when the *New York Times* devoted a special Sunday Magazine to the Constitution's Bicentennial,[1] it gave over four of its seven feature articles to lawyers (including Derrick Bell, Laurence Tribe, Yale Kamisar, and William Bradford Reynolds; one of the remaining three articles was written by a *Times* staffer). Needless to say, political scientists did not contribute.

Even if we accept the intellectually narrow construct of constitutionalism-as-law, a grave disservice is done when law is left solely to lawyers. While lawyers are most well schooled to practice law, the crucial matter of constitutional interpretation—meaning the

185

study of the law in its larger sense—is a realm wherein political science is uniquely situated to contribute. I will later offer two specific examples of the adverse consequences of leaving the Constitution to lawyers. As Louis Fisher wrote in his award-winning book, *Constitutional Dialogues*, "constitutional law is not a monopoly of the judiciary."[2] In a book aimed specifically at law schools, Fisher (along with coauthor Neal Devins) wrote: "Even a general understanding of American legal history does not support the view that courts are the predominant force in shaping the Constitution. Court judgments are regularly overturned by constitutional amendments, congressional statutes, state actions, and shifting social and political attitudes. Judges are merely one of many authoritative actors in the complicated process of constitutional change."[3] Just as the Constitution is not the sole province of lawyers and judges, the study of the Constitution is not, and ought not to be, left solely (or even primarily) to the legal profession.

The Study of Laws and Institutions in Political Science

Political science maintains long and deep roots in the study of institutional relationships and constitutional structures. An exemplar of this methodology is found in the study of the presidency. It is no coincidence that the foremost constitutional scholar of the first half of the twentieth century was a political scientist, Edward S. Corwin.[4] As Supreme Court Justice Benjamin Cardozo wrote to Corwin, "I find I have frequent occasion to draw upon your learning."[5] In turn, Corwin's most famous book, *The President: Office and Powers*, was, in his words, "a study in American public law" the thematic organization of which was the study of "the development and contemporary status of presidential power and of the presidential office under the Constitution."[6] Even in his day, Corwin provided and implemented the distinctive contribution of the political scientist when he wrote that his approach was "partly historical, partly analytical and critical."[7]

The behavioral revolution swept much institutional analysis aside, both in the discipline of political science and in the study of the presidency. All the more significant, then, has been the much-vaunted return to institutions of the last three decades. Foremost among political scientists leading this return was Louis Fisher,[8] who, like Corwin, has understood that political science, by its intellectual disposition, draws data from the historians and mechan-

ics from the lawyers in order to weave both with a politico-institu-
tional overlay that introduces a kind of coherence and vision to the
Constitution and its institutions that the other disciplines, by themselves, often struggle to achieve. Thus, the return to institutions
underscores political science's unique position—and, I would further argue, obligation—to study its central concern, the state. That
it continues to flag in this obligation is reflected in the observation
of one political scientist that, at least in the realm of presidency
research, "the ranks of 'legalists' studying the presidency have
been . . . thinly populated by political scientists since 1950 (despite
the rush to law school by so many of their students)."[9]

In this chapter, I take as my springboard Fisher's career-long
efforts to bring constitutional-institutional perspectives back into
political science and to bring political science perspectives into the
legal community by drawing on two disparate elements of constitutional interpretation in order to advance my own argument about
how constitutional analysis is generated. In both areas, a large and
influential body of constitutional interpretation has emerged, primarily from lawyers publishing in law journals. These two substantial and influential bodies of constitutional interpretation,
pertaining to a theory of the president's veto power from Article I,
section 7, and pertaining to the Second Amendment of the Bill of
Rights, have two traits in common: both arose primarily in and
through the writings of lawyers in law journals, and both are fa-
tally defective. While it may be overly facile on my part to attribute
the existence and influence of this defective body of literature to
traits appertaining to the legal profession, I nevertheless argue
that defective constitutional analysis too easily emerges when those
trained in the law maintain an analytic monopoly.

Case I: The Inherent Item Veto Dispute

For over a century, presidents and others have argued that
they should be granted item veto powers over legislation. That
argument took a unique twist during the Bush presidency when
the president announced in 1989 that he believed that the Constitution already provided for an item veto, and that he was contem-
plating the exercise of such a power. If Congress or others objected,
they could challenge the action in court, he proposed.

Setting aside the obvious fact that no president until Bush
ever claimed or exercised an item veto based on executive powers

enumerated in the Constitution,[10] let us for the moment accept the theoretical possibility that such a power lays concealed, like an unexploded bomb, within the confines of the Constitution.

Part of the legitimization of the inherent (also called unilateral, partial, or implicit) veto argument rests with the defective historical analysis of noted historian Forrest McDonald. The problems with McDonald's arguments are examined elsewhere.[11] Suffice it to say, however, that nothing from the American colonial period can be taken as lending support to the theory that an item veto was included, or meant to be included, in the 1787 Constitution.

Presidents might possess a unilateral item veto, proponents argue, because the legislative linking of disparate subjects through the attachment of riders under the heading "bill" would be viewed by the founders as an artifice for confounding an otherwise finely wrought legislative process. As early as 1965, Givens used this argument to propose that presidents should simply try an item veto, and let the courts resolve the dispute.[12] Clineburg asserts flatly that presidents may veto nongermane riders.[13] Writing more recently, Schroeder adapted this argument to propose that the courts had the power and standing to strike down laws containing "measures topically or operationally unrelated to the bills carrying them into law."[14] Riggs makes the same claim.[15]

Clineburg,[16] Glazier,[17] Haswell,[18] Crovitz,[19] Sidak and Smith,[20] Krasnow,[21] Schroeder,[22] and Rotunda and Nowak[23] all rely on the argument that the founders knew nothing of the rider problem, and therefore that this lack of knowledge justifies an item veto to restore the more pure and simple legislative process the founders allegedly envisioned. These writers further assert that the rider practice has in effect vitiated the potency of the regular veto.[24] If this assumption about what the founders knew is correct, it could be construed as support for the unilateral item veto. In point of fact, the founders were not only aware of the rider problem, but discussed it at considerable length in the Federal Convention.

The antecedents of the rider problem trace back to the British Parliament in the seventeenth and eighteenth centuries. As early as 1667, the House of Commons engaged in a process then referred to as "tacking." Based on the rule that the House of Lords could not amend money bills, the Commons would include in such bills nongermane riders that would not otherwise win acceptance from the Lords. The practice was used in 1692, 1698, and 1701.[25] In 1700, the House of Commons attached to a tax bill a rider annulling King William III's Irish land grants. Despite the resistance of

the House of Lords, not to mention the displeasure of the king, the bill was approved.[26] As keen students of British history and politics, the founders were fully aware of this history, as the federal debates make clear.[27]

The practice of tacking extended to the colonies as well. Colonial governors were instructed not to approve any colonial legislation that included riders. Even so, many legislatures attempted to attach such riders, which resulted in protracted political disputes that often delayed the allocation of funding for the colonies.[28]

During the Federal Convention, Pierce Butler argued on June 13 that both houses of Congress should have equal say over money bills because a failure to do so "will lead the latter [i.e. the House] into the practice of tacking other clauses to money bills."[29] Col. George Mason discussed a proposal by fellow Virginia delegate Edmund Randolph to mimic the British system, whereby the upper house (the Senate) would similarly be denied the ability to alter or amend money bills, as was true of the British House of Lords. Such a proposal, Mason said on August 13, would mean that "the Senate could not correct errors of any sort, & that it would introduce into the House of Reps. the practice of tacking foreign matter to money bills."[30] (Note that Butler and Mason used the British term "tacking.") Thus, the founders were familiar with the rider problem, although it was controversial then, as it is today.

Inherent item veto proponents similarly argue that, aside from the possibilities and consequences of riders, early legislation was limited to single subjects.[31] Modern legislation, by contrast, is often a complex conglomeration of diverse topics housed under the single title "bill." More significantly, modern appropriations often take the form of enormous omnibus appropriations bills when, many argue, early appropriations were limited to single subjects.

While it is certainly true that modern legislation is more likely to be composed of diverse elements, such legislation constitutes a single bill as much as a bill dealing with a single subject. Contrary to the claim that "separate legislative proposals in substance contained in the same Act are separately vetoable 'bills' regardless of the format or timing of introduction. . . .",[32] a bill quite simply is "any singular, entire piece of legislation in the form in which it was approved by the two Houses [of Congress]."[33]

Even if we set aside history and past practice, any effort to restrict the definition of "bill" to single subjects raises two serious problems. One is the practical problem of deciding which items do and do not belong together. The making of law and policy follows no simple formula, and the interconnectedness of matters addressed in legislation would render chaotic any effort to meaningfully enact a one-subject-per-bill rule. To reintroduce historical considerations, the founders discussed on a number of occasions the nature and complexities of bill construction, including the clear understanding that a "bill" could, and often did, incorporate more than one subject. As with the rider problem, the nature of bill construction was controversial, but was nevertheless well understood.

As for the use of omnibus appropriations bills, contrary to much erroneous supposition, this practice is not, as Louis Fisher has pointed out, a modern one. Indeed, the nation's first appropriations bill, passed in 1789, was an omnibus measure that incorporated the entire budget, made up of four lump sum dollar amounts covering the diverse subject areas of the Department of War, the "civil list," pensions for invalid individuals, and prior government expenditures. This omnibus appropriations process was used in 1790, 1791, 1792, and in 1793. In 1794, appropriations were split between two bills—one for the military, and the other for the rest of the government.[34]

Some legal authors have argued that the construction of the Presentment clause of the Constitution (Art. I, sec. 7) may provide for an item veto. Clause 2 of sec. 7 says that "Every bill" passing the House and Senate shall go to the president for final action. Yet confusion seems to arise, because if Clause 2 is so clear about what is to be done with bills, why, critics have asked, does the next paragraph (Clause 3) repeat this same directive by saying again that "Every Order, Resolution, or Vote to which the Concurrence of the Senate and House of Representatives may be necessary . . . shall be presented to the President. . . ."? This question takes on added significance because the framers were parsimonious and careful in their final construction of the Constitution in order to produce a stylistically cleaner and neater document. This included the excision of extraneous words and phrases.[35] According to Glazier, Clause 3 authorizes an item veto because "Congress may not subvert the veto by bunching legislation into something it calls 'one' bill."[36] Such a "bunching gambit" is in effect the ducking of presentment barred in sec. 7, Glazier asserts. Crovitz makes the same argument.[37]

Yet the reason for this apparent repetition in the Constitution is explained in the federal debates. Clause 3 "was added to avoid a situation in which Congress might seek to avoid presidential review of legislation by giving it some other name."[38] Considerable attention was focused at the convention on the concern that Congress might try to duck a veto by calling a bill something other than "bill" in order to avoid presentment entirely. Such ploys had been used repeatedly by colonial legislatures to duck vetoes by the British monarch's appointed governors. As Madison said at the convention, "if the negative of the President was confined to *bills*; it would be evaded by acts under the form and name of Resolutions, votes, &c."[39] (The specific reference to "the negative," i.e., the veto, arose because the veto clause was under discussion at the time.) Edmund Randolph concurred by offering a motion the next day "putting votes, Resolutions &c. on a footing with Bills."[40] There is no reason to believe that this wording means presidents can veto the constituent parts of legislation passed on for signature or veto.

In short, the proposition that a bill was meant to be a single subject only is false. Thus, presidents have no basis for subdividing that which is presented to them by Congress based on any meaning or implication arising from the Constitution. Moreover, presentment is not ducked at all because presidents are indeed presented with omnibus bills, multisubject bills, and bills with riders.

Beyond this, there is another important distinction justifying the existence and separation of the two paragraphs in Article I. Clause 2 is written as a set of directions *to the president*, carefully explaining executive options for dealing with legislation sent to the chief executive. Quite simply, it is the president's "how to" guide for handling enrolled bills. Clause 3, however, serves a different purpose, in that it speaks not to the president, but *to Congress*. The whole thrust of the paragraph is to caution Congress against using subterfuge of the sort used by colonial legislatures to thwart the executive's role in the legislative process laid out in the Constitution. In other words, it is a "thou shalt not" aimed at Congress (as is much of the succeeding Section 9 in Art. I).

The inherent item veto argument is predicated on a veritable parade of erroneous assumptions and assertions. As I have argued, there are no applicable colonial or early state precedents for the inherent veto argument; the founders were indeed aware of the rider and omnibus phenomena in the construction of legislation; they were also aware that bill construction could be limited to single subjects, but chose not to codify such a narrow definition.

Case II: The Second Amendment

Few parts of the Constitution are so often invoked, yet so little understood, as the Second Amendment. After sweeping away the polemic, the meaning in the Second Amendment is simple and clear. As the text itself says, "A well regulated Militia, being necessary to the security of a free State, the right of the people to keep and bear Arms, shall not be infringed." As debate concerning the amendment during the First Congress made clear, the amendment was added to allay the concerns of anti-Federalists and others who favored stronger states, that state sovereignty would be impinged by the new federal government, which had been given vast new powers over the use of military force. In other words, the inclusion of the Second Amendment embodied the Federalist assurance that the state militias would be allowed to continue as a military and political counterbalance to the national army at a time when military takeovers were the norm in world affairs. Debate during the First Congress dealt with the narrow military questions of the need to maintain civilian government control over the military, the military unreliability of militias as compared with professional armies, possible threats to liberties from armies versus militias, and whether to codify the right of conscientious objectors to opt out of military service (an early version of the amendment included such language).[41]

As four Supreme Court cases and nearly twenty lower federal court rulings have made clear, the Second Amendment pertains only to citizen service in a government-organized and regulated militia.[42] The abysmal performance of civilian (general) militias in the War of 1812 essentially ended the government's use of such forces to meet military emergencies. Instead, the government came to rely on the military draft. The select or volunteer militias used in the Civil War were institutionalized and brought under federal military authority as the National Guard early in the twentieth century. Further, even if the Second Amendment did pertain to personal weapons ownership or use, the court has refused to incorporate it, unlike most of the rest of the Bill of Rights, thereby limiting its relevance only to federal action. In any case, the Second Amendment provides no protection for personal weapons use, including hunting, sporting, collecting, or even personal self-protection.[43]

Yet despite the definitive nature of historical lessons and court rulings, some legal writers, publishing almost exclusively in law journals, have sought to spin out other interpretations of the Second Amendment. As with the inherent item veto debate, these authors have succeeded in finding legitimacy for a variety of erroneous and even nonsensical arguments concerning the meaning of the Second Amendment through publication in law journals. Even though these writings represent a minority view,[44] they are often used to justify public proclamation of imagined Second Amendment rights by such organizations as the National Rifle Association.[45] Law reviews have, in fact, been the primary breeding ground for these theories.

In order to study the development of alternate theories concerning the Second Amendment, I examined over 250 law journal articles published between 1912 and 1997, as cited in the *Index to Legal Periodicals*[46] (the standard reference work for articles in law journals), that offered significant commentary on the Second Amendment. Of these 250-plus articles, I culled through direct examination a list of 145 articles offering significant Second Amendment analysis. These were then categorized according to whether the articles subscribe to the "court" view, as summarized above, or the "individualist" view, which encompasses the alternate interpretations discussed below. The sheer size of this list, reprinted at the end of this chapter, gives the lie to two claims often made by those advancing new and novel interpretations: 1) that little to nothing of any consequential scholarly nature has been published on the Second Amendment, especially before the 1980s;[47] and 2) that the individual view was or is the prevalent one until recent critics saying otherwise (i.e. what is identified here as the "court" view) came along.[48]

As Table 1 makes clear, a total of thirty-nine articles were published in law journals from 1912 to 1979 on the meaning of the

Table 1

Law Journal Articles T aking "Court" and "Individualist" Views of the Second Amendment*

	Court	Individualist
1912–1959	11	0
1960–1969	11	3
1970–1979	8	6
1980–1989	17	21
1990–1997	23	45
Total	70	75

*Data compiled from articles listed in Appendix. Coded and compiled by the author. Articles cited in the *Index of Legal Periodicals,* 1887–November 1997.

Second Amendment. Of these, only nine took the individualist view, with the very first such article appearing in 1960 (all of these articles and their categorization appear at the end of this chapter). Since 1980, there has indeed been a significant increase in the number of articles published on the Second Amendment, especially those taking an individualist view. The fact that unusual or bizarre legal theories are able to find a home in law journals comes as little surprise when one realizes that there are, by one recent count, over eight hundred such journals.[49] Surely no other academic discipline boasts such a vast publishing arena. The sheer article appetite generated by so many journals, most of which are run by students, is surely a primary catalyst to the problems described here.

Leaving aside the question of author motivations and the inclination of academics to offer unusual or counterintuitive arguments for the sake of intellectual jousting, and the political cloud that hangs over the gun control issue,[50] one can identify a few common critiques of the existing Second Amendment law and its interpretation. Let me emphasize again that these theories arise almost entirely from legal scholars publishing in law journals.

The "Individualist" Critique

Some argue that the Second Amendment really bestows every American citizen with a right to have guns, aside from or in addition to the militia principle.[51] This argument is usually supported by plucking key phrases from court cases and colonial or federal debate that emphasize the right of all Americans to carry guns.

This analysis has two problems. First, it often relies on supporting quotes accidentally or willfully pulled out of context that, when examined in context, support the verdict of history and the courts.[52] Gun ownership was undeniably an important, even vital component of colonial and federal life. But as a matter of constitutional law, the issue of the bearing of arms *as it pertained to the Constitution and the Bill of Rights* always came back to service in a government-organized and regulated military unit, and the balance of power between the states and the federal government, as reflected in the two most important historical sources, the records of the Constitutional Convention and those of the First Congress when the Bill of Rights was formulated.

Second, the definition of the citizen militias at the center of this debate has always been limited to men roughly between the ages of eighteen and forty-five.[53] That is, it has always excluded a majority of the country's adult citizens—men over forty-five, the infirm of all ages, and all women. Therefore, it is not, and never has been, a right enjoyed by all citizens, unlike other Bill of Rights protections such as free speech, religious freedom, or right to counsel.[54]

Selective Analysis

Other critiques of the prevailing view tell only part of the Second Amendment story, leaving aside or misconstruing the whole matter of incorporation, for example,[55] or ignoring the actual developments in national defense between colonial times and the present.[56] Obviously, the American system of national defense today is very different from that envisioned by the founders. One might therefore argue that the courts or Congress have deviated from the principles upon which the country is founded by not insuring that Americans today be armed, and thus suggesting that governmental leaders have somehow betrayed the country's principles.[57] Yet this argument ignores two centuries of development and the organic nature of the Constitution. After all, the original Constitution countenanced slavery; made no provision for an air force; could not have foreseen the need to protect citizens from electronic surveillance. Yet we accept that these matters can and should be dealt with within the constitutional framework. Some constitutional structures that have not been altered, such as the electoral college, operate in a way entirely different from what the founders envisioned.[58] Nevertheless, we accept these developments because they arise from changing needs, with political consensus, and (as necessary) the blessing of the courts. So, too, with the Second Amendment; that is, the fact that the nation's military and defense structure is very different from that of the eighteenth century is by itself no condemnation of the current system, and nothing in the Second Amendment requires states or the federal government to employ old-style citizen militias to meet military needs. Indeed, a constitutional system incapable of adapting to changing circumstances is probably one that cannot survive the test of time. Still other critics simply object to the courts' Second Amendment rulings, often expressing unvarnished frustration or dismay.[59]

Self-Defense

Critics also argue that the principle of personal self-protection or self-defense is (or ought to be) covered by the Second Amendment.[60] In doing so, some of this analysis intermixes the defense needs of early Americans (against Indians, or predators, for example) with modern personal self-defense against robberies, assaults, rapes, intrusions into people's homes, or other life-threatening circumstances. Yet the Second Amendment by design and interpretation has nothing to do with these very real modern-day threats, but rather with the threats confronted by armies and militias.

This does not mean that the law affords no legal protection to individuals who engage in personal self-defense—far from it. American and British common law has recognized and legally sanctioned personal self-defense for hundreds of years, prior to and independent of the Second Amendment. But it arises from the area of criminal law, not constitutional law.[61] The Second Amendment is as superfluous to legal protection for personal defense or defense of the home today as it was two centuries ago.

The "Right of Revolution" and Oppression

An additional challenge to the militia view argues that the Second Amendment does or should protect the ownership of arms for everyone because of an innate "right of revolution," or as a mechanism to keep the country's rulers responsive to the citizens.[62] While these theories pose interesting intellectual questions about the relationship between citizens and the state, they do not translate into meaningful policies for modern America. Most citizens recognize the importance of nonviolent political expression and the exercise of democratic values through elections, public opinion, and the interest group process, rather than by pointing guns (whether by threat or deed) at congressional leaders or the White House. Few Americans approve of those few individuals and groups in America that actively pursue something resembling a right of revolution—the Ku Klux Klan, the skinheads, the Branch Davidians, Los Angeles rioters, or Timothy McVeigh. As legal scholar Dean Roscoe Pound noted, a "legal right of the citizen to wage war on the government is something that cannot be admitted. . . . In the urban industrial society of today a general right to bear efficient arms so as to be enabled to resist oppression by the government would mean that gangs could exercise an extra-legal rule which would defeat the whole Bill of Rights."[63] In any event, any so-called right of revolution is carried out against the government, which means against that government's Constitution as well, including the Bill of Rights and the Second Amendment. One cannot carry out a right of revolution against the government while at the same time claiming protections within it.[64]

Along these lines, others have argued that traditionally oppressed groups, such as women and African Americans, should aggressively claim for themselves a right to bear arms.[65] Blacks in particular have been subject to race-based violence for hundreds of years, and were undeniably denied arms "as a means of racial oppression."[66] Yet the key handicap for blacks and other oppressed groups has not been the denial of Second Amendment rights in particular, but the denial of *all* basic Bill of Rights freedoms, not to mention denial of the basic common law principle of self-defense.

Getting It Wrong

The most flawed of these critiques are those that willfully distort the legal and historical record. To pick a particularly flagrant example, produced by legal staff, a report of the Subcommittee on the Constitution of the Senate Judiciary Committee, published in 1982 under the chairmanship of gun control foe Orrin Hatch (R-UT), stated that the Supreme Court "has only three times commented upon the meaning of the second amendment";[67] erroneously omitting *U.S. v Cruikshank* (1876) and *Presser v Illinois* (1886) entirely, the discussion mentioned *Dred Scott v Sandford* (1857), *U.S. v Miller* (1939), and *Lewis v U.S.* (1980). *Dred Scott*,[68] a pre-Civil War case that dealt with the question of whether a slave could assert citizenship rights after living in freedom, was cited in the Senate committee report because it "indicated strongly that the right to keep and bear arms was an individual right; the Court noted that, were it to hold free blacks to be entitled to equality of citizenship, they would be entitled to keep and carry arms wherever they went."[69] The foolishness of an argument predicated on a court case that ruled against the rights of blacks at a time when slavery was still legal indicates why the concern over blacks carrying guns expressed by the justices arose in the first place. Moreover, *Dred Scott* was handed down at a time when general militias still existed in theory. It was later overruled by the passage of the Thirteenth and Fourteenth Amendments. By any standard, it does not stand as law, and is irrelevant to the interpretation of the Second Amendment. The Senate report also omits the primary finding of *Miller*, and misrepresents the *Lewis* case.[70] Yet the report that offered this and other comment as competent legal analysis has been widely reprinted and quoted by sympathetic legal writers.

Regardless of one's feelings about gun control, the cause of rational policy debate is only throttled by the proliferation of bad analysis.

The desire to treat the Second Amendment as a constitutional touchstone by gun control opponents is understandable, given the "rights talk" that pervades American political discourse and the enormous political legitimacy that accompanies anything dubbed constitutional. Such claims are, however, without historical, constitutional, or legal foundation. In short, the Second Amendment poses no obstacle to gun control as it is debated in modern America.

Conclusion

One problem with leaving the Constitution to lawyers is that political and historical variables are too easily given short shrift because legal analysts are trained to focus more on internal legal and logical consistency than on broader political context. A second and related problem is that intellectual gamesmanship over the Constitution seems to find singularly free rein in legal publications. For example, Haswell argues in the inherent item veto debate that, regardless of the validity of the merits of the inherent item veto theory, it is good for the presidency to attempt such a procedure. "Win or lose, the President stands to gain by attempting a partial veto. The 'bully pulpit' of the Presidency would be illuminated by the glow of publicity arising out of the constitutional litigation which would likely ensue. . . ."[71] This a-constitutional recommendation is troubling not only because it comes from a lawyer, but because it treats proper or successful exercise of executive power as directly proportionate to the amount of litigation it generates. Absent a bona fide emergency, action should be predicated *only* on a firm legal basis, which Haswell himself admits is absent in this case. Academics of all fields generate arguments, but (in the case of political science) good argumentation cannot be cut loose from political and historical context. Without that context, Haswell's argument makes some sense. Yet when context is injected, the consequences of Haswell's argument become readily apparent. If it is good for the presidency to claim and exercise a constitutional power for which the justification is at best tenuous, why stop with the veto? Why not encourage the president to devote the resources of the Justice Department to the development and implementation of other new theories for more expansive use of other presidential powers, and let the courts arbitrate if challenges arise? In fact, the nation has undergone just such presidential experimentation. Its consequences precipitated such crises as Watergate (constitutionally justified as a feasible use of executive authority and executive privilege) and Iran-contra (constitutionally justified as a proper use of presidential foreign policy power). The constitutional paradigm suggested by Haswell is nothing less than an application of chaos theory to the Constitution. The only "glow" arising from such suspect executive action is the brief light accompanying the Constitution's immolation.

Sidak and Smith propose a different, if parallel justification for their advocacy of the inherent item veto based on the same kind of intellectual gamesmanship. At the start of their article, they note that since the courts have never ruled on this matter, it is still an open legal question: "reasonable minds differ on this constitutional question—as they do on abortion, the War Powers Resolution, affirmative action, the death penalty, and many other constitutional issues."[72] By indiscriminately blending these issues together, they attempt to reduce and thus equalize a wide mix of political and policy disputes using the "reasonable minds differ" standard. This intellectual relativism is allowable for issues like affirmative action and the death penalty, where reasonable minds do differ, and where the most important consideration is the normative inclination of the public will over the course of national policy. The item veto dispute, however, is not, insofar as it is a matter of constitutional interpretation, one to be decided at the polls. It is one to be resolved by a careful weighing of legal, historical, and political evidence, and although reasonable minds might differ, the facts in this case speak clearly about what is true. In other words, reasonable minds may differ, but reasonable people can also be wrong. When political and historical context are ignored in the analysis, the "reasonable minds differ" standard retains credibility. But when political and historical context are given their due, the shallow insincerity of the "reasonable minds" standard becomes apparent.[73] Facts are facts, and some arguments are simply wrong, reasonable minds notwithstanding.

The "reasonable minds" standard has an added pernicious consequence. It infers that a social-scientific weighing of evidence cannot lead to a clear conclusion as long as reasonable people (note— not reasonable arguments) stand against that conclusion. The articles cited in this chapter that defend the inherent item veto theory and many pertaining to the Second Amendment are full of waffling phrases like the "reasonable minds" touchstone. All seek to find cracks of daylight by raising reasonable-doubt questions in the prevailing wisdom; i.e., 'since we do not know for sure what the founders knew, our interpretation is as valid as any other.' The critical flaw is that this conclusion is supported primarily by a conscious argumentative style designed to create doubt (which of course is the basis of the adversary system in American law), rather than to find the truth by amassing and weighing evidence cast in broader historical-political perspective.

One finds similar argumentation in the debate over the Second Amendment. Sanford Levinson, for example, states in a widely cited article published in the *Yale Law Journal* that "It is not my style to offer 'correct' or 'incorrect' interpretations of the Constitution."[74] Yet he then procceds to do just that, seeking to call into question the conventional understanding of the Second Amendment. In the process, he asserts that the Second Amendment is an expression of republicanism that does and should take citizen participation beyond peaceful, constitutional means:

> . . . just as ordinary citizens should participate actively in governmental decisionmaking through offering their own deliberative insights, rather than be confined to casting ballots once every two or four years for those very few individuals who will actually make decisions, *so should ordinary citizens participate in the process of law enforcement and defense of liberty rather than rely on professional peacekeepers, whether we call them standing armies or police* [emphasis added].[75]

In short, Levinson offers as a bona fide constitutional argument the proposition that vigilantism and citizen violence, including armed insurrection, against the government are legal, proper, and even beneficial activities within the Second Amendment umbrella. The idea that vigilantism and armed insurrection are as constitutionally sanctioned as voting is a proposition of such absurdity that one is struck more by its boldness than by its pretensions to seriousness.

A perfect real world application of the citizen behavior extolled by Levinson is the case of Karen Mathews, clerk-recorder for Stanislaus County, California, who in 1994 was beaten, kicked, and stabbed because she refused to record several illegal documents, including fictitious "common law" liens, against property owned by local government officials and agents of the IRS. The attack on Mathews was part of a coordinated campaign by members of a group called the Juris Christian Assembly, an extremist group of tax protestors with ties to so-called militias who sought to intimidate and harass government officials by attempting to serve and execute such bogus liens. In California alone, clerk-recorders in forty-nine of the state's fifty-eight counties reported harassment.[76] Anti-government groups have applied intimidation tactics, including trials in so-called "common law courts," with increasing frequency. While I am sure that Levinson would deplore this instance of lawlessness, it is a precise, logical, and even necessary consequence of his generally bizarre argument.

I do not mean to suggest that social scientists are paragons of objectivity, whereas legal scholars are amoral intellectual shills. Rather, the two disciplines involve different emphases in training, intellectual style, and objectives. Lawyers are trained to be advocates; social science training, despite its limitations and flaws, emphasizes exploration. These differences, I argue, help to explain the pyramid-like growth of the inherent veto argument and the proliferation of alternate theories of the Second Amendment in law journals and other legal publications.

A third problem with the analysis criticized here is its source—law reviews. As is well known, most law reviews are not subject to the customary peer review process found in most disciplines. That is, with one exception,[77] all of the articles advancing the inherent item veto argument appeared in prominent law journals, which are governed by student-run law review boards and which do not rely on peer review. Nearly all of the Second Amendment arguments discussed here also arose in law journals. Peer review is a process subject to legitimate criticisms, including cronyism and an innate conservatism stemming from the fact that manuscript review is usually conducted by those who have already published in an area, meaning that they are likely to view new or unorthodox ideas with suspicion. Even so, an article that might pass muster for a law review because it is logically argued and extensively footnoted would be less likely to win approval from a peer-reviewed journal if the argument itself is flawed in conception. Those doing the review for social science journals are most likely to be familiar with the full range of arguments in a given field or subfield. The law students who serve on law reviews and who engage in editorial review simply do not possess, and cannot be expected to possess, the knowledge and expertise of those who have researched and published in a field.[78] As Shea notes, "Law reviews are unique in lacking a peer-review system."[79] I do not mean this to be a sweeping indictment of law journals. Law reviews and the legal community have produced much excellent scholarship, and they are also keenly aware of the problems and shortcomings associated with these student-run publications. Indeed, they have engaged in much soul-searching over the criticisms raised here, as well as related questions.[80]

Political science has a long and distinguished tradition of the study of constitutionalism and the law. That tradition was neglected with the rise of behavioralism, and although it has received renewed attention in the return to institutions, the cases of the inherent item veto and the Second Amendment underscore the incompleteness of political science's ballyhooed "return" to institutions. The study of institutions is more than an intellectually significant avenue of research. It represents, I argue, a special obligation owed by the discipline to proper understanding of the state and its policy apparatus. Further, political science needs to construct a more systematic dialogue with legal scholars. Scholars like Edward Corwin and Louis Fisher provide exemplars in this regard. Political science would do well to reacquaint itself with the intersection of law and politics.

Appendix:
Coding of "Court" (C) and "Individualist" (I) Law Journal Articles

1912
C   "The Constitutional Right to Keep and Bear Arms and Statutes Against Carrying Weapons." *American Law Review* 46(September–October 1912): 777–79.

1913
C   "Right to Bear Arms." *Law Notes* 16(February 1913): 207–8.

1915
C   Emery, L.A. "The Constitutional Right to Keep and Bear Arms." *Harvard Law Review* 28(March 1915): 473–77.

1928
C   McKenna, D.J. "The Right to Keep and Bear Arms." *Marquette Law Review* 12(Fall 1928): 138–49.

1934
C   Brabner-Smith, J. "Firearm Regulation." *Law and Contemporary Problems* 1(October 1934): 400–14.

1939

C   Montague, W. "Second Amendment, National Firearms Act."
     Southern California Law Review 13(November 1939): 129–
     30.

C   "Second Amendment." *St. John's Law Review* 14(November
     1939): 167–69.

1940

C   Breen, V., et al. "Federal Revenue as Limitation on State
     Police Power and the Right to Bear Arms—Purpose of Leg-
     islation as Affecting its Validity." *Journal of the Bar Associa-
     tion of Kansas* 9(November 1940): 178–82.

C   Weiner, F.B. "The Militia Clause of the Constitution." *Harvard
     Law Review* 54(December 1940): 181–220.

1941

C   Haight, G.I. "The Right to Keep and Bear Arms." *Bill of
     Rights Review* 2(Fall 1941): 31–42.

1950

C   "Restrictions on the Right to Bear Arms: State and Federal
     Firearms Legislation." *University of Pennsylvania Law Re-
     view* 98(May 1950): 905–19.

1960

I   Hays, S.R. "The Right to Bear Arms, A Study in Judicial
     Misinterpretation." *William and Mary Law Review* 2(1960):
     381–406.

1965

C   Fletcher, J.G. "The Corresponding Duty to the Right of Bear-
     ing Arms." *Florida Bar Journal* 39(March 1965): 167–70.

I   Sprecher, Robert A. "The Lost Amendment." *American Bar
     Association Journal* 51(June/July 1965): 554–57, 665–69.

1966

C   Feller, P.B., and K.L. Gotting. "The Second Amendment: A
     Second Look." *Northwestern University Law Review* 61(March/
     April 1966): 46–70.

C   Rohner, R.J. "The Right to Bear Arms: A Phenomenon of
     Constitutional History." *Catholic University Law Review*
     16(September 1966): 53–84.

1967

C   "Firearms: Problems of Control." *Harvard Law Review*
      80(April 1967): 1328–46.

C   Mann, J.L. II. "The Right to Bar Arms." *South Carolina Law
      Review* 19(1967): 402–13.

I   Olds, N.V. "Second Amendment and the Right to Keep and
      Bear Arms." *Michigan State Bar Journal* 46(October 1967):
      15–25.

C   Riseley, R.F. Jr. "The Right to Keep and Bear Arms: A Nec-
      essary Constitutional Guarantee or an Outmoded Provision
      of the Bill of Rights, *Albany Law Review* 31(January 1967):
      74–87.

1968

C   Mosk, S. "Gun Control Legislation: Valid and Necessary."
      New York Law Forum 14(Winter 1968): 694–717.

1969

C   "Constitutional Limitations on Firearms Regulation." *Duke
      Law Journal* 18(August 1969): 773–801.

C   Grundeman, A. "Constitutional Limitations on Federal Fire-
      arms Control. *Washburn Law Journal* 8(Winter 1969): 238–
      47.

C   Levine, R.B., and D.B. Saxe. "The Second Amendment: The
      Right to Bear Arms." *Houston Law Review* 7(September 1969,
      1–19.

C   Sheppard, E.H. "Control of Firearms." *Missouri Law Review*
      34(Summer 1969): 376–96.

1970

I   McClure, J.A. "Firearms and Federalism." *Idaho Law Re-
      view* 7(Fall 1970): 197–215.

1971

C   Levin, J. "Right to Bear Arms: The Development of the
      American Experience." *Chicago-Kent Law Review* 48(Fall–
      Winter 1971): 148–67.

C   McCabe, M.K. "To Bear or to Ban—Firearms Control and the
      'Right to Bear Arms.' " *Journal of the Missouri Bar* 27(July
      1971): 313–28.

1972

C   Edwards, G. "Commentary: Murder and Gun Control." *Wayne Law Review* 18(July–August 1972): 1335–42.

1973

C   Wallitsch, T.A. "Right to Bear Arms in Pennsylvania: The Regulation of Possession." *Duquesne Law Review* 11(Summer 1973): 557–75.

1974

I   Hardy, D.T., and J. Stompoly. "Of Arms and the Law." *Chicago-Kent Law Review* 51(Summer 1974): 62–114.

C   Riley, R.J. "Shooting to Kill the Handgun: Time to Martyr Another American 'Hero.'" *Journal of Urban Law* 51(1974): 491–524.

I   Weiss, J.A. "A Reply to Advocates of Gun-Control Law." *Journal of Urban Law* 52(1974): 577–89.

1975

C   Weatherup, R.G. "Standing Armies and Armed Citizens: An Historical Analysis of the Second Amendment." *Hastings Constitutional Law Quarterly* 2(Fall 1975): 961–1001.

1976

I   Caplan, D.I. "Restoring the Balance: The Second Amendment Revisited." *Fordham Urban Law Journal* 5(Fall 1976): 31–53.

I   Whisker, J.B. "Historical Development and Subsequent Erosion of the Right to Keep and Bear Arms." *West Virginia Law Review* 78(Fall 1976): 171–90.

1977

C   Jackson, M.H. "Handgun Control: Constitutional and Critically Needed." *North Carolina Central Law Journal* 8(Spring 1977): 189–98.

C   Santee, J.C. "Right to Keep and Bear Arms." *Drake Law Review* 26(1976–77): 423–44.

1978

I   Caplan, D.I. "Handgun Control: Constitutional or Unconstitutional?—A Reply to Mayor Jackson." *North Carolina Central Law Journal* 10(Fall 1978): 53–58.

1980

I Cantrell, C.L. "The Right to Bear Arms: A Reply." *Wisconsin Bar Bulletin* 53(October 1980): 21–26.

C Elliott, R.L. "Right to Keep and Bear Arms." *Wisconsin Bar Bulletin* 53(May 1980): 34–36.

1981

I Halbrook, S.A. "Jurisprudence of the Second and Fourteenth Amendments." *George Mason University Law Review* 4(Spring 1981): 1–69.

1982

C Ashman, M.C. "Handgun Control by Local Government." *Northern Kentucky Law Review* 10(1982): 97–112.

C Benedict, M. "Constitutional Law—Second Amendment Right to Bear Arms—Quilici v. Village of Morton Grove." *Akron Law Review* 16(Fall 1982): 293–301.

C Bernardy, P., and M.E. Burns. "Of Lawyers, Guns, and Money: Preemption and Handgun Control." *University of California at Davis Law Review* 16(Fall 1982): 137–66.

I Caplan, D.I. "Right of the Individual to Bear Arms: A Recent Judicial Trend." *Detroit College Law Review* (Winter 1982): 789–823.

I Dowlut, R., and J.A. Knoop. "State Constitutions and the Right to Keep and Bear Arms." *Oklahoma City University Law Review* 7(Summer 1982): 177–241.

C Freibrun, E.S. "Banning Handguns: Quilici v. Village of Morton Grove and the Second Amendment." *Washington University Law Quarterly* 60(Fall 1982): 1087–1118.

I Gardiner, R.E. "To Preserve Liberty—A Look at the Right to Keep and Bear Arms." *Northern Kentucky Law Review* 10(1982): 63–96.

I Gottleib, A.M. "Gun Ownership: A Constitutional Right." *Northern Kentucky Law Review* 10(1982): 138–54.

I Halbrook, S.P. "To Keep and Bear Their Private Arms: The Adoption of the Second Amendment, 1787–1791." *Northern Kentucky Law Review* 10(1982): 13–39.

C   Klunin, K.F. "Gun Control: Is It a Legal and Effective Means of Controlling Firearms in the United States?" *Washburn Law Journal* 21(Winter 1982): 244–65.

C   Pierce, D.R. "Second Amendment Survey." *Northern Kentucky Law Review* 10(1982): 155–62.

1983

C   Barrett, S.R. Jr. "The Right to Bear Arms and Handgun Prohibition: A Fundamental Rights Analysis." *North Carolina Central Law Journal* 14(1983): 296–311.

C   Bass, H.I. "Quilici v. Village of Morton Grove: Ammunition for a National Handgun Ban." *DePaul Law Review* 32(Winter 1983): 371–97.

I   Dowlut, R. "The Right to Arms: Does the Constitution or the Predilection of Judges Reign?" *Oklahoma Law Review* 36(Winter 1983): 65–105.

I   Halbrook, S.A. "Tort Liability for the Manufacture, Sale, and Ownership of Handguns?" *Hamline Law Review* 6(July 1983): 351–82.

I   Kates, D.B. "Handgun Prohibition and the Original Meaning of the Second Amendment." *Michigan Law Review* 82(November 1983): 204–73.

I   Malcolm, J.L. "The Right of the People to Keep and Bear Arms: The Common Law Tradition." *Hastings Constitutional Law Quarterly* 10(Winter 1983): 285–314.

C   Spannaus, W. "State Firearms Regulation and the Second Amendment." *Hamline Law Review* 6(July 1983): 383–90.

1985

I   Halbrook, S.P. "The Right to Bear Arms in the First State Bills of Rights: Pennsylvania, North Carolina, Vermont, and Massachusetts." *Vermont Law Review* 10(Fall 1985): 255–320.

1986

C   Beschle, D.L. "Reconsidering the Second Amendment: Constitutional Protection for a Right of Security." *Hamline Law Review* 9(February 1986): 69–104.

I   Halbrook, S.P. "What the Framers Intended: A Linguistic Analysis of the Right to 'Bear Arms.'" *Law and Contemporary Problems* 49(Winter 1986): 151–62.

I   Hardy, D.T. "Armed Citizens, Citizen Armies: Toward a Jurisprudence of the Second Amendment." *Harvard Journal of Law and Public Policy* 9(Summer 1986): 559–638.

C   Hunt, M.T. "The Individual Right to Bear Arms: An Illusory Public Pacifier?" *Utah Law Review* (1986): 751–79.

I   Kates, D.B. "The Second Amendment: A Dialogue." 49 *Law and Contemporary Problems* 49(Winter 1986): 143–62.

I   Shalhope, R.E. "The Armed Citizen in the Early Republic." *Law and Contemporary Problems* 49(Winter 1986): 125–41.

1987

C   Carlson, P.E. "Quilici and Sklar: Alternative Models for Handgun Control Ordinances." *Washington University Journal of Urban and Contemporary Law* 31(Winter 1987): 341–72.

I   Hardy, D.T. "The Second Amendment and the Historiography of the Bill of Rights." *The Journal of Law and Politics* 4(Summer 1987): 1–62.

I   Lund, N. "The Second Amendment, Political Liberty, and the Right to Self-Preservation." *Alabama Law Review* 39(Fall 1987): 103–30.

1989

C   Brown, W. "Guns, Cowboys, Philadelphia Mayors, and Civic Republicanism: On Sanford Levinson's 'The Embarrassing Second Amendment.'" *The Yale Law Journal* 99(December 1989): 661–67.

C   Callaghan, M.O. "State v. Buckner and the Right to Keep and Bear Arms in West Virginia." *West Virginia Law Review* 91(Winter 1988–89): 425–49.

I   Dowlut, R. "Federal and State Constitutional Guarantees to Arms." *University of Dayton Law Review* 15(Fall 1989): 59–90.

C   Ehrman, K.A., and D.A. Henigan. "The Second Amendment in the Twentieth Century: Have You Seen Your Militia Lately?" *University of Dayton Law Review* 15(Fall 1989): 5–58.

I   Halbrook, S.P. "Encroachments of the Crown on the Liberty of the Subject: Pre-Revolutionary Origins of the Second Amendment." *University of Dayton Law Review* 15(Fall 1989): 91–124.

I   Levinson, S. "The Embarrassing Second Amendment." *The Yale Law Journal* 99(December 1989): 637–59.

C   Udulutch, M. "The Constitutional Implications of Gun Control and Several Realistic Gun Control Proposals." *American Journal of Criminal Law* 17(Fall 1989): 19–54.

1990

I   Bordenet, B.J. "The Right to Possess Arms: The Intent of the Framers of the Second Amendment." *University of West Los Angeles Law Review* 21(1990): 1–30.

I   Moncure, T.M. "Who is the Militia—the Virginia Ratifying Convention and the Right to Bear Arms." *Lincoln Law Review* 19(1990): 1–25.

I   Morgan, E.C. "Assault Rifle Legislation: Unwise and Unconstitutional." *American Journal of Criminal Law* 17(Winter 1990): 143–74.

I   Tahmassebi, S.B. "Gun Control and Racism." *George Mason University Civil Rights Law Journal*, 2(Winter 1990): 67–99.

1991

I   Amar, A.R. "The Bill of Rights as a Constitution." *The Yale Law Journal* 100(March 1991): 1131–1210.

C   Calhoun, C. "Constitutional Law—Eleventh Circuit Interprets Firearms Owners' Protection Act to Prohibit Private Possession of Machine Guns." *Suffolk University Law Review* 25(Fall 1991): 797–804.

I   Cottrol, R.J., and R.T. Diamond. "The Second Amendment: Toward an Afro-Americanist Reconsideration." *The Georgetown Law Journal* 80(December 1991): 309–61.

C   Dobray, D., and A.J. Waldrop. "Regulating Handgun Advertising Directed at Women." *Whittier Law Review* 12(1991): 113–30.

I   Halbrook, S.P. "The Right of the People or the Power of the State: Bearing Arms, Arming Militias, and the Second Amendment." *Valparaiso University Law Review* 26(Fall 1991): 131–207.

C   Henigan, D.A. "Arms, Anarchy and the Second Amendment."
       Valparaiso University Law Review 26(Fall 1991): 107–29.

I   Moncure, T.M. Jr. "The Second Amendment Ain't About
       Hunting." *Howard Law Journal* 34(1991): 589–97.

C   O'Donnell, M.T. "The Second Amendment: A Study of Recent
       Trends." *University of Richmond Law Review* 25(Spring 1991):
       501–18.

C   Scarry, E. "War and the Social Contract: Nuclear Policy,
       Distribution, and the Right to Bear Arms." *University of Penn-
       sylvania Law Review* 139(May 1991): 1257–1316.

C   Williams, D.C. "Civic Republicanism and the Citizen Militia:
       The Terrifying Second Amendment." *The Yale Law Journal*
       101(December 1991): 551–615.

1992

I   Amar, A.R. "The Bill of Rights and the Fourteenth Amend-
       ment." *Yale Law Journal* 101(April 1992): 1193–1284.

I   Johnson, N.J. "Beyond the Second Amendment: An Individual
       Right to Arms Viewed Through the Ninth Amendment."
       Rutgers Law Journal 24(Fall 1992): 1–81.

I   Kates, D.B. "The Second Amendment and the Ideology of
       Self-Protection." *Constitutional Commentary* 9(Winter 1992):
       87–104.

C   O'Hare, R.A. Jr., and J. Pedreira. "An Uncertain Right: The
       Second Amendment and the Assault Weapon Legislation Con-
       troversy." *St. John's Law Review* 66(Winter 1992): 179–206.

I   Wagner, J.R. "Gun Control Legislation and the Intent of the
       Second Amendment: To What Extent Is There An Individual
       Right to Keep and Bear Arms?" *Villanova Law Review*
       37(1992): 1407–59.

1993

C   Blodgett-Ford, S. "Do Battered Women Have a Right to Bear
       Arms?" *Yale Law and Policy Review* 11(1993): 509–60.

C   Bogus, C.T. "Race, Riots, and Guns." *Southern California
       Law Review* 66 (May 1993): 1365–88.

I   Halbrook, S.A. "Rationing Firearms Purchases and the Right
       to Keep Arms: Reflections on the Bills of Rights of Virginia,

West Virginia, and the United States." *West Virginia Law Review* 96(Fall 1993): 1–83.

I   Martire, P.V. "In Defense of the Second Amendment: Constitutional & Historical Perspectives." *Lincoln Law Review* 21(1993): 23–37.

I   Quinlan, M.J. "Is There a Neutral Justification for Refusing to Implement the Second Amendment or Is the Supreme Court Just 'Gun Shy'?" *Capital University Law Review* 22(Summer 1993): 641–92.

1994

C   Fox, K.A., and N.C. Shah. "Natural Born Killers: The Assault Weapon Ban of the Crime Bill—Legitimate Exercise of Congressional Authority to Control Violent Crime or Infringement of a Constitutional Guarantee?" *St. John's Journal of Legal Commentary* 10(Fall 1994): 123–50.

I   Kates, D.B. "Gun Control: Separating Reality From Symbolism." *Journal of Contemporary Law* 20(1994): 353–79.

I   Reynolds, G.H. "The Right to Keep and Bear Arms Under the Tennessee Constitution: A Case Study in Civic Republican Thought." *Tennessee Law Review* 61(Winter 1994): 647–73.

I   Van Alstyne, W. "The Second Amendment and the Personal Right to Arms." *Duke Law Journal* 43(April 1994): 1236–55.

I   Vandercoy, D.E. "The History of the Second Amendment." *Valparaiso University Law Review* 28(Spring 1994): 1007–39.

C   Walsh, T.J. "The Limits and Possibilities of Gun Control." *Capital University Law Review* 23(1994): 639–66.

1995

C   Aborn, R.M. "The Battle Over the Brady Bill and the Future of Gun Control Advocacy." *Fordham Urban Law Journal* 22(Winter 1995): 417–39.

C   Ballinger, J. "Torts: Torts and Gun Control: Sealing Up the Cracks and Helping Licensed Dealers Avoid Sales to Unqualified Buyers." *Oklahoma Law Review* 48 (Fall 1995): 593–625.

C   Blodgett-Ford, S. "The Changing Meaning of the Right to Bear Arms." *Seton Hall Constitutional Law Journal* 6(Fall 1995): 101–88.

I   Capezza, M. "Controlling Guns: A Call for Consistency in Judicial Review of Challenges to Gun Control Legislation." *Seton Hall Law Review* 25 (1995): 1467–95.

I   Cottrol, R.J., and R.T. Diamond. " 'Never Intended to be Applied to the White Population': Firearms Regulation and Racial Disparity—The Redeemed South's Legacy to a National Jurisprudence?" *Chicago-Kent Law Review* 70(1995): 1307–35.

I   Denning, B.P. "Can the Simple Cite Be Trusted?: Lower Court Interpretations of United States v. Miller and the Second Amendment." *Cumberland Law Review* 26(1995–96): 961–1004.

I   Dennis, A.J. "Clearing the Smoke From the Right to Bear Arms and the Second Amendment." *Akron Law Review* 29(Summer 1995): 57–92.

I   Dennis, W.G. "A Right to Keep and Bear Arms? The State of the Debate." *Washington State Bar News* 49(July 1995): 47–54.

C   Dougherty, C. "The Minutemen, The National Guard, and the Private Militia Movement: Will the Real Militia Please Stand Up?" *John Marshall Law Review* 28(Summer 1995): 959–85.

C   Dunlap, C.J. Jr. "Revolt of the Masses: Armed Civilians and the Insurrectionary Theory of the Second Amendment." *Tennessee Law Review* 62(Spring 1995): 643–77.

I   Funk, T.M. "Gun Control and Economic Discrimination: The Melting-Point Case-in-Point." *The Journal of Criminal Law and Criminology* 85(Winter 1995): 764–806.

I   Garcia, M.I. "The 'Assault Weapons' Ban, the Second Amendment, and the Security of a Free State." *Regent University Law Review* 6(Fall 1995): 261–98.

I   Halbrook, S.P. "Congress Interprets the Second Amendment: Declarations By a Co-Equal Branch on the Individual Right to Keep and Bear Arms." *Tennessee Law Review* 62(Spring 1995): 597–641.

I   Halbrook, S.P. "Personal Security, Personal Liberty, and 'the Constitutional Right to Bear Arms': Visions of the Framers for the Fourteenth Amendment." *Seton Hall Constitutional Law Journal* 5(Spring 1995): 341–434.

I   Halbrook, S.P. "Second-Class Citizenship and the Second Amendment in the District of Columbia." *George Mason University Civil Rights Law Journal* 5(Summer 1995): 105–78.

C   Herz, A.D. "Gun Crazy: Constitutional False Consciousness and Dereliction of Dialogic Responsibility. *Boston University Law Review* 75(January 1995): 57–153.

I   Johnson, N.J. "Shots Across No Man's Land: A Response to Handgun Control, Inc.'s, Richard Aborn." *Fordham Urban Law Journal* 22(Winter 1995): 441–51.

I   Kopel, D.B., and R. E. Gardner. "The Sullivan Principles: Protecting the Second Amendment from Civil Abuse." *Seton Hall Legislative Journal* 19 (1995): 737–75.

C   Littman, R.J. "Gun-Free Schools: Constitutional Powers, Limitations, and Social Policy Concerns Surrounding Federal Regulation of Firearms in Schools." *Seton Hall Constitutional Law Journal* 5(Spring 1995): 723–70.

I   Reynolds, G.H. "A Critical Guide to the Second Amendment." *Tennessee Law Review* 62(Spring 1995): 461–512.

I   Reynolds, G.H., and D.B. Kates. "The Second Amendment and States' Rights: A Thought Experiment." *William and Mary Law Review* 36(August 1995): 1737–68.

C   Romano, T.E. "Firing Back: Legislative Attempts to Combat Assault Weapons." *Seton Hall Legislative Journal* 19(1995): 857–93.

I   Shelton, G.L. "In Search of the Lost Amendment: Challenging Federal Firearms Regulation Through the 'State's Right' Interpretation of the Second Amendment." *Florida State University Law Review* 23(Summer 1995): 105–39.

C   Tobia, J.S. "The Brady Handgun Violence Prevention Act: Does It Have a Shot At Success?" *Seton Hall Legislative Journal* 19(1995): 894–920.

1996

I   Barnett, R.E., and D.B. Kates. "Under Fire: The New Consensus on the Second Amendment." *Emory Law Journal* 45(Fall 1996): 1139–1259.

I   Bursor, S. "Toward a Functional Framework for Interpreting the Second Amendment." *Texas Law Review* 74(April 1996): 1125–51.

I   Denning, B.P. "Palladium of Liberty? Causes and Consequences of the Federalization of State Militias in the Twentieth Century." *Oklahoma City University Law Review* 21(Summer/Fall, 1996): 191–245.

I   Denning, B.P., and G.H. Reynolds. "It Takes a Militia: A Communitarian Case for Compulsory Arms Bearing." *William and Mary Bill of Rights Journal* 5(Winter 1996): 185–214.

I   Docal, R. "The Second, Fifth, and Ninth Amendments—The Precarious Protectors of the American Gun Collector." *Florida State University Law Review* 23(Spring 1996): 1101–43.

I   Larish, I.A. "Why Annie Can't Get Her Gun: A Feminist Perspective on the Second Amendment." *University of Illinois Law Review* (1996): 467–508.

I   Larizza, R.J. "Paranoia, Patriotism, and the Citizen Militia Movement: Constitutional Right or Criminal Conduct?" *Mercer Law Review* 47(Winter 1996): 581–636.

I   Lund, N. "The Past and Future of the Individual's Right to Arms." *Georgia Law Review.* 31(Fall 1996): 1–76.

C   Polesky, J.E. "The Rise of Private Militia: A First and Second Amendment Analysis of the Right to Organize and the Right to Train." *University of Pennsylvania Law Review* 144(April 1996): 1593–1642.

I   Szczepanski, K.D. "Searching for the Plain Meaning of the Second Amendment." *Buffalo Law Review* 44(Winter 1996): 197–247.

1997

C   Dowd, D.W. "The Relevance of the Second Amendment to Gun Control Legislation." *Montana Law Review* 58(Winter 1997): 79–114.

C   Harman, R. "The People's Right to Bear Arms—What the Second Amendment Protects: An Analysis of the Current Debate Regarding What the Second Amendment Really Protects." *Whittier Law Review* 18(Winter 1997): 411–44.

I   McAfee, T.B. "Constitutional Limits on Regulating Private Militia Groups," *Montana Law Review* 58 (Winter 1997): 45–78.

I   Powe, L.A. Jr. "Guns, Words, and Constitutional Interpretation." *William and Mary Law Review* 38(May 1997): 1311–1403.

Notes

1. "The Great Voyage: Two Hundred Years of the Constitution," *The New York Times Magazine*, 13 September 1987.

2. Louis Fisher, *Constitutional Dialogues* (Princeton, N.J.: Princeton University Press, 1988), p. 3.

3. Louis Fisher and Neal Devins, *Political Dynamics of Constitutional Law* (St. Paul, Minn.: West, 1996), p. 1.

4. Corwin actually received his doctoral degree in history from the University of Pennsylvania in 1905, but this came at a time when political science was not yet a fully formed discipline. As a faculty member at Princeton, Corwin was a founding member of the Politics Department, of which he was the first chair, and where he was later named the McCormick Professor of Jurisprudence. Political science can thus rightly claim Corwin for itself. See Glenn H. Utter and Charles Lockhart, eds., *American Political Scientists* (Westport, Conn.: Greenwood Press, 1993), p. 52.

5. Quoted in Richard Loss, ed., *Presidential Power and the Constitution* (Ithaca, N.Y.: Cornell University Press, 1976), p. ix.

6. Edward S. Corwin, *The President: Office and Powers* (New York: New York University Press, 1957), p. vii.

7. Corwin, *The President*, p. vii.

8. See his first book, *President and Congress* (New York: Free Press, 1972), in which Fisher examined the two branches of government pertaining to legislative power, spending power, taxation, and war power. At a time when most political science was obsessed with political dynamics behind formal power (following, most importantly, Richard Neustadt's

paradigm from *Presidential Power*), here was Fisher urging his readers to return to the Constitution, the Federalist Papers, and the legal-structural arrangements that gave rise to these institutions and modern policy disputes.

9. Stephen J. Wayne, "Approaches," in *Studying the Presidency*, ed. by George C. Edwards III and Stephen J. Wayne (Knoxville, Tenn.: University of Tennessee Press, 1983), pp. 25–26. While I would concede that political science has focused more aggressively on institutions since 1983, the point of this chapter is precisely that it continues to lag far behind in areas that continue to be dominated by the legal community.

10. The unilateral item veto idea won wide attention after the publication of an article in the *Wall Street Journal* in 1987 (Steven Glazier, "Reagan Already Has Line-Item Veto," December 4, 1987), but it was met with skepticism by the Reagan administration. See David Rapp, "Does Reagan Already Have a Line-Item Veto?" *CQ Weekly Report*, May 14, 1988, pp. 1284–85. In a fifty-four-page memorandum prepared by Charles Cooper, head of Reagan's Office of Legal Counsel, the inherent item veto argument was rejected. See "Memorandum for the Attorney General Re: The President's Veto Power," U.S. Department of Justice, Office of Legal Counsel, July 8, 1988. Past presidents have at times exercised considerable creativity, as when President Andrew Jackson signed a bill in 1830, but at the same time sent a message to Congress (after the House had recessed) that restricted the scope of the bill. President Tyler did something similar. See Louis Fisher, *Constitutional Conflicts Between Congress and the President* (Lawrence, Kans.: University Press of Kansas, 1997), pp. 132–33. President Bill Clinton won a qualified item veto power—really enhanced rescission—by congressional enactment in 1996. He exercised the power in 1997, which was then declared unconstitutional in 1998. See Robert J. Spitzer, "The Item Veto Dispute and the Secular Crisis of the Presidency," *Presidential Studies Quarterly* (Fall 1998).

11. See Robert J. Spitzer, "The Constitutionality of the Presidential Line-Item Veto," *Political Science Quarterly* 112(Summer 1997): 261–84.

12. Richard A. Givens, "The Validity of a Separate Veto of Nongermane Riders to Legislation," *Temple Law Quarterly* 39(Fall, 1965): 60–64. See rejoinder to Givens by Richard A. Riggs, "Separation of Powers: Congressional Riders and the Veto Power," *University of Michigan Journal of Law Reform* 6(Spring, 1973): 735–59.

13. William A. Clineburg, "The Presidential Veto Power," *South Carolina Law Review* 18(1966): 753.

14. Thomas Stefan Schroeder, "Original Understanding and Veto Power," *Journal of Law and Politics* 7(Summer 1991): 760.

15. Riggs, "Separation of Powers," p. 738.

16. Clineburg, "The Presidential Veto Power," pp. 752–53.

17. Stephen Glazier, "The Line-Item Veto," in *Pork Barrels and Principles* (Washington, D.C.: National Legal Center for the Public Interest, 1988), p. 10.

18. Anthony Haswell, "Partial Veto Power—Does the President Have It Now?" *Federal Bar News and Journal* 36(March/April, 1989): 142, 144.

19. Gordon Crovitz, "The Line-Item Veto," *Pepperdine Law Review* 18(1990): 43.

20. J. Gregory Sidak and Thomas A. Smith, "Four Faces of the Item Veto," *Northwestern University Law Review* 84(Winter 1990): 467.

21. Diane-Michele Krasnow, "The Imbalance of Power and the Presidential Veto," *Harvard Journal of Law and Public Policy* 14(Spring 1991): 584, 601.

22. Schroeder, "Original Understanding and Veto Power," pp. 759, 784–85.

23. Ronald D. Rotunda and James E. Nowak, *Treatise on Constitutional Law*, 4 vols. (St. Paul, Minn.: West, 1992): I, 757.

24. Judith A. Best also makes this argument. See "The Item Veto: Would the Founders Approve?" *Presidential Studies Quarterly* 14(Spring, 1984): 183–88.

25. Thomas Pitt Taswell-Langmead, *English Constitutional History* (Boston: Houghton-Mifflin, 1946), pp. 613–14.

26. Paul R.Q. Wolfson, "Is a Presidential Item Veto Constitutional?" *Yale Law Journal* 96(March, 1987): 841.

27. Indeed, one convention delegate, John Rutledge, complained that the convention relied too much on British law and practice, exhibiting "a blind adherence to the British model." See Max Farrand, *The Records of the Federal Convention*, 4 vols. (New Haven, Conn.: Yale University Press, 1966) II, p. 279.

28. Paul R.Q. Wolfson, "Is a Presidential Item Veto Constitutional?" *Yale Law Journal* 96(March 1987): 843. Frank W. Prescott and Joseph F. Zimmerman note that New York's colonial governor was forbidden by royal instruction from approving acts that included riders on appropriations bills. See *The Politics of the Veto of Legislation in New York State*, 2 vols. (Washington, D.C.: University Press of America, 1980), I, 2.

29. Farrand, *The Records of the Federal Convention of 1787*, I, p. 233.

30. Farrand, *The Records of the Federal Convention*, II, p. 273. Much of the subsequent discussion on that August day dealt with the extent to

which the founders should or should not follow the British example. That discussion alone makes clear that the founders well understood the British system. In comments offered the same day, James Wilson expressed a similar concern that "The House of Reps. will insert the other things in money bills, and by making them conditions of each other, destroy the deliberate liberty of the Senate." (II, p. 275)

31. Clineburg, "The Presidential Veto Power," p. 753; Russell M. Ross and Fred Schwengel, "An Item Veto for the President?" *Presidential Studies Quarterly* 12(Winter, 1982): 67–68; Krasnow, "The Imbalance of Power and the Presidential Veto," p. 601.

32. Haswell, "Partial Veto Power," p. 142.

33. Anthony Gressman, "Observation: Is the Item Veto Constitutional?" *North Carolina Law Review* 64(April, 1986): 819. According to Henry C. Black, a bill in legislation is "The draft of a proposed law from the time of its introduction in a legislative house through all the various stages in both houses. . . . The form of a proposed law before it is enacted into law by a vote of the legislative body." *Black's Law Dictionary* (St. Paul, Minn.: West, 1983), p. 87. Rappaport's examination of the meaning of bill in the eighteenth century in both Britain and America supports the conclusion that even then bill meant "a draft of a law containing whatever provisions the author deemed desirable." Michael B. Rappaport, "The President's Veto and the Constitution," *Northwestern University Law Review* 87(Spring, 1993): 762.

34. Louis Fisher, "The Item Veto—a Misconception," *Washington Post*, February 23, 1987; Fisher, "The Presidential Veto," in *Pork Barrels and Principles*, p. 22.

35. Max Farrand, *The Framing of the Constitution of the United States* (New Haven, Conn.: Yale University Press, 1913), p. 179.

36. Glazier, "The Line-Item Veto," p. 11.

37. Crovitz, "The Line-Item Veto," pp. 45–46.

38. Robert J. Spitzer, "Presentation Clause," *Encyclopedia of the American Presidency*, 4 vols. (New York: Simon & Schuster, 1994), III, p. 1193.

39. Farrand, *The Records of the Federal Convention of 1787*, II, p. 301.

40. Farrand, *The Records of the Federal Convention of 1787*, II, p. 304. This is logical because the second paragraph of Section 7 begins "Every bill . . . shall, before it becomes a Law, be presented to the President. . . ." The next paragraph in the section begins with the "Every order" language to resolve the bill ambiguity problem. Madison had offered a hurried motion late in the day on August 15 to resolve the problem, but the impromptu attempt engendered confusion and was defeated. Early the next day, prob-

ably after consulting with Madison the previous night, Randolph offered the language that was included in the Constitution. As Randolph stated, the reference to orders, resolutions, and votes, applied not just to bills to be vetoed, but to all legislation presented to the president for final review (as indeed the clause reads).

41. Helen E. Veit, Kenneth R. Bowling, and Charlene Bangs Bickford, eds., *Creating the Bill of Rights* (Baltimore, Md.: Johns Hopkins University Press, 1991), pp. 182–84, 198–99. See also Robert J. Spitzer, "Door No. 1: Muskets? Or Door No. 2: Free Speech?" *The Christian Science Monitor*, 19 September 1997.

42. See *U.S. v Cruikshank*, 92 US 542 (1876); *Presser v Illinois*, 116 US 252 (1886); *Miller v Texas*, 153 US 535 (1894); and *US v Miller*, 307 US 174 (1939). The court acknowledged this line of cases in *Lewis v US*, 445 US 95 (1980).

43. These arguments are discussed in great detail in Robert J. Spitzer, *The Politics of Gun Control* (New York: Chatham House, 1998), Chap. 2. Personal self-defense is covered in common law and criminal law.

44. Some of these minority authors even admit that their views are not in line with most analyses. See for example Don B. Kates, "Handgun Prohibition and the Original Meaning of the Second Amendment," *Michigan Law Review* 82(November 1983): 206.

45. The NRA reprints and distributes copies of law journal articles that support a so-called individual rights interpretation of the Second Amendment.

46. These articles were culled from the *Index to Legal Periodicals* from its beginning in 1887 through the November 1997 issue in the *Index* under the subject headings "weapons" and "right to bear arms." This latter heading only appeared starting in Volume 31, 1991. No articles on the Second Amendment were referenced from 1887 through 1911. All articles cited in the Appendix to this chapter were first found in the *Index* and then personally examined by the author. Book reviews were omitted, and articles that either mentioned the Second Amendment only in passing, or that discussed the Second Amendment but took no position its meaning, were also omitted. I here express my gratitude to the Cornell University Law Library for the use of its facilities.

47. R.E. Barnett and D.B. Kates, "Under Fire: The New Consensus on the Second Amendment," *Emory Law Journal* 45(Fall 1996): 1141; R.G. Cottrol and R.T. Diamond, "The Second Amendment: Toward an Afro-Americanist Reconsideration," *The Georgetown Law Journal* 80(December 1991): 311; N.J. Johnson, "Beyond the Second Amendment: An Individual Right to Arms Viewed Through the Ninth Amendment," *Rutgers Law Journal* 24(Fall 1992): 72; Sanford Levinson, "The Embarrassing Second

Amendment," *Yale Law Journal* 99(December 1989): 658; N. Lund, "The Second Amendment, Political Liberty, and the Right to Self-Preservation," *Alabama Law Review* 39(Fall 1987): 226; G.H. Reynolds, "The Right to Keep and Bear Arms Under the Tennessee Constitution," *Tennessee Law Review* 61(Winter 1994): 647; G.L. Shelton, "In Search of the Lost Amendment," *Florida State University Law Review* 23(Summer 1995): 108–10.

48. R.E. Barnett and D.B. Kates, "Under Fire: The New Consensus on the Second Amendment," *Emory Law Journal* 45(Fall 1996): 1141; S. Bursor, "Toward a Functional Framework for Interpreting the Second Amendment," *Texas Law Review* 74(April 1996): 1126; D.B. Kates, "The Second Amendment and the Ideology of Self-Protection," *Constitutional Commentary* 9(Winter 1992): 361.

49. Rosa Ehrenreich, "Look Who's Editing," *Lingua Franca* (January/February 1996), 60.

50. For more on these questions, see Spitzer, *The Politics of Gun Control*.

51. For example, Stuart R. Hays, "The Right to Bear Arms, A Study in Judicial Misinterpretation," *William and Mary Law Review* 2(1960): 381–406; David I. Caplan, "The Right of the Individual to Bear Arms," *Detroit College of Law Review* 4(Winter 1982): 789–823; Robert E. Shalhope, "The Ideological Origins of the Second Amendment," *Journal of American History* 51(December 1982): 599–614; Robert J. Cottrol, "The Second Amendment: Invitation to a Multi-Dimensional Debate," in *Gun Control and the Constitution*, 3 vols. (New York: Garland, 1993), I, pp. ix–xi; Stephen Halbrook, *That Every Man Be Armed* (Oakland, Calif.: Independent Institute, 1984). An indication of the weakness of this argument is seen in an effort in 1989 to codify the "individualist" interpretation of the Second Amendment in a concurrent resolution introduced in the House of Representatives by Rep. Philip Crane (R-IL). It read in part: "Whereas the Framers of the second amendment to the Constitution and those who ratified the second amendment intended that the individual retain the right to keep and bear arms in order to protect life, liberty, and property and to protect our Nation from those who would attempt to destroy our freedom: Now, therefore, be it Resolved . . . That it is the sense of the Congress that the Constitution provides that all individual citizens have the right to keep and bear arms, which right supersedes the power and authority of any government." No such resolution would be necessary if the verdict of history, law, and the courts supported this proposition to begin with. See Subcommittee on Crime, Judiciary Committee, House of Representatives, "Semiautomatic Assault Weapons Act of 1989," 101st Cong., 1st sess., hearings April 5 and 6, 1989 (Washington, D.C.: Government Printing Office, 1989), pp. 53–54.

52. To pick an example, Stephen P. Halbrook quotes Patrick Henry's words during the Virginia ratifying convention as saying, "The great object

is, that every man be armed. . . . Every one who is able may have a gun."
("To Keep and Bear Their Private Arms," *Northern Kentucky Law Review*
10[1982]: 25) This quote would seem to support the view that at least some
early leaders advocated general popular armament aside from militia
purposes. Yet here is the full quote from the original debates: "May we not
discipline and arm them [the states], as well as Congress, if the power be
concurrent? so that our militia shall have two sets of arms, double sets of
regimentals, &c.; and thus, at a very great cost, we shall be doubly armed.
The great object is, that every man be armed. But can the people afford to
pay for double sets of arms, &c.? *Every one who is able may have a gun.*
But we have learned, by experience, that, necessary as it is to have arms,
and though our Assembly has, by a succession of laws for many years,
endeavored to have the militia completely armed, it is still far from being
the case." (emphasis added) It is perfectly obvious that Henry's comments
are in the context of a discussion of the militia, and the power balance
between the states and Congress. This quote is from Jonathan Elliot,
*Debates in the Several State Conventions on the Adoption of the Federal
Constitution*, 4 vols. (Washington, D.C.: Clerk's Office of the District Court,
1836), III, p. 386. Similar analytic problems can be found in Kates, "Handgun Prohibition and the Original Meaning of the Second Amendment," pp.
204–273. Many other such examples as this can be found; space limits
constrain the presentation of additional illustrations.

53. See 10 USC 311 (1983). Current code lists the lower age as 17; in
colonial times, the age range was of necessity wider.

54. This also puts to rest the assertion of some that the phrase "the
people" in the Second Amendment somehow means all of the people, as is
the case when the phrase appears in other parts of the Bill of Rights.
Obviously, the Second Amendment is talking about only those people who
could serve in a militia, as the Supreme Court made clear in *Presser*. This
argument is raised in Cottrol, "The Second Amendment," pp. xxxi–xxxii;
and Robert Dowlut, "The Right to Bear Arms," *Oklahoma Law Review*
36(Winter 1983): 93–94. In *Fresno Rifle & Pistol Club v Van De Kamp*, the
court of appeals rejected the idea that the phrase "the people" had the
same, uniform meaning throughout the Bill of Rights (965 F.2d 723; 9th
Cir. 1992); No. 91-15466, at 5938–39.

Some law journal articles have asserted that a 1990 Supreme Court
case, *U.S. v Verdugo-Urquidez* (494 US 259), ruled that the phrase "the
people" in the Second Amendment meant all citizens. See for example
William Van Alstyne, "The Second Amendment and the Personal Right to
Bear Arms," *Duke Law Journal* 43(April 1994): 1243, n.19; Shelton, "In
Search of the Lost Amendment." Such interpretations are false, as the
Verdugo-Urquidez case has nothing to do with interpreting the Second
Amendment. In fact, the case deals with the Fourth Amendment issue of
whether an illegal alien from Mexico was entitled to constitutional protec-
tion regarding searches. In the majority decision, Chief Justice Rehnquist

discussed the meaning of the phrase "the people," given that the phrase appears not only in several parts of the Bill of Rights, but also in the Constitution's preamble, in order to determine its applicability to a noncitizen. Rehnquist speculated that the phrase "seems to have been a term of art" probably pertaining to people who have developed a connection with the national community. Rehnquist's speculations about whether the meaning of "the people" could be extended to a noncitizen and his two passing mentions of the Second Amendment in that discussion, shed no light, much less legal meaning, on this amendment.

55. Stephen P. Halbrook, for example, claims that the *Presser* case "plainly suggests that the second amendment applies to the States through the fourteenth amendment" when in fact the court said precisely the opposite. "To Keep and Bear Their Private Arms," *Northern Kentucky Law Review* 10,1(1982): 85. Sanford Levinson asks why the *Cruikshank* and *Presser* cases should be considered as legal precedent, since they occurred before the Supreme Court began the incorporation process in 1897. The obvious answer is because the courts have chosen not to incorporate the Second Amendment and still consider the two cases binding precedent. "The Embarrassing Second Amendment," 653. Robert J. Cottrol mentions but fails to acknowledge the significance of the incorporation principle in his discussion. "The Second Amendment," p. xxiii–xxiv. Some argue that the Fourteenth Amendment should be used to incorporate the Bill of Rights in totality, even though the courts have refused to do so. See for example Akhil Reed Amar, "The Bill of Rights and the Fourteenth Amendment," *Yale Law Journal* 101(April 1992): 1193–1284.

56. For example, David C. Williams extols "the corruption-battling functions" of militia service and the bearing of arms, arguing that such service "trained one in a life of virtue, both self-sacrificing and independent." Yet this characterization bears no relationship to the actual behavior of militias during the Revolution or after. "Civic Republicanism and the Citizen Militia: The Terrifying Second Amendment," *Yale Law Journal* 101(1991): 556, 579–81.

57. Cottrol, "The Second Amendment," p. xxxv; Lund, "The Second Amendment, Political Liberty, and the Right to Self-Preservation," 103–111; Kates, "The Second Amendment and the Ideology of Self-Protection," 87–104.

58. Judith V. Best, *The Case Against Direct Election of the President* (Ithaca, N.Y.: Cornell University Press, 1975).

59. Cottrol, for example, says that the Supreme Court has shown "reluctance" to examine Second Amendment questions. ("The Second Amendment Debate," p. xxxii.) Levinson says analysts "marginalize" the amendment. ("The Embarrassing Second Amendment," p. 640.) Lund says that the Supreme Court has "ignored" the Second Amendment, and that the

courts are "uncomfortable" with it. ("The Second Amendment, Political Liberty, and the Right to Self-Preservation," p. 103.)

60. See for example David I. Caplan, "Restoring the Balance: The Second Amendment Revisited," *Fordham Urban Law Journal* 5(Fall 1976): 52; Dowlut, "The Right to Arms," p. 67; Kates, "The Second Amendment and the Ideology of Self-Protection,"; and Lund, "The Second Amendment, Political Liberty, and the Right to Self-Preservation," pp. 118, 130.

61. See Joel Samaha, *Criminal Law* (Minneapolis, Minn.: West, 1993), Chap. 6.

62. Robert E. Shalhope says the Second Amendment protects weapons possession for Americans in part "for the purpose of keeping their rulers sensitive to the rights of the people." Would this make, say, Lee Harvey Oswald, John Wilkes Booth, David Koresh, and Timothy McVeigh true democrats? "The Ideological Origins of the Second Amendment," *Journal of American History* 69(December 1982): 614. See also Halbrook, *That Every Man Be Armed*, pp. 68, 194–195; Lund, "The Second Amendment, Political Liberty, and the Right to Self-Preservation," pp. 111–116; Reynolds, "The Right to Keep and Bear Arms Under the Tennessee Constitution," 647–73; and Van Alstyne, "The Second Amendment and the Personal Right to Arms," 1243.

63. Quoted in Keith Ehrman and Dennis Henigan, "The Second Amendment in the Twentieth Century," *University of Dayton Law Review* 54(1989): 54, n. 354. See also Wendy Brown, "Guns, Cowboys, Philadelphia Mayors, and Civic Republicanism: On Sanford Levinson's 'The Embarrassing Second Amendment,'" *Yale Law Journal* 99(December 1989): 661–667.

64. Stuart R. Hays goes so far as to cite with approval the Civil War as an instance of "the right to revolt when the laws of the government began to oppress. . . ." Whatever one thinks of that conflict, the effort of southern states to break away from the Union was not within the bounds of the Constitution, but was rather a threat to the Union's continued existence. "The Right to Bear Arms," p. 382.

65. See for example Cottrol and Diamond, "The Second Amendment: Toward an Afro-Americanist Reconsideration," 309–361; and Stefan B. Tahmassebi, "Gun Control and Racism," *George Mason University Civil Rights Law Review* 1(Winter 1990): 67–99. Blacks were undeniably deprived of the fundamental right of self-protection, pertaining to but not limited to, weapons possession. Yet extension of weapons ownership to a subdominant group in society at a time when the group was deprived of most other basic freedoms and protections would in all likelihood be a formula for racial annihilation, as was the case with Native Americans. A discussion of women and the Second Amendment can be found in Jeffrey R. Stone, Richard A. Epstein, and Cass R. Sunstein, eds., *The Bill of Rights in the Modern State* (Chicago: University of Chicago Press, 1992).

66. Cottrol and Diamond, "The Second Amendment," p. 335.

67. Subcommittee on the Constitution, Judiciary Committee, Senate, "The Right to Keep and Bear Arms," 97th Cong., 2nd sess. (Washington, D.C.: Government Printing Office, February 1982), p. 14.

68. 60 US (19 How.) 393 (1857), at 417.

69. Subcommittee on the Constitution, "The Right to Keep and Bear Arms," p. 14.

70. In the *Lewis* case, the Senate report took Justice Blackmun's affirmation of *U.S. v. Miller* only to mean that convicted felons may be deprived of rights, when in fact Blackmun was affirming the militia-based understanding of the Second Amendment as it was laid out in *Miller*. Here is how the Senate report discussed *Lewis*: "a footnote in *Lewis v. United States*, indicated only that 'these legislative restrictions on the use of firearms'—a ban on possession by felons—were permissible. But since felons may constitutionally be deprived of many of the rights of citizens, including that of voting, this dicta reveals little." Subcommittee on the Constitution, "The Right to Keep and Bear Arms," p. 14. Here's the full quote from *Lewis*: "These legislative restrictions on the use of firearms are neither based upon constitutionally suspect criteria, nor do they trench upon any constitutionally protected liberties. See *United States v. Miller* . . . (the Second Amendment guarantees no right to keep and bear a firearm that does not have 'some reasonable relationship to the preservation or efficiency of a well regulated militia')." 445 US 90 (1980). Contrary to the Supreme Court's own rulings, the report also argues that *Cruikshank* has been rendered irrelevant because it occurred before the court began the incorporation process (p. 10).
To cite another example of bad analysis, Robert E. Shalhope says that of the four key Supreme Court cases, only *U.S. v. Miller* "relate[s] gun ownership to the militia." "The Ideological Origins of the Second Amendment," p. 600, n. 4. This is manifestly untrue, as *Presser* gives this extended attention, and *Cruikshank* makes reference to "internal police," a synonym for the militia (92 US 542, at 553). See Spitzer, *The Politics of Gun Control*, pp. 38–40.

71. Haswell, "Partial Veto Power," p. 145.

72. Sidak and Smith, "Four Faces of the Item Veto," p. 439.

73. During the Senate Judiciary Committee hearings on S. Res. 195 on June 15, 1994, Sen. Specter repeatedly asked those testifying against the inherent item veto if they could at least agree that "reasonable people may differ" on the question, perhaps as a way of constructing some kind of consensus to justify support for the proposal.

74. Levinson, "The Embarrassing Second Amendment," p. 642.

75. Ibid., pp. 650–51.

76. Karen Mathews, "The Terrorist Next Door," *New York Times*, 1 June 1997.

77. The exception is the *Pork Barrels and Principles* monograph, which is simply the published proceedings of a symposium sponsored by the National Tax Limitation Foundation and Citizens for America.

78. This complaint is often and increasingly heard about law reviews. See for example Christopher Shea, "Students v. Professors," *The Chronicle of Higher Education*, 2 June 1995, pp. A33–34.

79. Ibid., p. A34.

80. See for example, "Special Issue," *Akron Law Review* 30(Winter 1996); "Special Issue: Law Review Conference," *Stanford Law Review* 47(1995); "Symposium on Law Review Editing: The Struggle Between Author and Editor Over Control of the Text," *Chicago-Kent Law Review* 61(1994). The many criticisms leveled by legal scholars in these symposia and elsewhere do not include one raised here—that defective publishing practices may produce policy recommendations that encourage wayward public policy.

9

Commentary

Louis Fisher

When I learned that the annual American Political Science Association (APSA) meeting would have a panel dedicated to my writings, I had three thoughts. The first: undeniable evidence of aging. Second: for a person so honored, should I be deceased or at least retired? I satisfied neither qualification. Third: what could I possibly say in response to the authors of these papers?

I know the writers very well. Some I met when they were young scholars, just beginning to make a name for themselves. It has been a pleasure to see them contribute so much since that time. The other participants are closer to my age. They were established scholars when I first met them and continue to publish widely and perceptively on important issues. All of the contributors to this volume write with energy, thoughtfulness, and clarity.

The authors analyze *what* I have written. Their articles prompted me to wonder *why* I wrote what I did. What motivations and values pushed me? Do some common themes tie my articles and books together? How did one work lead to the next?

I'll admit to being somewhat suspicious, if not superstitious, about any effort to plumb motivations, or even results. I always felt that if I really learned what made me tick I'd stop ticking. I might interrupt or disrupt whatever caused me to do what I do. Much of my research and writing seems like second nature. A few years ago someone asked me why I was able to write so much. Was there any secret I could impart? I thought for a moment and replied: "I can't not write." If I looked at myself in the morning and said: "Lou, that's it. No more writing," it wouldn't change a thing. The writing factory seems to operate on its own.

Juggling Words and Sentences

I've wondered if a stuttering phase I went through as a child made me preoccupied with words and sentence structures. To have half a chance of speaking, a stutterer must form a sentence in advance, keeping troublesome sounds away from the front. After that sentence is launched, other thoughts are drafted, always ready to make last-second substitutions, switch clauses, and yank words that are too risky. Even in the 1940s I was doing wordprocessing. Block and move. Block and move. A strange way of talking and thinking. Even after the problem disappeared in my early teens, I still found myself tossing thoughts around, creating sentences in my head before I spoke, and finding pleasure in the vitality of words and sentences.

My fascination with words led to a lifelong interest in the origins of words and phrases. Although I never developed much fluency in other languages, I have spent a lot of time studying Arabic, French, German, Greek, Hebrew, Italian, Latin, Spanish, and Yiddish. I love to see connections, similarities, and borrowings.

What about the content of my writings? Why did I pick certain subjects? Unlike Bill Clinton and others who seem to know in childhood or adolescence what they will be as adults, I certainly had no early interest in government, budgeting, political science, or constitutional law. My father was basically a lobbyist and knew Congress and federal agencies quite well, so perhaps that was an influence. But my interests were elsewhere. First and foremost it was to be the successor to my boyhood idol, Ted Williams. That aspiration went nowhere (although in my daydreams I still hit them out of the park). Another ambition was to be an artist, which is what I was in grade school, high school, and college. I was always the one to do posters for events, artwork for the yearbook, and win ribbons in various art categories. Although as an adult I have continued to do some artwork, it is less with lines than with words. With words we can sculpt, creating what was not there before.

Finding a Discipline

Between my second and third year in college I did what all students do: picked a major. I eventually settled on chemistry, which I had never taken either in high school or college. Over the next two years I took four years of chemistry, physics, calculus, and scientific German, doing well enough to get a scholarship to Johns Hopkins. But I felt so self-conscious about being a "science major" that whenever I carved out three hours for chemistry, physics, calculus, or German, I set aside the identical block of time for novels, history, plays, poetry, and other nonscientific subjects. Unwittingly, I was building a foundation for something else.

Self-consciousness escalated at graduate school. You can't apply to graduate school by selecting chemistry. It has to be more specific, like physical chemistry or organic chemistry. Picking physical chemistry increased my discomfort about overspecialization. At Hopkins I was told that physical chemistry was too broad, and I needed to pick from a subset of five, so I selected atomic and molecular spectra. Deeper uneasiness, if not panic. At the end of my first month at Hopkins I was advised that atomic and molecular spectra was way too broad, and I needed to concentrate on something smaller. One of the professors in the chemistry department was working on phosphate bonds and it seemed natural that I would head in that direction. Natural except for a voice inside that screamed out at someone who had just turned twenty-two: "Get out! Run!" It was one of those pivotal times in life when it is best to obey the inner voice. I did.

After two years in the army, five months hitchhiking around Europe, and a year with Dow Chemical in Midland, Michigan, I found myself in New York City doing technical writing for an agency. Later I worked as editor of a trade magazine, learning more about writing and publishing but coming to understand that I didn't want to devote the rest of my life to technical writing. On most evenings I was running around town listening to Carl Tillich, Malcolm X, Walter Kaufmann, Michael Harrington, Irving Howe, and others, while attending lectures on Carl Jung, theosophy, Marxism, Karen Horney, humanism, socialism, existentialism from Tolstoy to Camus, and you name it. Stimulating but heading toward dilettantism. I needed a focus.

I took three undergraduate classes at the New School for Social Research: one in economics, another in political philosophy,

and a third in international relations. This interdisciplinary course-
work satisfied a breadth I needed. The inner voice was happy. I
was accepted into the New School graduate program in political
science.

In this second effort at graduate school, all eight cylinders
were working. If the professor assigned five books, I'd read ten or
fifteen. There couldn't have been a better mixture (or should I say
chemistry) between the New School and Lou Fisher. It was a delight to work closely with such people as Robert Heilbroner, Hans
Staudinger, Jacob Landynski, and Saul Padover. They were very
responsive and encouraging. I remember one day I took the subway
uptown to Heilbroner's apartment on Park Avenue to drop off the
latest chapter of my dissertation. By the time I returned to my
room on Eleventh Street, the phone was ringing. It was Heilbroner,
ready to give me helpful feedback. How exciting and energizing to
have that kind of support!

After the New School I taught for three years at Queens College, where I realized that my desire to apply what I know—or
what I *would* know—would draw me to Washington, D.C. My interests in separation of powers, constitutional law, federal budgeting,
and foreign affairs would not get very far in Flushing. Scholars like
Leonard White had impressed me. They studied government not
from the outside but from the inside.

A Career at CRS

In September 1970 I started work with the Congressional
Research Service (CRS). Again, that selection seems uncanny. There
couldn't have been a better fit than between CRS and Lou Fisher,
although I suppose some of my supervisors over the years have had
their doubts. But I was in my element: writing memos for Members
of Congress and their committees, testifying on various issues, writing committee reports and floor statements, and getting so charged
up by the daily activities that I would regularly cart materials
home and continue my work there. Actually, I never knew the
difference between working hours and nonworking hours. For me,
they were all the same. Only the location changed. Sometimes the
location did not change, because I would find myself leaving the
Library of Congress at two in the morning, still full of energy and
excitement. A labor of love without labor.

Much of my satisfaction comes from working with congressional staff and agency careerists. They are highly skilled and professional, putting in long hours to do the best job possible. In the Capitol Hill environment, titles (doctorates, etc.) mean nothing. These things count: accurate information, sound judgment, plain speaking, lucid writing, keeping your word. Pretending to know something you don't is deadly.

When my daughters, Ellen and Joanna, were quite young they would be asked the standard question: "And what do *you* want to be when you grow up?" The response was as weird as it was unexpected: "I want to work." They had no idea what work meant, but they knew it was something that kept Dad in good spirits.

My behavior was not very normal, balanced, or sane. I have never done very well by those standards. Even as a child I was impressed by a sentence from a book called *The Human Mind*: "The adjuration to be 'normal' seems shockingly repellent to me." Part of me was in touch with reality, perhaps a corner of my soul that constituted five percent. Late at night this exhausted and impatient companion would protest: "This doesn't make any sense. Get to bed! It is two in the morning." I would reply, with kindness and understanding: "You're right, but first let me finish this section."

Picking My Targets

What accounts for the subjects and themes in my books and articles? In part they give me the breadth and interrelatedness that I need. I take a subject as it is, a mix of politics, law, public administration, history, economics, international relations, philosophy, sociology. Wherever the subject leads I follow. It never made sense to me to study a branch of government by itself. Congress is connected to the president, to the judiciary, to local government, to foreign governments, and to whatever else it comes in contact with. The linkages fascinate me, much as the combination of elements that make up a molecule. I would build my own molecules in political science, adding whatever chains and benzene rings I needed.

Separation of powers became an umbrella to cover a multitude of interests. What keeps the branches together? What do they share, and what remains exclusive to one branch? When do they reach an accommodation, and when is it time to fight? How do things change over time? What is decided by judges? What is resolved outside the courtroom?

My first book was *President and Congress: Power and Policy* (The Free Press, 1972). The dedication: "To Paul H. Douglas, for setting and satisfying high standards, personal and public." Douglas came to the New School in 1966 after his defeat to Chuck Percy, having served in the U.S. Senate ever since 1949. I took classes with him and was attracted by his academic credentials, enthusiasm, and dedication to public service.

My topics reflect the value I place on the individual, free to grow and fulfill one's potential. That includes the right to participate in government and not be shut out by experts and the self-appointed, self-anointed elite. That value would influence my writings on budgeting, constitutional law, and foreign affairs, all of which are prone to exclusiveness: "We know best; stay out." I wanted in. More important, I wanted to open the door to citizens to give them a stake in their system, to make it less alien, to join government more closely to the public.

I hope in my work I have been consistent in warning against reliance on experts, including me. Think for yourself. Do your own homework. Don't rely on secondary sources. Go to the original. Never assume that experts know what they are talking about. Never.

Budgeting

The articles in this book focus on my writings on constitutionalism and politics. From the start, however, I was drawn to budgeting. When it comes to studying law, politics, and institutions, nothing is so fundamental as the appropriation and the spending of funds. By the time I arrived at CRS in 1970, I had published two articles on presidential impoundment of funds. Because of this work, much of my time at CRS was devoted to the impoundment controversies during the Nixon years. I sat behind Senator Sam Ervin during hearings to provide advice, wrote committee reports and floor dialogue on legislative intent, and participated in the drafting of the Budget Act of 1974. On July 22, 1974, two weeks before his resignation as president, I received a letter and ceremonial pen from Richard Nixon for my work on this legislation.

More and more I wondered: What happens to money after Congress appropriates it? How are funds impounded, transferred, reprogrammed, and hidden? After many articles and papers I was ready to complete *Presidential Spending Power* (Princeton University Press, 1975). In 1976, this book received the Louis Brownlow Book Award from the National Academy of Public Administration. Again I picked a New School professor for the dedication: "To Robert L. Heilbroner, for keeping alive in our time the discipline of political economy." I marveled at Heilbroner's ability to weave together—with his usual lucidity—complex, multidimensioned material.

Over the years I published articles on reprogramming of funds, the authorization-appropriation process, the Budget Act of 1974, annual authorizations, the item veto, continuing resolutions, the balanced budget amendment, and biennial budgeting. From 1983 to the present I have served as Associate Editor of *Public Budgeting & Finance*. In 1982, I received the National Distinguished Service Award from the American Association for Budget and Program Analysis "in recognition of outstanding academic contributions." In 1995, the Association for Budgeting and Financial Management presented me with the Aaron B. Wildavsky Award for "lifetime scholarly achievement in public budgeting."

When I look at the thirty-five times that I have testified before congressional committees, twenty-one appearances relate to some kind of budgeting dispute. Here are some of the subjects I covered in testimony: legislative control of executive spending discretion, committee prior-approval procedure for transferring funds between appropriations accounts, rescission and item-veto authority, the "inherent" item veto, the Gramm-Rudman-Hollings Bill, continuing resolutions, congressional budget process, the Balanced Budget Amendment, budget reform, executive lobbying with appropriated funds, covert spending, biennial budgeting, and the statutory options that are available after the Supreme Court's invalidation of the Line Item Veto Act of 1996. The friends I have in the world of budgeting generally have no idea that I also write on presidential power, constitutional law, and war powers.

In the early 1970s, I published a number of articles on secret spending and confidential spending. To me, covert spending offended the Constitution's Statement and Account Clause and the right of taxpayers to see how their money is spent. Covert spending also leads to deceptions in the legislative process because intelligence money has to be tucked away in various appropriations accounts. The issue continued to interest me, leading to testimony in 1993 before the House Intelligence Committee where I supported disclosure of the aggregate intelligence budget. A variety of factors led to the first disclosure in 1997 and again the next year. By 1999, the intelligence budget was again made secret.

Loch Johnson covers many of the problems of governmental secrecy, including impoundment, war powers, covert spending, Watergate, executive agreements, the Iran-Contra affair, and non-disclosure agreements. Presidents and executive officials end up engaging in a "shell game designed to fool the public and its surrogates in Congress." As Loch notes, only if Congress is willing to defend its prerogatives and check executive abuses can we safeguard democratic principles and assure accountability to the electorate. In recent decades, Congress has been far too passive and acquiescent.

A Political Scientist as Constitutional Lawyer[1]

Classes with Jacob Landynski and work on my dissertation had opened the door to constitutional law in its largest sense: not just decisions handed down by courts but the values and customs of a society and the actions of legislators and executives. Although political science by the 1960s had turned increasingly toward behavioralism and process when studying the courts, I was more drawn to the tradition of Edward Corwin and other nonlawyers who felt comfortable in analyzing the substance and reasoning of case law. If a chemist could study political science, why not law? I didn't see any prohibitive boundaries.

At CRS, I spent much of my time in the library of the American Law Division. Many of the attorneys were perplexed. Why would a political scientist spend his time in a law library? One day I finally figured out the proper response. I asked whether they were familiar with the two thousand-page annotated Constitution put out every ten years by CRS. They were. Did they know that Corwin wrote the first edition? Yes, they were well aware of that. Did they think Corwin was a lawyer? Of course he was, they said. How shattering for them to be told that Corwin was a historian. Over the years, I have been amused by attorneys who ask what law school I attended. One attorney was not deceived. He told me: "I know you didn't go to law school. You write too clearly."

I began to follow all of the major legal disputes among the branches, leading to a book for St. Martin's Press called *The Constitution between Friends: Congress, the President, and the Law*

(1978). This was the start of what would be many articles and books on constitutional interpretation outside the courts. After changing publishers, the book was renamed *Constitutional Conflicts between Congress and the President*, published by Princeton University Press. The last two editions have been with the University Press of Kansas. Throughout its editions it has kept the same dedication to my daughters: "To Ellen and Joanna: Too young to understand constitutionalism, but learning what is fair and just." For all of us, that learning is lifelong.

I did another book on separation of powers, called *The Politics of Shared Power: Congress and the Executive* (CQ Press, 1981). I got in trouble with the dedication: "To my parents, for staying out of the way, letting a child grow." I meant it as a compliment. I loved the free time I had for projects (indoors and out) and the solitude that allowed for daydreaming. But my mother said the dedication made her look negligent and irresponsible. The next edition read: "To my parents, for giving room to a child's curiosities" and remains the same in its fourth edition, published in 1998 by Texas A&M University Press.

Throughout this period, the claim that constitutional rights and liberties are decided solely by the courts seemed to me, on its face, preposterous. Judges supposedly give the "final word" or the "last word," and we sit back and nod our heads. Really silly, and yet that was the dominant model used by law schools and many political science departments. Three books were on their way. One was *Constitutional Dialogues: Interpretation as Political Process* (Princeton University Press, 1988), which I dedicated to C. Herman Pritchett. For this I won my second Louis Brownlow Book Award. Next on the agenda was my textbook on *American Constitutional Law*, dedicated to The New School for Social Research. The first two editions (1990 and 1995) were with McGraw-Hill. The third edition (1999) is with Carolina Academic Press. The third book, written with Neal Devins, was *Political Dynamics of Constitutional Law* (West Publishing, 1992, 1996), which we dedicated to the College of William and Mary, where Neal teaches in the law school and where I attended as an undergraduate and returned to teach part-time in the law school. These books emphasized three-branch interpretation, the freedom of states to reach independent results, and the responsibility of citizens to be part of the process of defining and shaping constitutional values.

Neal Devins puts the issue squarely in his article. The belief that Supreme Court decisions are the "last word" in constitutional disputes "is overly parochial, ultimately shortsighted, and factually inaccurate. The Court may be the ultimate interpreter in a particular case, but not always the larger issue of which that case is a part."[2] Neal makes a bigger point, however. The belief in judicial exclusivity, he says, would end up marginalizing the Constitution and lead to less stability, not more, in constitutional values. It makes no sense to think that judicial supremacy can coexist in a system of democracy and self-government.

In his article, Dean Alfange critiques the Court for its "arrogance" and examines federalism not as a separate category from separation of powers but rather as a subset of separation of powers. For if federalism consists of drawing a line between national and state authority, someone at the national level must do it. The choice, he says, is between Congress and the federal courts. Dean makes a convincing case that the lion's share of power goes to Congress, and that the Court invariably gets into trouble when it arrogates for itself the authority to issue final pronouncements on federalism.

Nancy Kassop provides further insight into the limits that operate on judicial power. It is historically and politically false to believe that courts are uniquely gifted as an institution to protect individual liberties and constitutional values. The last two centuries, as Nancy shows, reveal repeated failures on the part of the Court to safeguard minority rights. More often it is Congress, the president, and the general public who must intervene to protect vital constitutional interests and reverse wrongheaded judicial rulings. In the end, the "legitimacy of the courts depends on public acceptance."[3]

The article by Robert Spitzer identifies the deficiencies in law-school education that create errors and misconceptions in legal scholarship. Preparation to practice law, he warns, does not automatically translate into competence to interpret the Constitution. Law reviews are still excessively court-centered, deal inadequately with historical and political realities, and suffer from a common problem: they are student run and lack the quality-control checks that come from journals that are peer reviewed. Bob shows how these defects yield poor legal scholarship on the item veto and the Second Amendment.

My writings on constitutional law and the presidency led to a wonderful collaboration with Leonard Levy on the four-volume *Encyclopedia of the American Presidency* (1994), which won the Dartmouth Medal a year later, awarded by the American Library

Association. Armed with fax machines in our homes, we started the substantive process of identifying topics and writers. Soon we were sharing personal details about our youth, education, children (two daughters each), the books and movies we love, and various experiences in life, good and bad. A rich and valued friendship emerged.

War Powers and Foreign Affairs

During 1987, I served as research director for the House Iran-Contra Committee. Listening to testimony and reading documents exposed me more fully to the theory that foreign policy and national security were playthings of the executive branch, not to be interfered with by Congress. Just as the courts claimed they had the "last word," the president was supposedly the "sole organ" in external affairs, including the decision to go to war. I found this theory of government profoundly obnoxious on every front: law, history, and politics. After a series of articles and papers, I was ready to put together a book that challenged single-handed executive action: *Presidential War Power*, published by the University Press of Kansas in 1995.

Susan Schott of Kansas Press had reason to believe that *The New York Times* would review the book on May 7. They had called for a "checking copy"— a second copy they needed to verify quotations and page citations from the reviewer. Susan didn't know whether the review would be prominent or stuck somewhere in the back as a short entry. I told her I was headed to Oregon to spend time with Len Levy and his wife, Elyse. Susan had Len's fax number.

When I arrived at the airport, Len and Elyse were wildly enthusiastic, waving something in the air. Sure enough, it was the review in *The New York Times*. Not just a review but the *lead* review. It ran three pages and had illustrations. Our enthusiasm was somewhat dampened because the review had been passed onward through so many fax machines that by the time it reached Oregon, we couldn't read a single word. It looked a little bit like Hebrew, perhaps ancient Hebrew, but it more than satisfied us until we could buy the book review section a few days later.

Two of the authors in this book focus on war power issues. From the so-called legislative "reassertion" in the War Powers Resolution of 1973, there has been an almost uninterrupted pattern of legislative acquiescence ever since. Although the framers did not want the

238

power to go to war placed in the hands of a single individual, from Truman in Korea to Clinton in a series of military operations—including Iraq, Haiti, Bosnia, Sudan, Afghanistan, and Kosovo—the warmaking power is now effectively lodged in the president.

David Adler develops a number of these themes. As he demonstrates, the White House has progressed through a number of stages in articulating legal arguments to defend military initiatives by the president. Earlier, administrations offered a variety of arguments, often strained and tendentious, to give legal color to a president's actions. Dave points out that we have reached the current stage where the administration doesn't even bother going through the exercise of manufacturing legal and constitutional arguments. It just acts.

Michael Glennon hammers home the vital link between constitutionalism and foreign policy. Particularly since World War II, presidents and executive officials have acquired unprecedented power over war and foreign relations, with only an occasional bow or nod toward legal and constitutional standards. For the most part, Congress and the courts have been handmaidens to this transfer of power. But we cannot, Mike reminds us, "play constitutional hopscotch to reach a preordained policy outcome; . . . to do so weakens not only the Constitution but the foreign policy that is supposedly advanced."[4]

At some point I know the internal writing factory will come to a halt, opening more time for reading, tennis, watching old movies, foreign travel, and other pleasures. Right now the factory remains busy. The third edition of *American Constitutional Law,* has been published. Neal Devins and I will do a third edition of *Political Dynamics of Constitutional Law* and we have another book, *The Democratic Constitution,* just about complete. I have finished a book manuscript on *Congressional Abdication: War and Spending* for the Texas A&M University Press and have started work on *Congress and the Constitution,* to be published by Kansas. I usually have ten or so articles at various stages of production. The appearance of so much material continues to baffle me. Where does it come from? Shall I ever understand the source? Probably no need to.

Notes

1. Title of a snappish and generally sneering article by Raoul Berger, in the *Political Science Reviewer* for Fall 1980, responding to my critique

of four of his books. To underscore the hazards of political scientists who study law, the title is followed by these words of caution from Alexander Pope: "a little learning is a dangerous thing."

2. Neal Devins, "The Last Word Debate Revisited," p. 19 of ms.

3. Nancy Kassop, "The Courts and the Political Branches," p. 89 of manuscript.

4. Michael J. Glennon, "Diplomacy, Foreign Affairs, and Coordinate Review," p. 40 of manuscript.

Appendix:
Bibliography of Louis Fisher's Publications

Books:

1. **President and Congress: Power and Policy** (New York: The Free Press, 1972). Cloth issued in 1972, paperback in 1973.

   a) Pages 110–32 reprinted in Harry A. Bailey Jr., *Classics of the American Presidency* (Oak Park, Ill.: Moore Publishing Co., 1980), pp. 253–65.

   b) Pages 1–17 reprinted in *Political Economy and Constitutional Reform*, hearings before the Joint Economic Committee, 97th Cong., 2d Sess., pp. 477–503 (1983).

   c) Pages 2–27 reprinted in Christopher H. Pyle and Richard M. Pious, eds., *The President, Congress, and the Constitution* (New York: The Free Press, 1984), pp. 19–25.

2. **Presidential Spending Power** (Princeton, N.J.: Princeton University Press, 1975). Simultaneous cloth and paper editions. Adopted by the Library for Political and International Affairs. Louis Brownlow Book Award for 1976, given by the National Academy of Public Administration.

   a) Pages 202–28, 316–23, reprinted in *Whether Disclosure of Funds Authorized for Intelligence Activities is in the Public Interest*, hearings before the Senate Select Committee on Intelligence, 95th Cong., lst Sess., pp. 355–89 (1977).

241

b) Pages 75–77, 99–101, 122 reprinted in Thomas M. Franck and Michael J. Glennon, eds., *Foreign Relations and National Security Law* (St. Paul, Minn.: West Publishing Co., 1987), pp. 672–75; 1993 ed., pp. 753–55.

3. **The Constitution Between Friends: Congress, the President, and the Law** (New York: St. Martin's Press, 1978). Simultaneous cloth and paper editions.

a) Pages 7–15 reprinted in Thomas E. Cronin, ed., *Rethinking the Presidency* (Boston, Mass.: Little, Brown and Co., 1982), pp. 155–61.

b) Pages 166–68 reprinted in Thomas M. Franck and Michael J. Glennon, eds., *Foreign Relations and National Security Law* (St. Paul, Minn.: West Publishing Co., 1987), pp. 671–72; 1993 ed., pp. 751–52.

4. **Studies on the Legislative Veto** (Washington, D.C.: Government Printing Office, 1980). Editor and Contributor to committee print for the House Committee on Rules, 96th Cong., 2d Sess.

5. **The Politics of Shared Power: Congress and the Executive** (Washington, D.C.: Congressional Quarterly Press, 1981). Paperback. Second edition, 1987; third edition, 1993; fourth edition published in 1998 by Texas A&M University Press in simultaneous cloth and paper editions.

a) Third edition published in Arabic in Amman, Jordan, 1994.

b) Chapter 3 on Congress as Administrator reprinted in Frederick S. Lane, *Current Issues in Public Administration* (3d edition, 1986).

6. **Constitutional Conflicts between Congress and the President** (Princeton, N.J.: Princeton University Press, 1985). Substantially revised edition of **The Constitution Between Friends**. Simultaneous cloth and paper editions. New edition published in 1991 by University Press of Kansas in simultaneous cloth and paper editions; fourth edition published in 1997 by University Press of Kansas in simultaneous cloth and paper editions.

a) Pages 123–39 reprinted in *Computer Security Act of 1987*, hearings before the House Committee on Government Operations, 100th Congress, 1st Session (1987).

b) Pages 307–18, 323–26, reprinted in Alan Shank, *American Politics, Policies, and Priorities*, 5th ed. (Allyn and Bacon, 1988).

c) Pages 60–70 reprinted in John H. Garvey and T. Alexander Aleinikoff, eds., *Modern Constitutional Theory: A Reader* (West, 1989), pp. 208–14. Reprinted also in 1992 edition.

7. **Item Veto: State Experience and Its Application to the Federal Situation** (Washington, D.C.: Government Printing Office, 1986). Editor and Contributor to committee print for the House Committee on Rules, 99th Cong., 2d Sess.

8. **Constitutional Dialogues: Interpretation as Political Process** (Princeton, N.J.: Princeton University Press, 1988). Simultaneous cloth and paper editions.

9. **American Constitutional Law** (New York: McGraw-Hill, 1990, 1995). Third edition published by Carolina Academic Press in 1999.

10. **Constitutional Structures: Separated Powers and Federalism** [Volume 1 of **American Constitutional Law**] (New York: McGraw-Hill, 1990, 1995). Third edition published by Carolina Academic Press in 1999.

11. **Constitutional Rights: Civil Rights and Civil Liberties** [Volume 2 of **American Constitutional Law**] (New York: McGraw-Hill, 1990, 1995). Third edition published by Carolina Academic Press in 1999.

12. **The Political Dynamics of Constitutional Law** [with Neal Devins] (St. Paul, Minn.: West Publishing Co., 1992; second edition, 1996).

13. **Encyclopedia of the American Presidency** [with Leonard W. Levy], 4 vols. (Simon & Schuster, 1994). Published as a two-volume set in 1998.

14. **Presidential War Power** (Kansas City: University Press of Kansas, 1995). Simultaneous cloth and paper editions.

Book Chapters:

1. *War Powers: A Need for Legislative Reassertion*, in **The Presidency Reappraised**, edited by Rexford G. Tugwell and Thomas E. Cronin (New York: Praeger, 1974), pp 56–73.

2. *The President Versus Congress: Who Wins?* in **Has the President Too Much Power?** edited by Charles Roberts (Harpers Magazine Press, 1974), pp. 160–67.

3. *Impoundment of Clean-Water Funds: The Limits of Discretion,* in **Cases in American Politics**, edited by Robert L. Peabody (New York: Praeger, 1976), pp. 44–70.

   a) Reprinted in **Public Budgeting in Theory and Practice**, edited by Fremont J. Lyden and Marc Lindenberg (New York: Longman, 1983), pp. 145–72.

4. *History of Pay Adjustments for Members of Congress,* in **The Rewards of Public Service: Compensating Top Federal Officials** (Washington, D.C.: The Brookings Institution, 1980), pp. 25–52.

5. *Effect of the Budget Act of 1974 on Agency Operations,* in **The Congressional Budget Process After Five Years**, edited by Rudolph G. Penner (Washington, D.C.: American Enterprise Institute, 1981), pp. 149–73.

6. *Congress and the President in the Administrative Process: The Uneasy Alliance,* in **The Illusion of Presidential Government**, edited by Hugh Heclo and Lester Salamon (Boulder, Colo.: The Westview Press, 1981), pp. 21–43.

7. *Developing Fiscal Responsibility,* in **The Power of Govern: Assessing Reform in the United States**, edited by Richard M. Pious, Proceedings of the Academy of Political Science, Vol. 34, No. 2 (New York: Academy of Political Science, 1981), pp. 62–75.

8. *Making Use of Legal Sources,* in **Studying the Presidency**, edited by George C. Edwards III and Stephen J. Wayne (Knoxville, Tenn.: University of Tennessee Press, 1982), pp. 182–98.

9. *The Budgetary Process: How Far Have We Progressed?* in **Improving the Accountability and Performance of Government**, edited by Bruce L. R. Smith and James D. Carroll (Washington, D.C.: The Brookings Institution, 1982), pp. 75–83.

10. *Bureaucracy, Appropriations, and Budget,* published in Funk and Wagnalls' Encyclopedia.

11. *Presidential Impoundment,* in Volume Six of **The Guide to American Law**, edited by Harold Chase (West Publishing Company, 1984), pp. 127–28.

12. *The Budget Act of 1974: A Further Loss of Spending Control,* in **Congressional Budgeting: Politics, Process and Power** (Baltimore, Md.: Johns Hopkins University Press, 1984), pp. 170–89.

13. *Presidential Powers,* in **The American Presidency: A Policy Perspective from Readings and Documents**, edited by David C. Kozak and Kenneth N. Ciboski (Chicago: Nelson-Hall, 1985), pp. 15–45.

14. *Evolution of Presidential and Congressional Powers in Foreign Affairs,* in **Congress, the Presidency, and the Taiwan Relations Act**, edited by Louis W. Koenig, et al. (New York: Praeger, 1985), pp. 15–35.

   a) Reprinted in *Computer Security Act of 1987,* hearing before the House Committee on Government Operations, 100th Cong., 1st Sess. (1987), pp. 616–36.

15. *War Powers Resolution,* published by World Book Encyclopedia (1986).

16. *Legislative Veto, Emergency Powers, Presidential Ordinance-Making Power, Presidential Spending Power, Veto Power, Youngstown Sheet and Tube Co. v. Sawyer, President Truman, Executive Order 10340, and President Carter,* in **Encyclopedia of the American Constitution**, edited by Leonard W. Levy and Kenneth L. Karst (4 vols., Macmillan Company, 1987).

17. *Congress,* in **Encyclopedia of the American Judicial System**, edited by Robert J. Janosik (New York: Charles Scribner's, 1987), vol. III, pp. 958–71.

18. Various sections and chapters of **Iran-Contra Affair**, a joint congressional committee report, 100th Cong., 1st Sess. (November 1987).

19. Foreword to **The Presidential Veto: Touchstone of the American Presidency**, by Robert J. Spitzer (Albany, N.Y.: SUNY Press, 1988), pp. xi–xiii.

20. *Does the Supreme Court Have the Last Word on Constitutional Law?* in **E Pluribus Unum: Constitutional Principles and the Institutions of Government** (Latham, Md.: University Press of Virginia, 1988), pp. 166–90.

   a) Reprinted in part in the Congressional Record, March 17, 1992, by Senator Robert C. Byrd, pp. S3749–50 (daily ed.).

21. *The Presidential Veto: Constitutional Development,* published in **Pork Barrels and Principles: The Politics of the Presidential Veto** (National Legal Center, 1988), pp. 17–28.

22. *Separation of Powers in America: Theory and Practice,* in **Principles of the Constitutional Order: The Ratification Debates**, edited by Robert L. Utley, Jr. (Lanham, Md.: University Press of America, 1989), pp. 131–49.

23. *Micromanagement by Congress: Reality and Mythology,* in **The Fettered Presidency** (Washington, D.C.: American Enterprise Institute, 1989), pp. 139–57, with commentary at pp. 185–93.

    a) Reprinted in part in Foundations of Administrative Law, edited by Peter H. Schuck (New York: Oxford University Press, 1994), pp. 248–57.

24. *The Allocation of Powers: The Framers' Intent,* in **Separation of Powers in the American System**, edited by Barbara B. Knight (Fairfax, Va.: George Mason University Press, 1989), pp. 19–40.

25. *Does the President Have Too Much Power in Relation to Congress?* in **The American Democracy** by Thomas E. Patterson (New York: McGraw-Hill, 1990), p. 506.

26. *Congressional Supervision of the Executive Branch: The Necessity for Legislative Controls,* in **The Constitutional Bases of Political and Social Change in the United States** (New York: Praeger, 1990), pp. 43–61.

27. *The Legitimacy of the Congressional National Security Role,* in **The Constitution and National Security** (Washington, D.C.: National Defense University, 1990), pp. 243–58.

28. *Reagan's Relations with Congress,* in **The Reagan Presidency** edited by Dilys M. Hill, et al. (London: Macmillan Press, 1990), pp. 95–114.

29. Introduction to **Judicial Power** (New York: Macmillan Co., 1990).

30. *How Tightly Can Congress Draw the Purse Strings?* in **Foreign Affairs and the U.S. Constitution**, edited by Louis Henkin, Michael J. Glennon, and William D. Rogers (Ardsley-on-Hudson, N.Y.: Transnational Publishers, Inc., 1990), pp. 47–55.

31. *Relaciones Ejecutivo-Legislativas en Politica Exterior*, in **Derecho Constitucional Comparado, Mexico-Estados Unidos**, edited by James Frank Smith (Mexico: Universidad Nacional Autonoma de Mexico, 1990), Vol. II, pp. 917–33.

32. *Congress as Micromanager of the Executive Branch*, in **The Managerial Presidency**, edited by James P. Pfiffner (Pacific Grove, Cal.: Brooks/Cole Publishing Co., 1991), pp. 225–37.

33. *War Powers: The Need for Collective Judgment*, in **Divided Democracy**, edited by James A. Thurber (Washington, D.C.: Congressional Quarterly Press, 1991), pp. 199–217.

34. *The Constitution and Presidential Budget Powers: The Modern Era*, in **The Constitution and the American Presidency**, edited by Martin L. Fausold and Alan Shank (Albany, N.Y.: State University of New York Press, 1991), pp. 147–69, 292–95.

35. *The Separation Doctrine in the Twentieth Century*, in **Understanding Congress: Research Perspectives**, edited by Roger H. Davidson and Richard C. Sachs (Washington, D.C.: Government Printing Office, 1991.), pp. 135–49.

36. *Federalism and Shared Powers, Non-judicial Interpretation of the Constitution, The Senate Judiciary Committee, and The Item Veto*, published in Supplement I to **Encyclopedia of the American Constitution**, edited by Levy & Karst (New York: Macmillan, 1992).

40. *One of the Guardians, Some of the Time*, in **Is the Supreme Court the Guardian of the Constitution?** (Washington, D.C.: American Enterprise Institute, 1993), pp. 82–97.

41. *The Power of Commander in Chief*, in **The Presidency and the Persian Gulf War**, edited by Marcia Lynn Whicker, et al. (New York: Praeger, 1993), pp. 45–61.

42. *The Legislative Veto*, in **Encyclopedia of the American Legislative System** (New York: Charles Scribner's Sons, 1994), vol. III, pp. 1505–20.

43. *Baker Accord of 1989, Checks and Balances, Comptroller General, Fiscal Corporation Bill, Gag Orders, General Accounting Office, Impoundment, Impoundment Control Act, Incompatability Clause, Ineligibility Clause, INS v. Chadha (1983), Legislative Veto, Lobbying with Appropriated Money Act, Quasi-War of 1798,*

Spending Power, Unvouchered Expenditures, in **Encyclopedia of the American Presidency**, edited by Leonard W. Levy and Louis Fisher (New York: Simon & Schuster, 1994).

59. *Historical Survey of the War Powers and the Use of Force*, in **The U.S. Constitution and the Power to Go to War**, edited by Gary M. Stern & Morton H. Halperin (Greenwood Publishing, 1994), pp. 11–28.

60. Foreword to **Truman and the Steel Seizure Case: The Limits of Presidential Power**, by Maeva Marcus (Durham, N.C.: Duke University Press, 1994), pp. ix–xx.

61. *How Supreme Is the Supreme Court?* in **Governance V: Institutions and Issues**, edited by Kenneth W. Thompson (Lanham, Md.: University Press of America, 1994), pp. 3–23.

62. *Power of the Purse*, in **History of the United States House of Representatives, 1789–1994**, H. Doc. No. 103–324, 103d Cong., 2d Sess. (U.S. Government Printing Office, 1994), pp. 201–31.

63. *Constitutional Interpretation by Congress, Removal Power, Salaries, Twenty-Seventh Amendment, Nonstatutory Controls*, in **Encyclopedia of the United States Congress**, edited by Roger H. Davidson et al. (New York: Simon & Schuster, 1995).

68. *President Clinton as Commander in Chief*, in **Rivals for Power: Presidential-Congressional Relations**, edited by James A. Thurber (Washington, D.C.: Congressional Quarterly, 1996), pp. 214–31.

69. *The Spending Power*, in **The Constitution and the Conduct of American Foreign Policy**, edited by David Gray Adler and Larry N. George (Lawrence, Kans.: University Press of Kansas, 1996), pp. 227–40.

70. *Truman in Korea*, in **The Constitution and the Conduct of American Foreign Policy**, edited by David Gray Adler and Larry N. George (Lawrence, Kans.: University Press of Kansas, 1996), pp. 320–33.

71. *The Barbary Wars: Legal Precedent for Invading Haiti?* in **The Constitution and the Conduct of American Foreign Policy**, edited by David Gray Adler and Larry N. George (Lawrence, Kans.: University Press of Kansas, 1996), pp. 313–19.

72. *Budget, Management, and Personnel*, in **The Executive Office of the President**, edited by Harold C. Relyea (Westport, Conn.: Greenwood Press, 1977), pp. 99–130.

73. *Invitation to Struggle: The President, Congress, and National Security*, in **Understanding the Presidency**, edited by James P. Pfiffner and Roger H. Davidson (New York: Longman, 1997), pp. 262–72.

74. *The Law/Politics Dialogue: It's Not All Courts!* in **Handbook of Public Law and Public Administration**, edited by Philip J. Cooper and Chester I. Newland (Jossey-Bass, 1997), pp. 63–75.

75. *Without Restraint: Presidential Military Initiatives from Korea to Bosnia*, in **The Domestic Sources of American Foreign Policy**, 3d ed., edited by Eugene R. Wittkopf and James M. McCormick (New York: Roman & Littlefield, 1999), pp. 141–55.

76. *Constitutional and Political Basis of War and the Military*, to be published in the **Oxford Companion to American Military History** (New York: Oxford University Press).

77. *The War Power*, to be published in **The Constitution and Its Amendments** (New York: Macmillan Reference).

78. *Commander in Chief*, to be published in **The Constitution and Its Amendments** (New York: Macmillan Reference).

79. *Foreign and Defense Policy*, to be published in **Presidential Policymaking**, edited by Steven A. Shull (New York: Garland Publishing, 1998).

80. *Constitutional History, 1989–1998, Line-Item Veto*, and *Presidential War Powers*, to be published in **Encyclopedia of the American Constitution** (Supplement II) by Macmillan Reference in 1999.

83. *Congress as Co-Manager of the Executive Branch*, to be published in **The Managerial Presidency**, edited by James P. Pfiffner, 2nd edition.

Articles and Other Publications:

1. *Nixon at the Controls, **The New Leader**, December 16, 1968, pp. 8–10.

2. *Funds Impounded by the President: The Constitutional Issue,* **George Washington Law Review**, Vol. 38, No. 1, October 1969, pp. 124–37.

   a) Reprinted in *Executive Impoundment of Appropriated Funds,* hearings before the Senate Committee on the Judiciary, 92d Congress, 1st Session, pp. 120–33 (1971).

   b) Reprinted in *Impoundment Reporting and Review,* hearings before the House Committee on Rules, 93d Congress, 1st Session, Part I of 2 Parts, pp. 67–75 (1973).

3. *Federal Revenue Sharing: A Cautionary Word,* **The New Republic**, October 4, 1969, pp. 15–17.

   a) Placed in the Congressional Record, December 17, 1969, by Rep. William F. Ryan, pp. E10764–65 (daily ed.).

   b) Reprinted in *America in Crisis,* edited by Raymond L. Lee and Dorothy Palmer (Cambridge: Winthrop Publ., 1972), pp. 198–202.

4. *ABM: A Case Study in Deception,* **The Progressive**, November 1969, pp. 21–23.

   a) Placed in the Congressional Record, November 6, 1969, by Senator Thomas Eagleton, pp. S13860–62 (daily ed.).

5. *Presidential Tax Discretion and Eighteenth Century Theory,* **The Western Political Quarterly**, Vol. 23, No. 1, March 1970, pp. 151–65.

6. *The Politics of Impounded Funds,* **Administrative Science Quarterly**, Vol. 15, No. 3, September 1970, pp. 361–77.

   a) Reprinted in *Executive Impoundment of Appropriated Funds,* hearings before the Senate Committee on the Judiciary, 92d Congress, 1st Session, pp. 103–19 (1971).

   b) Reprinted in *Impoundment Reporting and Review,* hearings before the House Committee on Rules, 93d Congress., 1st Session, Part 1 of 2 Parts, pp. 54–67 (1973).

   c) Reprinted in *Public Administration,* 2d edition, edited by Robert T. Golembiewski (Rand McNally, 1973), pp. 135–55.

7. *Delegating Power to the President,* **Journal of Public Law**, Vol. 19, No. 2, 1970, pp. 251–82.

a) Reprinted in *Resolved: That the Powers of the Presidency Should be Curtailed,* H. Doc. No. 93-273, 93d Congress, 2d Session, pp. 258–82. (1974)

8. *Efficiency Side of Separated Powers,* **Journal of American Studies**, Vol. 5, No. 2, August 1971, pp. 113–31.

a) Reprinted in *Legislative Veto and the "Chadha" Decision,* hearings before the Senate Committee on the Judiciary, 98th Congress, 1st Session, pp. 135–53 (1983).

9. *Executive Shell Game: Hiding Billions from Congress,* **The Nation**, November 15, 1971, pp. 486–90.

a) Placed in the Congressional Record, November 11, 1971, by Senator J. William Fulbright, pp. S18232–34 (daily ed.).

10. *Presidential Spending Discretion and Congressional Controls,* **Law and Contemporary Problems**, Vol. 37, No. 1, pp. 135–72 (Winter 1972).

a) Reprinted in *Impoundment of Appropriated Funds by the President,* Joint Hearings before the Senate Committees on Government Operations and the Judiciary, 93d Congress, 1st Session, pp. 683–719 (1973).

b) Reprinted in *Improving Congressional Control of the Budget,* hearings before the Senate Committee on Government Operations, 93d Congress, 1st Session, pp. 541–78 (1973).

11. Review article of *Guide to the Congress of the United States,* by Congressional Quarterly, Inc., for **Harvard Journal on Legislation**, Vol. 10, No. 2, pp. 366–72 (February 1973).

12. *Impoundment Relies on Weak Arguments,* [Washington] **Sunday Star and Daily News**, February 25, 1973, p. C-2.

a) Placed in the Congressional Record, February 28, 1973, by Senator Edmund S. Muskie, pp. S3588–90 (daily ed.).

b) Placed in the Congressional Record, March 8, 1973, by Senator Hubert H. Humphrey, pp. S4313–15 (daily ed.).

13. *Big Government, Conservative Style,* **The Progressive**, March 1973, pp. 22–26.

14. *Power Struggle in Washington,* interviewed by **U.S. News & World Report**, April 23, 1973, pp. 64–69.

a) Placed in the Congressional Record, May 8, 1973, by Senator Sam J. Ervin, Jr., pp. S8518–22 (daily ed.).

b) Placed in the Congressional Record, May 15, 1973, by Senator Hubert H. Humphrey, pp. S9088–91 (daily ed.).

15. *Congressional Control of Budget Execution,* printed in **Committee Organization in the House** (Vol. 2 of 3, Part 3 of 3), panel discussions before the House Select Committee on Committees, 93d Congress, 1st Session, pp. 593–602 (June 1, 1973).

16. *Impoundment of Funds: Uses and Abuses,* **Buffalo Law Review**, Vol. 23, No. 1, Fall 1973, pp. 141–200.

a) Placed in the Congressional Record, February 4, 1974, by Senator Hubert H. Humphrey, pp. S1162–76 (daily ed.).

17. *Secret Spending: Dark Corners in the Budget,* **The Nation**, January 19, 1974, pp. 75–78.

18. *Congress, the Executive, and the Budget,* **The Annals**, Vol. 411, pp. 102–13 (January 1974).

19. *Reprogramming of Funds by the Defense Department,* **The Journal of Politics**, Vol. 36, No. 1, pp. 77–102 (February 1974).

a) Placed in the Congressional Record, June 3, 1974, by Senator James Abourezk, pp. S9422–28 (daily ed.).

20. *Democracy and Secret Funding,* **The Center Magazine**, Vol. VII, No. 2, (March/April 1974), pp. 54–56.

21. *The Changing Concept of Property,* **The Progressive**, April 1975, pp. 23–25.

22. *Senate Procedures for Authorizing Military Research and Development,* **Priorities and Efficiency in Federal Research and Development**, a compendium of papers submitted to the Subcommittee on Priorities and Economy in Government, Joint Economic Committee (October 29, 1976), pp. 20–45.

23. *The Supreme Court on Defamation,* **The Nation**, November 13, 1976, pp 485–87.

24. *The Senate's Legislative Power,* **Techniques and Procedures for Analysis and Evaluation**, a compilation of papers prepared for the Commission on the Operation of the Senate, 94th Congress, 2d Session, pp. 3–13 (Committee print, 1977).

a) Reprinted in *Congress and Public Policy: A Source Book of Documents and Readings,* edited by David C. Kozak and John D. Macartney (Homewood, Ill.: The Dorsey Press, 1982), pp. 374–81.

25. *Relationship Between the Senate and the Executive Branch,* **Committees and Senate Procedures**, a compilation of papers prepared for the Commission on the Operation of the Senate, 94th Congress, 2d Session, pp. 115–30 (Committee print, 1977).

26. *Confidential Funding: A Study of Unvouchered Accounts,* prepared for the House Budget Committee (Committee print, March 1977).

27. *Congressional Budget Reform: The First Two Years,* **Harvard Journal on Legislation**, Vol. 14, No. 3, April 1977, pp. 413–57.

28. *Flouting the Constitution,* **The Center Magazine**, November/December 1977, pp. 13–19.

29. *A Political Context for Legislative Vetoes,* **Political Science Quarterly**, Vol. 93, No. 2, Summer 1978, pp. 241–54.

30. *Raoul Berger on Public Law,* **Political Science Reviewer**, Vol. 8, Fall 1978, pp. 173–203.

a) Rebutted by Berger in *A Political Scientist as Constitutional Lawyer: A Reply to Louis Fisher,* Ohio State Law Journal, Vol. 41, No. 1, 1980, pp. 147–75.

b) Rebutted by Berger in *A Political Scientist as Constitutional Lawyer: A Reply to Louis Fisher,* Political Science Reviewer, Vol. 10, Fall 1980, pp. 387–423.

31. *Presidential Staffing—-A Brief Overview* [with Harold C. Relyea], prepared for the House Committee on Post Office and Civil Service, Committee print No. 95-17, 95th Congress, 2d Session, July 25, 1978.

32. *Protecting Civil Servants: There are Reasons and Precedents for Defining Job Rights as Property,* **The Washington Post**, Outlook Section, December 31, 1978, p. B3.

a) Placed in the Congressional Record, September 5, 1979, by Senator Orrin G. Hatch, pp. S11862–65 (daily ed.).

33. *Confidential Spending and Governmental Accountability,* **George Washington Law Review**, Vol. 47, No. 2, January 1979, pp. 347–85.

   a) Reprinted in *GAO Legislation,* hearings before the Senate Committee on Government Affairs, 96th Congress, 1st Session, pp. 29–68 (1979).

   b) Reprinted in *Public Disclosure of the Aggregate Intelligence Budget Figure*, hearings before the House Permanent Select Committee on Intelligence, 103d Congress, 2d Session, pp. 122–60 (1994).

34. *Grover Cleveland Against the Senate,* **Congressional Studies**, Vol. 7, No. 1, Spring 1979, pp. 11–25.

   a) Reprinted in The Congress of the United States, 1789–1989 (Brooklyn, N.Y.: Carlson Publishing Co., 1991), Title 10.

35. Review of Bruce Buchanan's *The Presidential Experience: What the Office Does to the Man,* **Political Science Quarterly**, Vol. 94, No. 3, Fall 1979, pp. 523–24.

36. *The Authorization-Appropriation Process in Congress: Formal Rules and Informal Practices,* **Catholic University Law Review**, Vol. 29, No. 1, Fall 1979, pp. 51–105.

37. Review of Larry Berman's *The Office of Management and Budget and the Presidency, 1921–1979,* **Political Science Quarterly**, Vol. 95, No. 1, Spring 1980, pp. 160–61.

38. *Delegating with Ambivalence: The Legislative Veto and Reorganization Authority* (with Ronald C. Moe), in **Studies on the Legislative Veto**, committee print for the House Committee on Rules, 96th Congress, 2d Session, pp. 164–247.

39. Review of Philip B. Kurland's *Watergate and the Constitution,* **Presidential Studies Quarterly**, Vol. X, No. 1, Winter 1980, pp. 129–31.

40. *Presidential Reorganization Authority: Is It Worth the Cost?* (with Ronald C. Moe), **Political Science Quarterly**, Vol. 96, No. 2, Summer 1981, pp. 301–18.

   a) Reprinted in *Reorganization Act of 1981,* hearing before the Senate Committee on Governmental Affairs, 97th Congress, 1st Session, pp. 53–63 (1981).

b) Reprinted in *Legislative Veto After Chadha,* hearings before the House Committee on Rules, 98th Congress, 2d Session, pp. 655–72 (1984).

41. *In Dubious Battle? Congress and the Budget,* **The Brookings Bulletin**, Vol. 17, No. 4, Spring 1981, pp. 6–10.

42. Review of Lance LeLoup's *The Fiscal Congress: Legislative Control of the Budget,* **American Political Science Review**, Vol. 75, No. 3, September 1981, pp. 776–77.

43. *Congress Can't Lose On Its Veto Power,* **Washington Post**, Outlook Section, February 21, 1982, pp. D1, D5.

   a) Placed in the Congressional Record by Rep. Trent Lott, February 22, 1982, pp. E428–430 (daily ed.).

   b) Placed in the Congressional Record by Rep. Elliott Levitas, February 23, 1982, pp. E501–502 (daily ed.).

   c) Placed in the Congressional Record by Senator Harrison Schmitt, March 23, 1982, pp. S2587–88 (daily ed.).

   d) Placed in the Congressional Record by Rep. Elliott Levitas, Deccember 1, 1982, pp. H8722–23 (daily ed.).

   e) Placed in the Congressional Record by Rep. Elliott Levitas, June 28, 1983, pp. E3218–19 (daily ed.).

44. *Research Tools for Public Law,* **Teaching Political Science**, Vol. 9, No. 3, Spring 1982, pp. 132–38.

45. Review of James I. Lengle's *Representation and Presidential Primaries: The Democratic Party in the Post-Reform Era,* **Political Science Quarterly**, Vol. 97, No. 2, Summer 1982, pp. 376–77.

46. *The Case for the Legislative Veto,* **National Law Journal**, January 16, 1983, pp. 13, 22.

   a) Reprinted in *Legislative Veto and the 'Chadha' Decision* hearings before the Senate Committee on the Judiciary, 98th Congress, 1st Session, pp. 154–56 (1983).

47. *Annual Authorizations: Durable Roadblocks to Biennial Budgeting,* **Public Budgeting & Finance**, Vol. 3, No. 1, Spring 1983, pp. 23–40.

48. *Congress and the Removal Power,* **Congress & the Presidency**, Vol. 10, No. 1, Spring 1983, pp. 63–77.

   a) Reprinted in *Divided Democracy,* edited by James A. Thurber, (Washington, D.C.: Congressional Quarterly Press, 1991), pp. 255–74.

49. Review of W. Taylor Reveley III's *War Powers of the President and Congress,* **Congress & the Presidency**, Vol. 10, No. 2, Autumn 1983, pp. 268–69.

50. *Chadha's Impact on the Budget Process,* **Public Budgeting & Finance**, Vol. 3, No. 4, Winter 1983, pp. 103–07.

51. *Legislative Vetoes, Phoenix Style,* **Extensions**, a Newsletter for the Carl Albert Center, Spring 1984, p. 2.

   a) Reprinted in *Courts, Judges & Politics,* edited by Walter F. Murphy and C. Herman Pritchett (New York: Random House, 1986), pp. 347–49.

52. *Constitutional Separation of Powers,* published as a monograph by the Philippine Bar Association in 1984.

53. *The Authorization Process; the Appropriation Process,* in *Issue Presentations Before the Rules Committee Task Force on the Budget Process,* House Committee on Rules, 98th Congress, 2d Session (Committee Print, October 1984), pp. 70–92.

54. *Constitutional Interpretation by Members of Congress,* **North Carolina Law Review**, Vol. 63, No. 4, April 1985, pp. 701–41.

   a) Reprinted in *Line Item Veto,* hearings before the Senate Committee on Rules and Administration, 99th Congress, 1st Session, pp. 111–52 (1985).

55. *Ten Years of the Budget Act: Still Searching for Controls,* **Public Budgeting & Finance**, Vol. 5, No. 3, Autumn 1985, pp. 3–28.

   a) Reprinted in *Government Budgeting: Theory, Process, and Politics,* by Albert C. Hyde (Pacific Grove, Cal.: Brooks/Cole Publishing Co., 1992).

56. *Judicial Misjudgments about the Lawmaking Process: The Legislative Veto Case,* **Public Administration Review**, Vol. 45, Special Issue, November 1985, pp. 705–11.

a) Reprinted in *Congress and Public Policy,* edited by David C. Kozak and John D. Macartney (Prospect Heights, Ill.: Waveland Press, 1990), pp. 425–34.

57. Review of Christopher H. Pyle and Richard M. Pious, eds., *The President, Congress, and the Constitution,* **Political Science Quarterly,** Vol. 100, No. 3, Fall 1985, pp. 511–12.

58. Review of John W. Macy, et al., *America's Unelected Government: Appointing the President's Team,* and Richard L. Schlott and Dagmar S. Hamilton, *People, Positions, and Power: The Political Appointments of Lyndon Johnson,* **Presidential Studies Quarterly,** Vol. XV, No. 4, Fall 1985, pp. 843–45.

59. Review of Edward S. Corwin, *The President: Office and Powers, 1787–1984,* Fifth Revised Edition by Randall W. Bland, et al., **Presidential Studies Quarterly,** Vol. XV, No. 4, Fall 1985, pp. 845–49.

60. *Scrutiny of Appointments by Parliament,* **Canadian Parliamentary Review,** Vol. 9, No. 1, Spring 1986, pp. 14–17.

61. *The Politics of Constitutional Law,* published as a monograph by the Philippine Bar Association and the International Law Association (Philippine Branch) in 1986.

62. *How Successfully Can the States' Item Veto be Transferred to the President?* (with Neal Devins), **Georgetown Law Journal,** Vol. 75, No. 1, October 1986, pp. 159–97.

a) Reprinted in *The Line-Item Veto,* hearing before the Senate Committee on the Judiciary, 101st Cong., 1st Sess. (1989), pp. 102–40.

63. *Impoundment: Here We Go Again,* **Public Budgeting & Finance,** Vol. 6, No. 4, Winter 1986, pp. 72–73.

64. *Congress and the Fourth Amendment,* **Georgia Law Review,** Vol. 21, No. 1, Special Issue 1986, pp. 107–70.

65. *The Item Veto—A Misconception,* **Washington Post,** February 23, 1987, p. A11.

a) Placed in the Congressional Record by Rep. Lawrence C. Smith, February 24, 1987, p. E587 (daily ed.).

b) Placed in the Congressional Record by Rep. Don Bonker, February 26, 1987, p. E651 (daily ed.).

c) Reprinted in *The Line-Item Veto,* hearing before the Senate Committee on the Judiciary, 101st Cong., 1st Sess. (1989), p. 101.

66. *Court's Narrow View on Role of Congress,* **San Francisco Chronicle**, March 18, 1987.

67. *Social Influences on Constitutional Law,* **Journal of Political Science**, Vol. XV, Nos. 1 and 2, Spring 1987, pp. 7–19.

68. Review of *the President, the Congress, and Foreign Policy,* by Edmund S. Muskie, et al., **Political Science Quarterly**, Vol. 102, No. 1, Spring 1987, pp. 114–15.

69. *The Administrative World of* Chadha *and* Bowsher, **Public Administration Review**, Vol. 47, No. 3, May/June 1987, pp. 213–19.

70. *Methods of Constitutional Interpretation: The Limits of Original Intent,* **Cumberland Law Review**, Vol. 18, No. 1, 1987–1988, pp. 43–67.

71. *Seven Ways to Reinvent the Budget Process,* **The New York Times**, September 27, 1987, p. E5.

72. *The Congress and the Courts,* **CRS Review**, January 1988, pp. 19–21.

73. Comments on a *Mini-Symposium on the Federal Executive Budget,* **Public Budgeting & Finance**, Vol. 8, No. 1, Spring 1988, pp. 100–03.

74. *Line-Item Imaginings* (with Ronald C. Moe), **The American Spectator**, August 1988, pp. 38–39.

75. *Constitutional Interpretation by the Congress,* **CRS Review**, September 1988, pp. 26–27.

76. *How to Avoid Iran-Contras,* review of *The President, the Congress, and Foreign Policy* by Edmund S. Muskie, et al., **California Law Review**, Vol. 76, pp. 939–60 (July 1988).

77. *Continuing Resolutions: Can't Live With 'em, Can't Live Without 'em,* **Public Budgeting & Finance**, Vol. 8, No. 2, Summer 1988, pp. 101–04.

78. Review of *The Cult of the Court,* by John Brigham and *The Supreme Court,* by William H. Rehnquist, **Presidential Studies Quarterly**, Vol. 18, No. 3, Summer 1988, pp. 601–04.

79. *Foreign Policy Powers of the President and Congress*, **The Annals**, Vol. 499, September 1988, pp. 148–59.

  a) Reprinted in *The Congress of the United States, 1789–1989* (Brooklyn, N.Y.: Carlson Publishing Co., 1991), Title 10.

80. *Lessons From the Iran / Contra Affair*, **International Practitioners Notebook** [International Law Association], No. 40, September 1988, pp. 8–9.

81. *Continuing Resolutions: Product of the Process?* in **A Call for Congressional Reform**, a publication of the House Republican Research Committee, U.S. Congress, 1988.

82. *Understanding the Role of Congress in Foreign Policy*, **George Mason University Law Review**, Vol. 11, No. 1, Fall 1988, pp. 153–68.

83. *The Foundations of a Scandal,* **Corruption and Reform**, Vol. 3, pp. 157–69 (1988).

84. Review of *How Washington Works: The Executive's Guide to Government,* by A. Lee Fritscher and Bernard H. Ross, **Public Administration Review**, Vol. 49, No. 1, January/February 1989, pp. 86–87.

85. *Legislative-Executive Relations: Search for Cooperation*, **CRS Review**, January 1989, pp. 10–11.

86. *Congressional Participation in the Treaty Process*, **University of Pennsylvania Law Review**, Vol. 137, No. 5, May 1989, pp. 1511–22.

87. Review of *Balanced Budgets & American Politics,* by James D. Savage, published in **American Political Science Review**, Vol. 83, June 1989, pp. 649–50.

88. Review of *Judges and Legislators: Toward Institutional Comity,* edited by Robert A. Katzmann **Governance**, Vol. 2, No. 3, July 1989, pp. 358–59.

89. *How States Shape Constitutional Law*, **State Legislatures**, Vol. 15, No. 7, August 1989, pp. 37–39.

  a) Reprinted in *H.R. 849 [Pocket Veto Issue]*, hearing before the House Committee on Rules, 101st Cong., 1st Sess., pp. 48–50 (1989).

90. *Looking for the Last Word*, **Legal Times**, August 7, 1989, pp. S14–S15. Also reprinted in:

   a) **New Jersey Law Journal**, Vol. CXXIV, No. 6, August 10, 1989, pp. 21, 25, under the title *Not Just the Justices: The Other Interpreters.*

   b) **The Recorder** [for the San Francisco Bay Area], No. 155, August 14, 1989, pp. 1, 13, under the title *Unpopular Rulings Part of "Constitutional Dialogues."*

   c) **The Connecticut Law Tribune**, Vol. 15, No. 33, August 21, 1989, pp. 20, 21, under the title *Interpreting the Constitution Isn't Just for the Courts.*

   d) **Texas Lawyer**, August 21, 1989, Section Three, pp. 10, 11, under the title *Mr. Justice Bush, Foley, Dole, Etc.*

   e) Reprinted in *H.R. 849 (Pocket Veto Issue)*, hearing before the House Committee on Rules, 101st Cong., lst Sess., pp. 46–47 (1989).

91. *When "The President Knew" Was No Defense*, **Los Angeles Times**, September 29, 1989, Part II, p. 7.

92. Review of *The Senate: 1789–1989*, by Robert C. Byrd, **Constitution**, Vol. 1, No. 5, Fall 1989, p. 70.

93. *Poindexter's Paper Victory in Iran-Contra*, **Legal Times**, October 30, 1989, pp. 25, 26, 27. Also reprinted in:

   a) **Manhattan Lawyer**, November 7, 1989—November 13, 1989, p. 14, under the title *Reagan's Orders Shouldn't Protect Poindexter in Trial Over Iran-Contra Misdeeds.*

   b) **Fulton County Daily Report**, Vol. 100, No. 214, November 1, 1989, pp. 8–9, under the title *The Buck Stops Elsewhere.*

   c) **New Jersey Law Journal**, Vol. CXXIV, No. 17, November 2, 1989, pp. 7, 18, under the title *Can Poindexter Paper Over His Responsibilities?*

94. *How Tightly Can Congress Draw the Purse Strings?* **American Journal of International Law**, Vol. 83, No. 4, October 1989, pp. 758–66.

   a) Reprinted in *Foreign Relations and National Security Law*, edited by Thomas M. Franck and Michael J. Glennon (St. Paul, Minn.: West Publishing Co., 1993), pp. 778–83.

95. *The Nature of Legislative Power,* **San Jose Studies**, Vol. 15, No. 3, Fall 1989, pp. 14–27.

96. *Congressional Access to Executive Branch Information: Lessons from Iran-Contra,* **Government Information Quarterly**, Vol. 6, No. 4, 1989, pp. 383–94.

97. Review of *Broken Purse Strings: Congressional Budgeting, 1974–1988,* by Rudolph G. Penner and Alan J. Abramson, **Political Science Quarterly**, Vol. 104, No. 4, Winter 1989–90, pp. 707–09.

98. *Congressional-Executive Struggles Over Information: Secrecy Pledges,* **Administrative Law Review**, Vol. 42, Winter 1990, pp. 89–107.

99. *Statutory Interpretations by Congress and the Courts,* **CRS Review**, January–February 1990, pp. 32–33.

100. *Is the Solicitor General an Executive or a Judicial Agent? Caplan's Tenth Justice,* **Law & Social Inquiry**, Vol. 15, No. 2, Spring 1990, pp. 305–20.

101. *Should Congress Grant Line Item Veto Authority to the President?* **Congressional Digest**, Vol. 69, No. 6–7, June–July 1990, pp. 187, 189, 191.

102. Review of *Invitation to Struggle: Congress, the President, and Foreign Policy,* 3d ed., by Cecil V. Crabb Jr. and Pat M. Holt, **Presidential Studies Quarterly**, Vol. XX, No. 3, Summer 1990, pp. 643–45.

103. Review of *National Security Constitution,* by Harold Koh, **Constitution**, Vol. 2, No. 3, Fall 1990, p. 73.

104. *Federal Budget Doldrums: The Vacuum in Presidential Leadership,* **Public Administration Review**, Vol. 50, No. 6, Nov.–Dec. 1990, pp. 693–700.

   a) Reprinted in *The Budget Process Reform Act of 1990,* hearings before the House Committee on Rules, 101st Cong., 2d Sess., pp. 139–46 (1990).

   b) Reprinted in *Governing,* edited by Roger H. Davidson and Walter J. Oleszek (Washington, D.C.: Congressional Research Service, 1992), pp. 497–510.

c) Reprinted in *The Balanced Budget Amendment*, Volume 1, hearings before the House Committee on the Budget, 102d Cong., 2d Sess., pp. 198–205 (1992).

105. *The Appropriations Power and the Necessary and Proper Clause*, **Washington University Law Quarterly**, Vol. 68, No. 3, 1990, pp. 632–39, 652–53.

106. *Separation of Powers: Interpretation Outside the Courts*, **Pepperdine Law Review**, Vol. 18, No. 1, 1990, pp. 57–93.

107. *The Curious Belief in Judicial Supremacy*, **Suffolk University Law Review**, Vol. XXV, No. 1, Spring 1991, pp. 86–116.

108. Review of *Constitutionalism, Democracy, and Foreign Affairs*, by Louis Henkin, **Political Science Quarterly**, Vol. 106, No. 1, Spring 1991, pp. 129–30.

109. Review of *Running on Empty*, by Lawrence Haas, **Public Budgeting & Finance**, Vol. 11, No. 3, Fall 1991, pp. 103–04.

110. Review of *A Very Thin Line: The Iran-Contra Affairs*, by Theodore Draper, **Constitution**, Vol. 3, No. 3, Fall 1991, p. 78.

111. *Another Legislative Veto Invalidated, But Others Survive*, **CRS Review**, September 1991, pp. 13–14.

112. *Adopt a Resolution* [judicial nomination process], **Legal Times**, October 7, 1991, pp. 26–27.

113. Review of *Order & Law*, by Charles Fried, **Public Interest Law Review**, 1992, pp. 128–34.

114. *The Effects of a Balanced Budget Amendment on Political Institutions*, **Journal of Law & Politics**, Vol. IX, No. 1, Fall 1992, pp. 89–104.

115. *Improved Development of Complex Tax Legislation*, **The American Journal of Tax Policy**, Vol. 10, No.2, Fall 1992, pp. 325–29.

116. Review of *The Constitution in Conflict*, by Robert Burt, **Legal Studies Forum**, Vol. XVI, No. 3, 1992, pp. 353–56.

117. *Should Congress Grant the President Line Item Veto or Expanded Rescission Authority?* **Congressional Digest**, Vol. 72, No. 3, February 1993, pp. 45, 47, 49, 51.

118. Review of *Repealing the War Powers Resolution: Restoring the Rule of Law in U.S. Foreign Policy,* by Robert F. Turner, in **Governance,** Vol. 6, No. 2, April 1993, pp. 289–90.

119. *Who Controls the Adminstrative State? A Debate on the Relationship between Congress and Government Agencies,* **Cumberland Law Review,** Vol. 23, No. 1, 1992–93, pp. 133–40.

120. *The Legislative Veto: Invalidated, It Survives,* **Law & Contemporary Problems,** Vol. 56, No. 4, Autumn 1993, pp. 273–92.

121. Review of *Crimes, Follies, and Misfortunes: The Federal Impeachment Process Trials,* by Eleanor Bushnell, and *Grand Inquests: The Historical Impeachments of Justice Samuel Chase and President Andrew Johnson,* by William H. Rehnquist, in **Congress & the Presidency,** Vol. 20, No. 1, Spring 1993, pp. 85–87.

122. *Laws Congress Never Made,* **Constitution,** Vol. 5, No. 3, Fall 1993, pp. 59–66.

123. Review of *Contest for Constitutional Authority: The Abortion and War Powers Debates,* by Susan Burgess, **The Review of Politics,** Vol. 55, No. 3, Summer 1993, pp. 531–33.

124. Review of *Political Questions / Judicial Answers: Does the Rule of Law Apply to Foreign Affairs?* by Thomas M. Franck, **American Political Science Review,** Vol. 87, No. 3, September 1993, pp. 791–92.

125. *The Gore Report on Budgeting* [with Albert J. Kliman], **Public Manager,** Winter 1993–94, pp. 19–22.

126. *The Balanced Budget Amendment: Risks to Political Institutions,* **PRG Report** [newsletter of the Presidency Research Group, The American Political Science Association], Vol. XVI, No. 1, Spring 1994, pp. 1, 4–6.

127. Review of *Between the Lines: Interpreting Welfare Rights,* by R. Shep Melnick, **Law and Politics Book Review,** Vol. 4, No. 5, May 1994, pp. 61–63.

128. *Congressional Checks on Military Initiatives,* **Political Science Quarterly,** Vol. 109, No. 5, Winter 1994–95, pp. 739–62.

129. *The Korean War: On What Legal Basis Did Truman Act?* **American Journal of International Law**, Vol. 89, No. 1, January 1995, pp. 21–39.

  a) Exchange of correspondence with Robert F. Turner, *American Journal of International Law,* Vol. 90, pp. 77–78, 261–62 (1996).

130. Review of *Less Than Meets the Eye: Foreign Policy Making and the Myth of an Assertive Congress,* by Barbara Hinckley, **American Political Science Review**, Vol. 89, No. 1, March 1995, pp. 207–08.

131. *Budget Reform Proposals in the NPR Report* [with Albert J. Kliman], **Public Budgeting & Finance**, Vol. 15, No. 1, Spring 1995, pp. 27–38.

132. *The Ubiquity and Ambiguity of Unfunded Mandates*, **Cornell Journal of Law and Public Policy**, Vol. 4, No. 2, Spring 1995, pp. 472–78.

133. *Clinton's Not King—War Is for Congress*, **National Law Journal**, June 19, 1995, pp. A21–A22.

134. *The 'Contract With America': What It Really Means*, **The New York Review of Books**, June 22, 1995, pp. 20–24.

135. Review of *Power Without Responsibility: How Congress Abuses the People Through Delegation,* by David Schoenbrod, **Public Administration Review**, Vol. 55, No. 4, July/August 1995, pp. 384–85.

136. *Symposium: The Constitutional Structure of National Government in the United States: Is It in a State of Crisis?* **Administrative Law Journal of the American University**, Vol. 9, No. 1, Spring 1995, pp. 14–20, 28, 32, 35–36.

137. *What Power to Send Troops?* **The New York Times**, Op-Ed, December 2, 1995, p. 21.

  a) Reprinted in the Congressional Record by Senator Joseph Inhofe, December 13, 1995, pp. S18465–66 (daily ed.).

138. *Government by Continuing Resolution: Smaller Is Inevitable*, **Los Angeles Times**, January 28, 1996, p. M2.

  a) Reprinted as *Government: Smaller Is Inevitable,* **Los Angeles Times**, Washington Edition, February 3, 1996, p. A3.

139. *The Bosnia Commitment*, **Legal Times**, March 11, 1996, pp. 22–23.

140. Review of *The Constitution as Political Structure,* by Martin H. Redish, **Journal of Legal Education**, Vol. 46, No. 1, March 1996, pp. 135–39.

141. *The Judge as Manager*, **Public Manager**, Vol. 25, No. 3, Fall 1996, pp. 7–10.

142. Review of *On Constitutional Ground,* by John Hart Ely, **Times Literary Supplement**, December 27, 1996, pp. 9–10.

143. *Have U.S. Courts Overreached?* **Los Angeles Times**, February 2, 1997, pp. M1, M6.

   a) Reprinted in **Newsweek: Education Program**, "Constitutional Issues in Modern Society," 1997, p. 24.

144. *White House Aides Testifying Before Congress*, in **Presidential Studies Quarterly**, Vol. 27, No. 1, Winter 1997, pp. 139–52.

145. Review of *War Powers: The President, the Congress, and the Question of War,* by Donald L. Westerfield, in the **American Political Science Review**, Vol. 91, No. 1, March 1997, pp. 204–05.

146. Review of *Congress and the Presidency: Institutional Politics in a Separated System,* by Michael Foley and John E. Owens, in **Political Science Quarterly**, Vol. 112, No. 1, Spring 1997, pp. 150–51.

147. *Judicial Independence and the Item Veto*, in **The Judges' Journal**, Vol. 36, No. 1, Winter 1997, pp. 18–21, 53.

   a) Reprinted in **Best of ABA Sections: General Practice, Solo & Small Firm Section**, Vol. 1, No. 2, Fall 1997, pp. 36–37.

   b) Reprinted in **Best of ABA Sections**, 1997, pp. 38–39.

148. *Presidential War Power*, to be published by the Miller Center of Public Affairs.

149. *Presidential Independence and the Power of the Purse*, **U.C. Davis Journal of International Law & Policy**, Vol. 3, No. 2, Spring 1997, pp. 107–41.

150. Review of *The Federal Impeachment Process,* by Michael J. Gerhardt, in **Congress and the Presidency**, Vol. 24, No. 2, Autumn 1997, pp. 222–24.

151. *Line Item Veto Act of 1996: Heads-up from the States*, in **Public Budgeting & Finance**, Vol. 17, No. 2, Summer 1997, pp. 3–17.

152. *Sidestepping Congress: Presidents Acting Under the UN and NATO*, **Case Western Reserve Law Review**, Vol. 47, No. 4, Summer 1997, pp. 1237–79.

153. Review of *The Power of Separation: American Constitutionalism and the Myth of the Legislative Veto,* by Jessica Korn, published in **Political Science Quarterly**, Vol. 112, No. 3, Fall 1997, pp. 523–24.

154. Review of *Courts and Congress,* by Robert A. Katzmann, **The Federal Lawyer**, Vol. 44, November/December 1997, pp. 70–72.

155. *Introduction: Reflections on Two Decades of Congressional Budgeting* [with Philip Joyce], **Public Budgeting & Finance**, Vol. 17, No. 3, Fall, 1997, pp. 3–9.

156. *Biennial Budgeting in the Federal Government*, **Public Budgeting & Finance**, Vol. 17, No. 3, Fall 1997, pp. 87–97.

157. *One Prosecutor Shouldn't Kill Off a Valuable Law*, **Los Angeles Times**, March 1, 1998, pp. M1, M6.

158. *The War Powers Resoluton: Time to Say Goodbye*, **Political Science Quarterly**, Vol. 113, No. 1, Spring 1998, pp. 1–20.

159. *Judicial Exclusivity and Political Instability* [with Neal Devins], **Virginia Law Review**, Vol. 84, No. 1, February 1998, pp. 83–106.

160. *Public Service as a Calling*, book review of *Archibald Cox: Conscience of a Nation,* by Ken Gormley, **Texas Law Review**, Vol. 76, No. 5, April 1998, pp. 1185–1217.

161. *Censure? Nice Try, But It Shouldn't Fly*, **Washington Post**, October 4, 1998, p. C3.

162. *Raoul Berger and Executive Privilege* [with Mark Rozell], **Presidential Studies Quarterly**, Vol. 28, No. 3, Summer 1998, pp. 687–92.

163. *Congress as the Grand Inquest*, **Extensions**, a Journal of the Carl Albert Congressional Research and Studies Center, Fall 1998, pp. 3–5.

164. *Military Action against Iraq*, **Presidential Studies Quarterly**, Vol. 28, No. 4, Fall 1998, pp. 793–98.

165. *Congressional Abdication: War and Spending Powers*, to be published in the **Saint Louis University Law Journal** in 1999.

Testimony Before Congressional Committees

1. June 15, 1973   *House Select Committee on Committees.* Subject: legislative control of executive spending discretion. Reprinted: "Committee Organization in the House," panel discussions before the House Select Committee on Committee, 93d Cong., 1st Sess., Volume 2 of 3, Part 1 of 3, pp. 92–123 (1973).

2. Feb. 20, 1980   *Senate Committee on Appropriations.* Subject: committee prior-approval procedure for the transfer to funds between accounts by the Agency for International Development. Reprinted: "Foreign Assistance and Related Programs Appropriations, Fiscal Year 1981," hearings before the Senate Committee on Appropriations, 96th Cong., 2d Sess., pp. 151–70 (1980).

3. Oct. 28, 1981   *House Committee on Government Operations.* Subject: to extend the authority of the President to reorganize executive agencies. Reprinted: "Reorganization Act of 1981 . . . ," hearings before the House Committee on Government Operations, 97th Cong., 1st Sess. 41–64 (1981).

4. July 20, 1983   *Senate Committee on the Judiciary.* Subject: legislative veto. Reprinted: "Legislative Veto and the 'Chadha' Decision," hearing before the Senate Committee on the Judiciary, 98th Cong., 1st Sess., pp. 112–56 (1983).

Appendix

5. Nov. 10, 1983   *House Committee on Rules*. Subject: legislative veto. Reprinted: "Legislative Veto After Chadha," hearings before the House Committee on Rules, 98th Cong., 2d Sess., pp. 225–32, 279–87 (1984).

6. Mar. 22, 1984   *House Committee on Rules*. Subject: legislative veto. Reprinted: "Legislative Veto After Chadha," hearings before the House Committee on Rules, 98th Cong., 2d Sess., pp. 633, 645–74 (1984).

7. May 14, 1985   *Senate Committee on Rules and Administration*. Subject: item veto. Reprinted: "Line Item Veto," hearings before the Senate Committee on Rules and Administration, 99th Cong., 1st Sess., pp. 80–152 (1985).

8. May 20, 1985   *Senate Committee on Rules and Administration*. Subject: item veto. Reprinted: "Line Item Veto," hearings before the Senate Committee on Rules and Administration, 99th Cong., 1st Sess., pp. 189–204 (1985).

9. Oct. 17, 1985   *House Committee on Government Operations*. Subject: Gramm-Rudman-Hollings Bill. Reprinted: "The Balanced Budget and Emergency Deficit Control Act of 1985," hearing before the House Committee on Government Operations," 99th Cong., 1st Sess., pp. 197–232 (1985).

10. Mar. 17, 1987   *House Committee on Government Operations*. Subject: executive privilege. Reprinted: "Computer Security Act of 1987," hearings before the House Committee on Government Operations, 100th Cong., 1st Sess., pp. 439–53, 616–54 (1987).

11. Dec. 16, 1987   *House Republican Research Committee*. Subject: continuing resolutions. Reprinted: "A Call for Congressional Reform," a publication of the House Republican Research Committee, 1988.

12. Apr. 11, 1989   *Senate Committee on the Judiciary*. Subject: item veto. Reprinted: "The Line-Item Veto," hearings before the Senate Committee on the Judiciary, 101st Cong., 1st Sess., pp. 292–305 (1989).

13. July 26, 1989   *House Committee on Rules*. Subject: pocket veto. Reprinted: "H.R. 849," hearing before the House Committee on Rules, 101st Cong., 1st Sess., pp. 32–54 (1989).

14. Mar. 21, 1990   *House Committee on Rules*. Subject: congressional budget process. Reprinted: "The Budget Process Reform Act of 1990," hearings before the House Committee on Rules, 101st Cong., 2d Sess., pp. 125–50 (1990).

15. May 9, 1990   *House Committee on the Judiciary*. Subject: pocket veto. Reprinted: "Pocket Veto Legislation," hearing before the House Committee on the Judiciary, 101st Cong., 2d Sess., pp. 71–84, 91–92, 95–114 (1990).

16. May 11, 1992   *House Committee on the Budget*. Subject: Balanced Budget Amendment. Reprinted: "The Balanced Budget Amendment (Volume 1)," hearing before the House Committee on the Budget, 102d Cong., 2d Sess., pp. 185–205, 219–38 (1992).

17. Sept. 25, 1992   *House Committee on Rules*. Subject: Rescission and item-veto authority. Hearing before the House Committee on Rules, 102d Cong., 2d Sess. (1992). "Legislative Line-Item Veto Proposals," hearings before the House Committee on Rules, 102d Cong., 2d Sess., pp. 300–10 (1992).

18. Mar. 10, 1993   *House Committee on Government Operations*. Subject: expedited rescission authority. Reprinted: "Expedited Rescission Authority for the President," hearing before the Subcommittee on Legislation and National Security, House Committee on Government

Operations, 103d Cong., lst Sess. pp. 129–42, 151–56 (1993).

19. Mar. 23, 1993   *Joint Committee on the Organization of Congress.* Subject: budget reform. Reprinted: "Budget Process: Testimony of Hon. Anthony Beilenson and a Panel of Experts," hearing before the Joint Committee on the Organization of Congress, 103d Cong., lst Sess., pp. 20–23, 32–38, 52–60 (1993).

20. Apr. 15, 1993   *Joint Committee on the Organization of Congress.* Subject: budget reform. Participant in a "Roundtable on Congressional Budget Reform" to discuss a range of proposals and recommendations. Not reprinted.

21. Feb. 17, 1994   *Senate Committee on Appropriations.* Subject: Balanced Budget Amendment. Reprinted: "Balanced Budget Amendment—S.J. Res. 41," hearings before the Senate Committee on Appropriations, 103d Cong., 2d Sess., pp. 275–89, 304–14 (1993).

22. Feb. 23, 1994   *House Permanent Select Committee on Intelligence.* Subject: disclosing aggregate intelligence budget. Reprinted: "Public Disclosure of the Aggregate Intelligence Budget," hearings before the House Permanent Select Committee on Intelligence, 103d Cong., 2d Sess., pp. 109–60, 205–18 (1994).

23. June 15, 1994   *Senate Committee on the Judiciary.* Subject: inherent line-item veto. Reprinted: "Line Item Veto: The President's Constitutional Authority," hearing before the Senate Committee on the Judiciary, 103d Cong., 2d Sess., pp. 200–05 (1994).

24. Oct. 5, 1994   *Senate Committee on the Budget.* Subject: Rescission, item-veto authority. Reprinted: "Legislative Line-Item Veto Authority," hearing before the Senate Committee on the Budget, 103d Cong., 2d Sess., pp. 60–67 (1994).

25. Jan. 24, 1995   *Senate Committee on the Judiciary.* Subject: constitutional amendment for an item veto. Reprinted: "The Line-Item Veto: A Constitutional Approach," hearing before the Senate Committee on the Judiciary, 104th Cong., 1st Sess. 75–81, 83–86 (1995).

26. Feb. 23, 1995   *Senate Committee on Governmental Affairs.* Subject: item veto bills. Reprinted: "S.4 and S.14, Line-Item Veto," hearing before the Senate Committee on Government Affairs, 104th Cong., 1st Sess. 28–31, 35–40, 79–84 (1995).

27. May 1, 1996   *House Committee on Banking and Financial Services.* Subject: recess appointments and presidential removal power. Reprinted: "The Termination of Mr. Robert H. Swan as a Member of the Board of the National Credit Union Administration," hearing before the House Committee on Banking and Financial Services, 104th Cong., 2d Sess. (1996).

28. May 15, 1996   *House Committee on Government Reform and Oversight.* Subject: executive lobbying with appropriated funds (H.R. 3078). Reprinted: "H.R. 3078, Federal Agency Anti-Lobbying Act," hearing before the House Committee on Government Reform and Oversight, 104th Cong., 2d Sess. 163–74, 178–82 (1996).

29. Feb. 13, 1997   *Senate Committee on the Budget.* Subject: biennial budgeting. Reprinted: "Concurrrent Resolution on the Budget for Fiscal Year 1988" (Vol. III of III), hearings before the Senate Committee on the Budget, 105th Cong., 1st Sess. 97–103 (1997).

30. Apr. 23, 1997   *Senate Committee on Governmental Affairs.* Subject: biennial budgeting. Reprinted: "S. 261—Biennial Budgeting and Appropriations Act," hearing before the Senate Committee

on Governmental Affairs, 105th Cong., 1st Sess. 25–28, 31–34, 36–40, 102–11 (1997).

31. Jan. 29, 1998   *House Committee on the Judiciary*. Subject: "Congress, the Court, and the Constitution."

32. Feb. 4, 1998   *Senate Select Committee on Intelligence*. Subject: whistle-blowing by employees in the intelligence community.

33. Feb. 11, 1998   *Senate Select Committee on Intelligence*. Subject: whistle-blowing by employees in the intelligence community.

34. May 20, 1998   *House Permanent Select Committee on Intellgence*. Subject: whistle-blowing by employees in the intelligence community.

Contributors

David Gray Adler (Ph.D. Utah, 1982) is Professor of Political Science at Idaho State University. He is the author of *The Constitution and the Termination of Treaties*, and is coeditor of *The Constitution and the Conduct of American Foreign Policy*. He has contributed articles and essays on the Constitution and foreign policy to various books and journals, including *Political Science Quarterly*, *Presidential Studies Quarterly*, and the *Encyclopedia of the American Presidency*.

Dean Alfange Jr. (Ph.D. Cornell, 1967) is Professor of Political Science at the University of Massachusetts, Amherst, where he has taught since 1967. While there, he served for five years as Dean of the Faculty of Social and Behavioral Sciences and as Acting Vice-Chancellor for Academic Affairs. He has been a visiting scholar at Yale Law School and Stanford Law School. Four of his articles have appeared in the *Supreme Court Review*, and others have appeared in the *University of Pennsylvania Law Review*, the *Cornell Law Review*, the *George Washington Law Review*, and elsewhere.

Neal Devins (J.D. Vanderbilt, 1982) is Ernest W. Goodrich Professor of Law and a lecturer in Government at the College of William and Mary. His books include *Shaping Constitutional Values: The Supreme Court, Elected Government, and the Abortion Dispute, Political Dynamics of Constitutional Law* (second edition, with Louis Fisher), *Redefining Equality* (with Davison Douglas), *Public Values, Private Schools, Federal*

273

Abortion Politics: A Documentary History (with Wendy Watson), *Elected Branch Influence in Constitutional Decisionmaking,* and *Government Lawyers.* He has written over fifty articles on constitutional law, civil rights, and administrative law. He has testified before Congress on the separation of powers, and has lectured before the American Association of Law Schools, the American Bar Association, the American Education Research Association, and the Brookings Institution. In 1992, he became the first law professor to be named an Alumni Fellow by William and Mary. Prior to joining the faculty, he served as Assistant General Counsel to the U.S. Commission on Civil Rights and as Project Director for the Vanderbilt Institute for Public Policy Studies.

Louis Fisher (Ph.D. New School for Social Research, 1967) is a senior specialist in separation of powers with the Congressional Research Service of the Library of Congress. He began work with CRS in 1970 and served as research director of the House Iran-Contra Committee in 1987, writing major sections of the final report. His numerous publications and awards are listed in the Appendix of this book. He has taught at Queens College, Georgetown University, American University, Catholic University, Indiana University, Johns Hopkins University, the College of William and Mary law school, and the Catholic University law school. He has been active with the Central and East European Law Initiative (CEELI) of the American Bar Association, traveling to Bulgaria, Albania, and Hungary to assist constitution-writers, participating in CEELI conferences in Washington, D.C., with delegations from Bosnia-Herzegovina, Lithuania, Romania, and Russia, and serving on CEELI "working groups" on Armenia and Belarus. As part of CRS delegations, he traveled to Russia and Ukraine to assist on constitutional questions. He has been invited to speak in Albania, Australia, Bulgaria, Canada, the Czech Republic, England, Germany, Greece, Holland, Israel, Macedonia, Malaysia, Mexico, the Philippines, Romania, Russia, Slovenia, Taiwan, and Ukraine.

Michael J. Glennon (J.D. Minnesota, 1973) is Professor of Law at the University of California, Davis, law school. Prior to going into teaching law, he was Legal Counsel to the Senate Foreign Relations Committee. His books include *Constitutional*

Diplomacy, Foreign Affairs and the U.S. Constitution (coedited with Louis Henkin and William D. Rogers), *When No Majority Rules*, and *Foreign Relations and National Security Law* (with Thomas Franck). He has also authored numerous articles on constitutional issues, has testified before the International Court of Justice in *Nicaragua v. United States of America* (1986), and has appeared as a witness before a number of congressional committees. Professor Glennon served as a consultant to the Senate Judiciary Committee on treaty interpretation and to the Senate Foreign Relations Committee on revision of the War Powers Resolution. In 1981, he was awarded the Certificate of Merit by the American Society of International Law, and in 1984, he was presented the Deak Prize presented by the Society for the best article by a younger author to appear that year in the *American Journal of International Law*. He was cocounsel to 110 congressional plaintiffs in *Lowry v. Reagan* (1988), challenging the violation of the War Powers Resolution in the Persian Gulf and authored the amicus curiae brief for the American Civil Liberties Union in *Dellums v. Bush* (1990), challenging the president's power to make war without prior congressional authorization.

Loch K. Johnson (Ph.D. University of California, Riverside, 1969) is a Regents Professor of Political Science at the University of Georgia and the author of several books, including *A Season of Inquiry, America As a World Power*, and *Secret Agencies*. He has won the Certificate of Distinction from the National Intelligence Study Center, the V.O. Key Prize from the Southern Political Science Association, the Josiah Meigs Award for Excellence in Teaching from the University of Georgia, and the Creative Research Medal, also from Georgia. From time to time, he has served in the federal government, most recently as special assistant to the chairman of the Presidential Commission on Intelligence.

Nancy Kassop (Ph.D. New York University, 1984) is Associate Professor of Political Science at the State University of New York, College at New Paltz, where she teaches courses in American government and politics, the presidency, and constitutional law. She has published articles and presented papers on subjects including the separation of powers, the presidency, constitutional law, and reproductive rights. She has contributed four articles in separate volumes for Hofstra University's presidential conferences, including those devoted to Nixon, Carter, Reagan, and Bush. Her most recent article is "The Bush Administration's Approach to Separation of Powers." In 1997, she received the Teacher of the Year Award for the College of Liberal Arts and Sciences at New Paltz.

Robert J. Spitzer (Ph.D. Cornell, 1980) is Distinguished Service Professor of Political Science at the State University of New York, College at Cortland. His books include *The Presidency and Public Policy, The Right to Life Movement and Third Party Politics, The Presidential Veto* (SUNY Press), *The Bicentennial of the U.S. Constitution, President and Congress, Media and Public Policy,* and *The Politics of Gun Control* (second edition). He is also Series Editor for the book series "American Constitutionalism" for SUNY Press. Spitzer is the author of over 100 articles and papers appearing in many journals and books on a variety of American politics subjects. He served as a member of the New York State Commission on the Bicentennial of the U.S. Constitution and has also testified before Congress on several occasions. He has won the Founder's Award for Best Paper on the Presidency presented at the American Political Science Association's Annual Conference, and has twice won Cortland's DiGiusto Award for Outstanding Service to Students.

Case Index

Subject and Name Index

281

Date Due